Uncharted

TRACKING POP

SERIES EDITORS: JOCELYN NEAL, JOHN COVACH,
ROBERT FINK, AND LOREN KAJIKAWA

RECENT TITLES:

UNCHARTED

Creativity and the Expert Drummer

Bill Bruford

University of Michigan Press

Ann Arbor

Published in the United States of America by the
University of Michigan Press
Manufactured in the United States of America
⊗ Printed on acid-free paper

2021   2020   2019   2018   4   3   2   1

A CIP catalog record for this book is available from the British Library.

Library of Congress Cataloging-in-Publication Data

Names: Bruford, Bill, author.
Title: Uncharted : Creativity and the expert drummer / Bill Bruford.
Description: Ann Arbor : University of Michigan Press, [2018] | Series: Tracking
    pop | Includes bibliographical references and index.
Identifiers: LCCN 2017039628| ISBN 9780472073788 (hardcover : alk. paper) |
    ISBN 9780472053780 (pbk. : alk. paper) | ISBN 9780472123674 (e-book)
Subjects: LCSH: Drum set—Performance. | Popular music—Philosophy and aesthetics.
Classification: LCC ML1035 .B78   2018 | DDC 786.9/143—dc23
LC record available at https://lccn.loc.gov/2017039628

Cover credit: Photograph by Claude Dufresne, 2006.

To Carolyn and our family

Foreword

If there is a thread that connects Bill Bruford's extraordinary musical career to the considerable achievement of writing this book, it is an ability to communicate a host of complex ideas, elegantly and coherently. There was a polymetric quality to his playing—a capacity to set up vivid, plural rhythms within a single framework—and this capacity to juggle different ideas without missing a beat remains undiminished, though now with different purpose—that of communicating *about* beats rather than *with* them.

Actually, this book is not so much about beats as those who make them. There will be some people picking up this book, perhaps expecting a relatively easy-going account of great drummers and their playing, who may need to sit down and listen to an Earthworks track, a King Crimson improvisation or two, before reminding themselves that Dr. Bruford, as a player and scholar, does not do easy-going. He made and continues to make demands of us—listeners (as was) and now readers. In the introduction to the book, Bill makes two "principal assertions: that (a) experience, the outcome of prolonged and accumulative interaction with environment, is generated by action; and that (b) the way to the human mind is through its cultural products and artifacts." This sentence should be enough to alert most readers that this is no ordinary book about drumming.

All this is not to say that Bill is making unreasonable demands. He is fully aware, as he outlines in his introduction, that different readers may want to focus on particular parts of the book, dependent on their reason for picking up the volume in the first place. I would urge anyone coming to this book from knowing Bill's music to trust in him as an author as they did in him as a player; there are so many ideas and perspectives articulated in this book that it takes us well beyond what it means to be a drummer, important as that is.

The book, at its heart, has a simple question, "what do drummers do," but in presenting this simple question brings action theory, cultural psychology, systems theories of creativity, and not least, the self-reports of some of the finest players in contemporary music, all to bear on the answering of this question. What makes the book particularly rich, in my view, is that it not only sheds light on the creativity of drumming and drummers but offers ideas and models that could be used in a wider analysis. It contributes to the increasingly important area of performance research and adds to the theorization of creativity in subtle and insightful ways.

The idea of creative practice in music may, at first glance, seem tautologous, but psychological research over recent decades has shown how complex, and poorly understood, is the notion of creativity across human action. One can trace this interest in the analysis of creativity to American research in the 1950s. At that point, when operationalism was becoming hugely influential in education, business management, and psychology more generally, researchers were motivated to measure creativity in a not dissimilar way to intelligence—tests of creativity were designed and applied in a thoroughly instrumental way. With the demise of behavioral psychology and the turn toward cognition as the central preoccupation of psychologists, so came a richer and more nuanced turn in the study of what it means to be creative. The work of Keith Sawyer, Mihaly Csikszentmihalyi, Pamela Burnard, and most tellingly, Vlad Glăveanu all inform this book's construction of a rich theoretical model of musical creativity—the integration of the creative "action context" of drumming, with a taxonomy of mechanisms that drive the creative impetus, and a model through which cultural meaning may circulate within communities of practice.

In addition to the book's rigorous dissection of creativity in drumming and its many facets, it serves a wider purpose in challenging some persistent shibboleths around drumming, drummers, and popular music more broadly. Although the book wisely avoids any crude apologetics or defense of the work of drummers—the reflective awareness, skills, and musical intelligence of the book's informants make the case fairly effortlessly. Bill rightly places the work of drummers within the context of a "culture's organizing ideology"—an ideology in which drumming is marked as "a breed apart and a breed below." Rather than taking Simon Frith's approach to the difficulty of talking about creativity—shot through as it is with ideological baggage— which is to suggest that we don't use the "C" word, Bill uses the term to draw out a set of careful thematic distinctions between different forms of creative practice, and he establishes a frame through which we can ask critical questions of creativity in drumming, without ditching the word altogether.

A central theme of the book, established early in the work, is to find a way to describe and understand the sometimes very different practices of drumming within a panoptic model. Bill uses the comparison between Max Roach and session drummer, Blair Sinta, to confront this. In doing so, he sets this up with the idea of a continuum of practice between the functional and the compositional, which very crudely could be paraphrased as thinking or acting within or outside the box. Crucially though, while exploring how drummers work within and without established boundaries, Bill allows that both ends of this continuum are rich in creativity. Not always the same things going on for Roach and Sinta but both very definitely creative. This is important because it takes us beyond the sometimes irritating and simplistic ideology that privileges particular genres as being inherently more or less creative; Bill is nudging us toward an idea of possibility without recourse to a crude notion of better/worse. And that doesn't mean a relativist position here. Bruford is clear that Roach is in a class of his own but this cannot and should not diminish the work of a great studio player such as Sinta.

Part of what makes this a great read is Bill's insight into areas of drum expertise that would fall below the radar of most. He describes, in relation to Chad Wackerman's account of working for James Taylor, that a necessary skill of drummers is to assess the locus of *actual* rather than *nominal* leadership. This shapes part of an extended dissection of the variety of forms of collaborative work, the nature of leadership, and musical roles. Compulsory reading for all bandleaders, perhaps.

Where the book contributes most in terms of creativity theory is the detailed set of chapters on what might be described as the mechanics of the drummer's creative work, formulated as a model of *Selection, Difference, Communication, and Assessment* (SDCA). Under each of these headings, Bill picks out the dimensions that go toward a creative performance. The forensic detail with which the book addresses each of these dimensions is powerful. I think there are any number of insights that can be gleaned from this model but particularly striking for me was the sense of power that the drummers in the book perceived in themselves and in their capacity to affect the direction and outcome of the music (in stark contrast to the way in which drummers may often be characterized). Perhaps more surprising was the way in which players saw communication more in terms of the expression of different experience rather than, say, emotion (which is taken to be the *sine qua non* of art music performance)—a useful contribution to the general literature on performance and genre.

There might be some for whom this study of creativity in music provokes an anxiety. For musicians, the fear can be that an analysis or explanation of what they do may close down their direct, unmediated involvement in their playing—that thinking too much about what they do will stop them from doing it. If there is an anxiety there, it should be dispelled by the depth of reflection and thought that goes into the responses of Bill's interviewees. Extraordinarily nuanced comments about the art of drumming are on every page. Not that this indicates any sort of party line on what it means to be a drummer. All of the players interviewed, from Peter Erskine to Cindy Blackman Santana, take up sometimes very different positions about where creativity resides, about what and how drummers communicate when they play, and much besides. One of the strengths of the writing and the book's theoretical position is to be able to accommodate the often disparate reports of players. It would be a little too easy to carve creativity up (as opposed to theorize it) and Bill Bruford overcomes this— allowing many different voices to support his understanding of the plural, relational nature of creative work on a drum kit.

While there was a brief temptation to begin this foreword with some spectacularly drole drummer joke, I forewent this noble contribution to humor for a number of reasons—first, this might have alienated a big proportion of the book's readership at a stroke; secondly and much more importantly, it would have done a serious injustice to a book that is a masterful contribution to our understanding of creativity, and a compelling account of what it takes and means to be a drummer.

Mark Doffman
Faculty of Music
University of Oxford
May 2017

Contents

Acknowledgments

Sometime during 2010, Professor Stephen Goss at the University of Surrey offered me an honorary degree. The celebrated guitarist Jimmy Page had been a recent recipient, he said. I was flattered but hesitant. There were some things I wanted to explore, I said, about creativity and the psychology of music performance. Could I explore them through doctoral study at the University, and actually earn the degree? His face clouded ominously. "Oh, so you want to do it the *hard* way," he said.

I thought I knew something of the "how" and a little of the "why" musicians do the things they do, but evidently not enough. Over the course of a decade a professional sclerosis had become increasingly debilitating to the point where I was unable to continue in the drum community in which I had strained every fiber to contribute over four decades. Why was I unable to function? The answer, I now know, is both simple and profound: because I could no longer hear what came next. How many others have experienced this sort of interior malfunction? Provoked into seeking answers, I edged from poacher to game-keeper and began to research the psychological world of the expert popular musician.

I am much indebted to Professor Goss and Dr. Chris Elliott, M.B.E. for inserting the idea of a turn to academia into my mind, and to Dr. Jonathan Little and Dr. Gareth Dylan Smith for suggesting the possibility of its realization. Making sense of the world is a tricky enough business; making sense of others making sense of the world is doubly so. My thanks go also to my supervisory team of Professor Allan Moore, Dr. Milton Mermikides, and Dr. Matthew Peacock at the University of Surrey for their patience, calmness, and wisdom during that particular endeavor; to Dr. Alison Yeung Yam Wah and Dr. Dawn Duke of the University Researcher Development team who offered much needed guidance to this novice researcher; and to the expert drummers who gave generously of their time and without whose perceptions of creativity this study would not have been possible: Cindy Blackman Santana, Peter Erskine, Martin France, Mark Guiliana, Dylan Howe, Ralph Salmins, Asaf Sirkis, Thomas Strønen, and Chad Wackerman.

My editor at the University of Michigan Press, Mary Francis, was an ever-patient guide through an exhaustive peer-review process. My thanks go to her and her editorial assistant Jenny Geyer. Special thanks are due also to my production editor Kevin Rennells for scrutiny of the work at a forensic level of detail, and the Tracking Pop series editors Lori Burns, Albin Zak and, in particular, John Covach. The book would have been a lesser document without John's helpful advice. Thank you also to Professor Vlad Petre Glăveanu for permission to reproduce the model of human experience in chapter 1, and to Claude Dufresne for the photographic image that graces the book's cover.

Finally, I would like to thank my family for their long-standing support for some of my wilder imaginings, the most recent of which you hold in your hands.

University of Surrey
September 2017

Introduction

Setting Up

When you and I look each other in the eye, count to four, and strike a drum or play notes together, we engage in an elemental millennia-old human occupation that connects us and makes us feel good on many levels. One explanation for this is that the combined outcome appears to be greater than the sum of its components. The micro-discrepancies in our respective performances ensure a degree of unrepeatable uniqueness in the collective outcome. No one else is likely to do it the same way with the same result. We like it, we do it again, and we may try to make it in some way better or different. We find meaning in this process, and the process is its own reward.[1] Such a starting point holds good for almost all intra-human, real-time music engagement, the exploration of which in the world of the expert drummer is in essence what this book is about.

The title of this volume conveys a presumption that drummers experience something called creativity, and not the least of its aims is to test the veracity of that presumption. What part (or parts) of the action described above, if any, might be described as creative? What meaning might such an attribution carry for you, me, or any listener? The current wide interest in creativity has focused attention on the process of popular music creation. If creativity does indeed lie at the heart of the modern economy, as scientists, authors, and government agencies maintain,[2] benefit should arise from the clearest possible understanding of its many manifestations. Popular music has been designated as part of the creative arts industry by policy makers in both government and academia, but the extent to which its instrumental practitioners are *actually* creative has rarely been interrogated, and their understanding of the experience of creativity even less so.

Most studies of the psychology of artistic creation have hitherto taken place within the visual, literary, and plastic arts. The products and processes of these domains, subject to revision and unveiling at the creator's command and often after a lengthy process of incubation and realization, offer units of analysis that presumably stand still long enough to permit effective scrutiny. By contrast, studies of artistic creativity whose usefulness, functionality, and validation are construed as being "in the moment" are perhaps more hazardous to undertake. Dancers', actors', and musicians' perceptions of creativity are tempered by the immediacy of the (usually) collaborative moment in which they must communicate significant difference, literally *perform*. The meager work on musicians' experiences[3] of performance has so far been produced predominantly from within the classical tradition and typically examines students or early career professionals performing on pitched instruments. Questionable transference of findings to other traditions suggests a need for the scope to be broadened: accordingly, my focus here is on the experiences of a cadre of peak-career, internationally renowned experts performing on unpitched[4] instruments within the popular music tradition.

The link between creativity and the popular music instrumentalist is casually assumed but little examined, and, as we shall see, creativity is not always welcome in performance. The water is perennially muddied by the conflation of creativity and popularity, with the continued insistence on a spurious and unproven connection between the two. Much invention in popular music is devoted to reaffirmation: the production of what listeners (and producers) already have, expect, or know. Rather less effort is devoted to the production of what people do not have, do not expect, or do not know, an activity that generally welcomes, and may require, creativity. Leaving aside for a moment the vexed question of what exactly creativity might be, and the many ways in which it might be, drummers are generally not associated with the phenomenon by those outside the music community. Within the music community, we are, on the contrary, very much associated with it, and, as the narrative will show, very much associate ourselves with it. How this disjunction came to be will be a central concern as the story unfolds.

I like what musicians do, and I believe that what we do is, in the broadest sense, useful; it matters to us and to the music in which we do it. It may also be highly creative, an assertion that the following pages will provide considerable evidence to support. The book will show how drummers enact creative performance, and how that creativity is socially and psychologically constructed, covert, and downplayed. It further aims to embolden those popular instrumentalists who have yet to engage with the idea that they could be creative, and indeed, should they wish to be useful musicians, have an obligation to engage their creative imagination and highest sensibilities for as much of the time as possible. In some respects this microlevel analysis of the way people make sense of their practice is an advocacy for the power of human performance. It calls for a reconsideration of the inestimable value of the vagaries of messy intra-human performance to performer, listener, and popular music alike.

Rationale, Scope, and Objectives

The focus, then, is on the musician rather than the music. I want to suggest some answers to fundamental questions about drummers, a community of which I am a member. What do we do and why do we do it? Is there anything creative about it? If so, how do we achieve and experience that creativity, and how might it inform our practice? Who attributes creativity? Who counts? More elusive still might be answers to other questions: What are drummers for, if not to be creative? How might an instrumental culture with an ideology as disparaging as that of the drum culture shape practitioners' attitudes?

To begin to answer these questions, I develop a synthesis of thinking from creativity studies and cultural psychology to illuminate aspects of creativity and meaning in drummer performance. Adopting Caroline Palmer's proposition that "each performer has intentions to convey"[5] I contend that (a) the performer hopes to effectively convey those intentions by means of the expression of experience; and (b) such an expression may be assessed by others as significant and hence creative. Viewed through an action-theoretical lens, I shall show how drummers experience creativity through significant "mediated action in context." Mediated action may be taken forward to become full experience, the communicative performance of which has the potential to be assigned creative significance.[6] These ideas inscribe the DNA of the book's theoretical background into one particularly dense sentence, the contents of which I shall unpack as the discussion develops. They turn out to be much more easily digestible than they first appear.

The book purports to be neither a study of music creativity in general, nor a study of how drummers experience creativity—that cannot be known. It is, rather, a study of how they *report* that experience, how they attach meaning to it, and how any such meaning might inform practice. It lies in the context of a recentering of music performance,[7] one dimension of which is that performance in popular music might be creative in meaningful ways. It is intended to be a significant addition to the creativity discourse in two respects. First, documenting and interpreting the insights of experts provides useful information as much for music educationalists and professional drummers as creativity theorists and those interested in the psychology of music performance. Educationalists, for instance, might wish to inculcate a greater appreciation of what it means and feels like to collaborate creatively in music, a discipline too heavily geared to the acquisition of technical ability as a creative tool, too little geared to the acquisition of the collaborative skills without which that tool is rendered far less potent.

Second, analysis of actions and action-choices taken at the level of the individual musician are important in illuminating the way people in general make meaning from their participation in change through creative action. Viewed in this context, action becomes the means by which we understand the individual drummer in the drum culture and the individual musician in the broader culture. Keith Negus and Michael Pickering's interpretation of creativity as a process that brings experience into meaning and significance forms a solid foundation upon which I can begin to build my argument.[8] From there I develop the proposition that creative music performance involves processes of selection, differentiation, communication, and assessment situated within a complex matrix of people, action, and artifacts—the *situation*.[9] Creativity resides in the ability to effect and communicate significant difference in a particular performance in a particular music situation; in brief, I argue that drummers derive creative meaning from making the music work and making it matter.

The work is based upon an action-theoretical thematic analysis of the "in the moment" collaborative creativity of a cohort of expert drummers. Building upon my findings, I explore perceptions of creativity within this group of mature peak-career practitioners in order to better understand the experience of the phenomenon as it arises within the immediacy of high-level popular music performance. I explain how drummers conceptualize, achieve, and interpret creativity in music performance, how we construct and communicate difference, and how we assess the significance of that difference. Taken together, the outcomes should help to cast light on and correct multiple historical misunderstandings of the behaviors, motivations, and intentions of our rhythmic specialists, leading to an improved understanding of the experience of creativity in popular music instrumental performance.

The Expert Perspective

This book is informed by the perceptions of a cohort of expert Western kit drummers. The term "Western kit drummer," abbreviated to "drummer," is used throughout to mean those European or North American practitioners who perform upon the Western drum kit. The ascription of

"Western" indicates only that the instrument in question was developed in the West, its pedagogy and practice were developed by Westerners, and it tends to be applied primarily within the ever-changing stylistic borders of Western popular music. While it is in frequent use in multiple ways in other cultures, my investigation is confined to the European and North American spheres of performance practice, in part to retain a sharp focus on the community of which I have professional experience, and in part because insufficient time and resources were available to investigate the phenomenon of creative drum performance in all its pan-global manifestations. After approximately a century of development, a collection of some seven instruments appears to have emerged as the norm for a standard "kit": a snare drum, two tom toms, and two cymbals, all played with the hands; a hi-hat and bass drum, both typically foot-operated. However, any number of additions or variations may be appended in the endless hunt for sonic difference. The origins, history, and development of the drum kit have been well described elsewhere,[10] but it is important to highlight one aspect of its use. The instrument is played seated with some combination of all four limbs in play. This definition therefore precludes the small army of percussionists who play percussion instruments with two hands only.

All the drummers in the study qualify as experts. Common understandings take expertise to be the acquisition of some special skills or knowledge by training, study, or practice. Regarding performance, such skills might include, importantly, interpretative techniques. Ralf Krampe and Anders Ericsson distinguish an "eminent" performer, one who "irrevocably changes and expands the known possibilities for a given instrument or repertoire," from an expert. Eminence, they suggest, "lies beyond the mere acquisition of skills and interpretative techniques," sufficient of which qualify the performer as "expert." Of all the drummers whose work is discussed here in depth, Max Roach alone, I contend, has achieved eminence: I return to his case shortly. Long beyond competence and proficiency, our interviewees' practice is typically masterful and, where necessary, virtuosic.[11]

Although it was not a criterion for participation, all interviewees stated that they had undergone the lengthy period of knowledge and skill acquisition without which some propose that no one can make contributions to a domain. This is variously expressed at the "ten year rule"[12] or the "ten thousand hour rule."[13] Extensive international-level experience was evidenced by the participant having led a music ensemble in multiple performances of his or her music and the production of at least one commercially available recording.[14] The thinking here was that production of contemporary work for commercial release in the name of the practitioner would embody performances that necessarily required the creative exercise of choice and control and afforded the freedom to exercise them.

By delimiting this exploration to the perceptions of a group of mature, peak-career participants, I was able to shine a light onto previously unrevealed areas and aspects of popular music performance. Young, immature drummers beginning their careers typically have insufficient experience of any performance, creative or otherwise, and are thus unlikely to have formed robust perceptions of the phenomenon—their views have been sought elsewhere.[15] The selection of the nine experts to be interviewed prioritized the widest possible range of ethnicities, styles, and contexts to capture the broadest possible picture of contemporary drummer performance:

- Cindy Blackman Santana (Carlos Santana, Lenny Kravitz, Herbie Hancock)[16]
- Peter Erskine (Weather Report, Steely Dan, Helsinki Philharmonic Orchestra)
- Martin France (John Taylor, Kenny Wheeler, NDR Radio Orchestra)
- Mark Guiliana (David Bowie, Brad Mehldau, Avishai Cohen)
- Dylan Howe (Ian Dury, Wilco Johnson, Steve Howe)
- Ralph Salmins (Van Morrison, the Waterboys, Paul McCartney)
- Asaf Sirkis (Tim Garland, Larry Coryell, Gwilym Simcock)
- Thomas Strønen (Bugge Wesseltoft, Tomasz Stanko, Trondheim Jazz Orchestra)
- Chad Wackerman (Frank Zappa, James Taylor, Allan Holdsworth)

A brief biography of each participant may be found in appendix A.

• In situating myself within this group of experts I am obliged to offer a brief declaration of interest. Historically, my own 41-year career as a drummer encompassed the comparatively leisurely shifts from pre- to postdigital domains, from a music industry to a music business, from the elite performer to the democratization of practice, from "all-in-a-room-together" to the "stay-home" drummer,[17] from "heel down" on the bass drum pedal to the balletic "heel up" as the music became louder, more assertive. I navigated these rapids with some efficiency, but with an increasing sense of anxiety as the river of change flowed ever faster. In a reckless youth I welcomed music performance with open arms because I knew it all. A little more than four decades later I dreaded performance to the point where, certain in the knowledge that I knew nothing, I was unable to function meaningfully. Far from the gilded certainties of ignorance, performance had become incomprehensibly difficult and insuperably so.

Unable to see where one had turned into the other, I called a halt and decided to look at things from another perspective. I stepped back out of practice to try to understand better what had made me stop. Consultations with others introduced me to the substantial literature on the psychology of performance and performance anxiety, and before long I was exploring the topic, and its close cousin the psychology of creative performance, within the corpus of experts whom I have introduced above. In this way, the origins of the book emerged organically from an ongoing and very personal sense of needing to know, or at least understand better, how drummers' cultural psychology determines what we do.

The above is important to understanding the relationship between the researcher and the researched. Rather than adopt the cultural anthropological methodology of participant observation, my approach was what Barbara Tedlock calls "the observation of participation" in which I both experienced and observed my own and others' co-participation in the construction of meaning.[18] My position as interlocutor was that of the knowledgeable tour guide, able to ask the right questions and analyze and interpret the answers, but it demanded careful negotiation lest I lay myself open to charges of subjectivity. Being acutely tuned-in to the experiences and meaning systems of others while being aware of how one's own biases and preconceptions may be influencing what one is trying to understand—to "indwell"—is no easy matter.[19] When the ethnographer is, in Stephen Cottrell's words, "part of the plot,"[20] balancing the emic (insider) and etic (outsider) perspectives creates a particular tension. A partial resolution was afforded by adopting the "complete-member" researcher perspective, seen as both "insider and outsider rather than insider or outsider."[21] A keen awareness of these issues and as to exactly whose meaning was emerging from the data required constant vigilance in order to gain knowledge about the socially shared meaning that forms the behaviors of the interviewees.

The central focus of the book, then, lies more in trying to understand the meaning people attach to particular performance events, less in whether participant accounts are accurate reflections of actual events. Since the data upon which it is based arose from an analysis of experience, the methodological thrust was to elicit insight rather than find solutions—the purpose being not to prove something, but rather to learn something and communicate that learning. Ference Marton suggests that in the same way as the botanist finds and classifies undiscovered species of plants, the phenomenographer discovers and classifies previously unspecified ways in which people think about a certain aspect of reality, in this case, drummers and the experience of creativity.[22] To achieve this I had to gain access to drummers' lived experience. This cannot, however, be studied directly, in part because "language, speech and systems of discourse mediate and define the very experience we attempt to describe."[23] It is important to remember that what was available for investigation was the *representation* of the experience of drummer creativity, not the experience itself. Only after interpretation using an appropriate methodology might such representations lead to better understanding. This line of thinking led to a common qualitative sampling strategy, that of studying a relatively small number of special cases of expert practitioners—a good source of learned lessons. I hoped that the characteristics of the semi-structured anonymous interview,[24] disinterested and focused on experience, might encourage a higher level of disclosure and forthrightness than is conventionally the case in the "career" interview. (See appendix B for the interview questions.)

Careful observation and interviews with expert practitioners may permit informed hypotheses about how some drummers at certain times and in specific places construe notions of creativity. I interpret such material through three theoretical positions: John Dewey's theories of art as the production, expression, and communication of experience; systemic theories of creativity propagated most notably by Mihaly Csikszentmihalyi and extended by Vlad Petre Glăveanu; and the action-theoretical approaches of Ernst Boesch and Glăveanu, which combine to help situate significance within mediated action. In taking this approach, we can begin to understand how meaning informs change in practice.

In linking ideas from creativity theory to those of cultural psychology, the book capitalizes on a strand of thinking within the latter that identifies mind and culture as fundamentally interdependent and dynamic, and identifies the circular feedback loop between the individual and culture as the principal informant in the meaning-making process. Extending the work of scholars such as Boesch and Glăveanu to music performance, creativity and meaning may be seen as connected through the construct of "significant situated action." Further, I employ the thinking of Etienne Wenger to position drummers as a "community of practice"[25] enfolded within the drum culture, a community that largely determines and shapes drummer action. Positioning action at the center of a web of relationships between lived experience, interpretation, and meaning, and integrated with domain-level cultural variables (drum culture expectations,[26] assessments of creativity, quality of ac-

tion), we may provide the single coherent picture of the experience of drummer creativity that this narrative aims to achieve.

Creativity and Music Performance

Creativity is a useful and valuable component of human cognition and psychological functioning. The history of the development of thinking on the
topic has been elegantly described by John Hope Mason, and several scholars have brought forward comprehensive reviews of the main trends in the
creativity literature.[27] Nevertheless, to understand its relationship to popular music instrumental performance we need to briefly review how we got
to where we are. Rather than highlight and debate differences in the creativity discourse, however, I confine myself to trying to seek out and apply the
key conceptions that usefully illuminate the methodology of the creative
drummer.

Broadly, contemporary creativity theory distinguishes between the Romantic person-centric approach found in earlier understandings of the phenomenon and more contemporary rationalist systemic approaches.[28] In the
latter view, creativity is seen as a dynamic system working on a larger scale
than that of the "lone genius" paradigm posited by the Romantic conception
and concomitant understandings. No longer a divine or mysterious process
in the gift of the gods and bestowed upon the lone genius, contemporary
thinking sees creativity as something that can be identified in us all: while
not everyone *will*, anyone *might* become creative in meaningful ways.[29] Far
from being the province alone of the highly gifted, we all share a cognitive
apparatus capable of creativity.[30] Only some, however, are given to employ
that apparatus in a manner likely to produce a creative act on a spectrum
ranging from the everyday sort of creativity employed by many, known as
"little-c" or "P" (psychological) creativity, to the novel, useful, and surprising
creativity accepted as such by a field of experts and in the gift of very few,
characterized as "Big-C" or "H" (historical) creativity.[31] Little-c creativity
includes everyday problem-solving and the ability to adapt to change, and
arguably the ability to play a musical instrument to a rudimentary standard.
Big-C creativity is far rarer, and is held to occur when a person solves a problem or creates an object that has a major impact on how we think, feel, and
live our lives.[32] In the domain of the drummer, for instance, it takes Big-C
creativity to change the way subsequent practitioners come to view the very
role and function of the instrument itself.

Current findings document creative music performance as a culturally situated human behavior characterized as recombinational, exploratory, or transformational (or a combination of these), with a component of problem finding or problem solving. It is less a discrete expression of individual will and more an activity constrained by and mediated between multiple actors and agencies. Music creativity is now seen as located within an interactive "network of people cooperating";[33] indeed, the idea that creativity might be seen, for example, as a purely neurological phenomenon now seems to be outflanked.[34] Systems theorists of creativity now join socioculturalists to argue persuasively that music creativity is seldom the result of individual action alone.[35] Many of these ideas are embodied in conceptions of creativity that coalesce around notions of novelty and usefulness (or value). Phillip McIntyre's definition of the phenomenon encapsulates many of these key components. For him, creativity is

> a productive activity whereby objects, processes and ideas are generated from antecedent conditions through the agency of someone, whose knowledge to do so comes from somewhere and the resultant novel variation is seen as a valued addition to the store of knowledge in at least one social setting.[36]

A drum performance may be characterized as a useful "valued addition" in any one or all of several ways: (a) in the microgenetic sense of furthering the measure or phrase of music at hand; (b) on a median level of gluing the performance together, perhaps with an irresistible groove; and (c) in the ontogenetic sense of redefining possible futures for the instrument and its practice across a lifespan.[37] The idea of novelty, however, is more problematic. It is frequently part of the musician's self-conception that she or he feels obliged to contribute to the performance in a way she or he perceives of as "new." While novelty may be one of the most important indicators of difference in a creative product,[38] it is not without contention and has limited use in music circles. If the drumming has not been derived, copied, imitated, or translated from any previous type of drumming (i.e., it is truly new), it would not be recognizable as drumming.[39] John Hope Mason asks a much better question—not "Is it new?" but "Does it matter?"[40]

Calls for the enrollment of some of these broad ideas into a general theory of music creativity have been raised only recently, music having hitherto been only infrequently viewed as an object of study in the creativity field. Increasingly, however, scholars have argued for greater critical attention to the topic and the meanings it is made to carry. Generally, there seems to be nothing in popular music that demands or requires that a performance be "creative," unless the mere activity possesses an intrinsic quality or qualities that answer to the definition of creativity. Instrumental performance has received minimal attention as an object of analysis, and is, as a consequence, poorly understood.[41] Creativity has been generally seen, by musicians at least, as a desirable phenomenon frequently governed by a sense of incompletion. For musician Art Farmer, "playing is generally a never-ending state of getting there."[42] Within the contemporary London music community surveyed by Cottrell, some saw music performance as craftsmanlike with the performer essentially re-creative or repetitive, as artisanal rather than artistic.[43] While traditional musicology seems to allow some performance analysis within jazz but not within rock, expert drummers themselves have diminishing interest in this mid-20th-century nomenclature, seen as either restrictive or irrelevant. We generally see creativity not as genre-specific (jazz, yes; grime, no), but rather in terms of the multiple possibilities for action contingent upon the degree of control available. The portfolio career of the 21st-century drummer might require some creativity at the morning "originals band" rehearsal, none at the afternoon recording session for a jingle, and plenty in the evening session of improvised music. Such a scenario implies ready access to, and avoidance of, the creative impulse, an idea developed in chapter 2 as a functional/compositional continuum (FCC) of control.

As contemporary music fragments into a plurality of micro-genres facilitated, mediated, and disseminated by digital technology, so the bordered and defined understandings and activities of yesterday's musicians blur and mutate in a process that demands more or less constant reevaluation of who is doing what, with what purpose, and to what effect.[44] Fundamental to an understanding of the performer in this regard is her or his relationship to the composer. The composer and composition have a long history of having been privileged, most notably by composers, over the performer and performance. Historically, music creativity has been seen as residing within the individual and made manifest in the creation of the composition rather than its production or performance.[45] This dichotomy has led to the notion that the former act is creative and the latter re-creative, with profound resonances for instrumental practice. Contemporary performers tend to equate creativity with putting something of yourself into the music, an idea that would have sat uncomfortably with those composers from the classical tradition who required that the performer put nothing of herself or himself into the performance. Arnold Schoenberg deemed the performer to be "totally unnecessary except as his interpretations make the music understandable to an audience unfortunate enough not to be able to read it in print." Pierre Boulez has provided further evidence of the denigration of the instrumentalist with his comment that "instrumentalists do not possess invention—otherwise they would be composers." Bruce Ellis Benson has produced a partial list of classical composers for whom the performer existed only as their "mouthpiece"; at best as a "necessary evil" whose "function was to serve the composer."[46]

Within popular music, too, creativity is not always welcome.[47] Theodore Gracyk recommends that the drummer *find* a central rhythm rather than create one.[48] Musicians frequently work in areas such as traditional music that do not readily welcome creativity, seen as standing in opposition to or tension with traditionalism. Stadium rock, theatrical shows, touring ballets, tribute bands, and circuses generally require a stable, repeatable, standardized product on which others (fellow performers, dancers, actors, jugglers, listeners, and promoters) may depend. While nevertheless acknowledging that some of their strongest experiences may have been in public performance, some musicians choose to avoid its complexities altogether, teaching or performing only in private collaboration. Any level of creativity is unlikely should the drummer decide to hide, avoid, or disable the creative impulse, momentarily or over time, for reasons of accommodation, getting the job done. Dictionary definitions of "uncreative," while tending to circulate around the absence of imagination or original ideas, make little mention of the deliberate avoidance of such ideas.[49] The extent to which the popular instrumentalist may operate on a continuum of personal creativity, able to turn it on or off like a tap, remains clouded.

While to some extent the performer remains the mouthpiece of the composer, she or he appears to be moving closer to the epicenter of music creativity. Process and product are now construed as being embodied within performance, generally understood as the means by which the musical idea is realized and transmitted to the listener, as a step in a process. In his exposition of what he calls "musicking," Christopher Small observes that without performance, there *is* no music.[50] The sociocultural approach has sought to reposition the locus of music creativity *away* from the person or product and *toward* processual aspects such as those of collaboration and interaction. The perpetual revision now easily afforded by a technology unavailable to earlier composers tends to discourage the fixing of the text, and allows for audience and performer input in what is essentially a test procedure (or remix). In this way, composition comes to be a form of "processual object continually redefined through performance."[51] Among the young postmodern, postclassical academy art musicians Pamela Burnard interviewed, the composition tended to be seen as existing *in the per-formance*, with the recording a documentation that individuates the work.[52] Current thinking, then, takes music less as an object, more as an activity with others in which creativity is seen as a set of decisions and choices.[53] Göran Folkestad prioritizes the *process* of music creation rather than the completed product. This, he suggests, has the benefit of focusing attention on the creator's perspective; it is not the music itself that is the focus but the practice of music creation.[54]

What Counts?

Anecdotally there seems to be some agreement about the extension or scope of creative music performance; we all seem to have an opinion on what it is and who manifests it. Nicola Benedetti is surely more creative than the fiddler in the pub, the late Nina Simone more creative than Robbie Williams, an improvising jazz group more creative than a tribute band. But there is some confusion as to why this might be, not least, quite probably, among Benedetti, Simone, and Williams. If creativity is seen as a prerequisite for the production of musical art, it follows that where art lies, there lies creativity. If the medium of musical art lies primarily in deviation from the fixed and regular, as Carl Seashore suggests,[55] the question then arises as to who promotes these deviations. Instrumentalists on unpitched or semi-definitely pitched instruments have a long history of being seen initially as noisemakers and subsequently as inherently less creative than instrumentalists on pitched instruments.[56] Looked at another way, within current Western popular music there appears to be unequal creative potential lying dormant within the process of drumming and, for example, the process of guitaring.

Most studies of music performance concern themselves with Western tonal music from the classical tradition, the availability of notation providing relatively unambiguous performance goals. The principal topics tend to be the measurement of performance, contributions concerning models of performance, and performance planning and practice.[57] Engagement with the issue of performance creativity is notable by its absence. Matters tend to become more confused in the underexplored world of unnotated music performance where the goals may be flexible, shifting, even negotiated live during the course of the performance, as is the practice in some jazz.[58] Indeed, the term "performance" itself remains ambiguous. It embodies understandings of both the end product (which may be captured in material form) and the process. Extreme understandings count theatrical live performance alone,[59] but most include recordings, as the primary form in which the audience consumes popular music. In the light of a variety of couplings with music technology, and the consequent blurring of a clear distinction between live and programmed performance, locating what "counts" as creativity in music performance is problematic. What lasts? What haunts?

In the case of the Western kit drummer, I qualify his or her performance as a "playable" performance whose essential characteristics are that it is able to be performed in real time (or in one "pass" in recording studio jargon); that it constitutes the "whole" of that player's contribution to that composition; that it has the clear authorship of one identifiable drummer; that it affords the possibility of creative expression; and that it is addressed to another.[60] Following from this, the term "performance" is interpreted throughout as live performance, understood as the studio recording of a playable performance or the live theatrical rendition of one. Other theatrical appearances in the form of, for example, miming to a playback or the inputting of data in the construction of unplayable performances do not afford the possibility of creative expression in the sense here intended.

Such a delimitation of course runs the risk of ignoring the rapid advance of music technology in the postdigital ecology of music invention, in which one salient feature is the replacement of the primary intra-human relationship with that between the (frequently lone) human and music technology. Finding meaning in the quality of a "perfect" product rather than an "imperfect" process, the discourse here characterizes intra-human music creation as slow, unreliable, unpredictable, unrepeatable, noisy, and potentially unaffordable. The new paradigm promises a shiny new world in which these unpleasant characteristics have been removed and replaced with their opposites: speed, reliability, predictability, repeatability, quietude, and affordability. Humans trying to be creative in a room together, probably in front of onlookers, can be messy, hot, malodorous, and sometimes ineffectual, but may change the course of popular music. British progressive rock groups of the 1970s often rehearsed for extended periods in confined, windowless basements without air-conditioning. It seemed to me that the reason these gatherings so frequently broke up in disagreement and rancor had as much to do with the lack of fresh air and natural light as anything to do with the music. Data input, on the other hand, perfumed and neutered, affords infinite nondegradable attempts at perfection, decreases creative risk, increases certainty of outcome, and may have equally potent effect. What's not to like?

Structure

This introduction has set out the rationale, scope, and objectives of the book, and offered an overview of the relationship between creativity and music performance. Chapter 1 explains the philosophical and theoretical background to this study of mind in culture. Drawing from existing models, it outlines a selective subset of four dimensions of creativity to serve as a conceptual framework within which to explore the creative actions of the interviewees. Individual and collaborative drummer performance is examined in terms of selection, differentiation, communication, and assessment (the SDCA framework) in chapters 4, 5, 6, and 7, respectively. Dewey's pragmatist philosophy of art as experience and Boesch's action-theoretical approach are called upon to underpin two principal assertions: that (a) experience, the outcome of prolonged and accumulative interaction with environment, is generated by action; and that (b) the way to the human mind is through its cultural products and artifacts.

In other words, we musicians are what we do, and what we do is embedded in a complex social matrix of people, action, and artifacts. Interpreted as the outcome of interaction with environment, culture's utility as a concept here is that it both regulates action and provides a framework for meaning-making; cultural psychology becomes the process by which meaning is made. In this way the dominant drum culture shapes the mind of the individual and her or his actions in turn shape the culture. This process is depicted in an integrated model of the circulation of meaning (IMCM) to show how action generates lived experience, which is interpreted and assigned meaning, in turn informing further action. This idea supports both the transformative nature of action and my own view that drummer creativity is best understood in terms of significant situated action in context.

In chapter 2, we see how individual drummer creativity is constrained by the determination of musical material and control over its performance. The freedom to select from possible options is governed by the individual's perceived position on a functional/compositional continuum (FCC) of control, an artificial thinking tool that frames much of the following discussion on drummer-practice. The terms "continuum of control," "functional practice," and "compositional practice" are defined, elaborated, and connected to the drummer's decision-making process. Chapter 3 draws upon participant perceptions to situate functional performance in the contexts of (a) performing *for* a leader, and (b) performing *with* a leader. The nuanced creativity demanded for success in both contexts plays out in the case study of drummer Blair Sinta. Compositional performance is positioned in two further contexts of (c) performing *as* a leader and (d) *without* a leader, illustrated in the case study of Max Roach. The chapter concludes with a survey of perceptions of difference between "live" and "studio" performance.

Interviewee Ralph Salmins's observation that the "biggest challenge" facing the drummer with sticks in hands is choosing *what and what not to play* acts as the theme of chapter 4, which addresses the first dimension of the SDCA model, that of selection. The first section considers issues of agency and control, constraints of genre, style, and conformity, and technical, environmental, and ethical constraints, before going on to explain how the negotiation of these constraints informs meaning-making. In the second section, the choice of *how and how not to play* (i.e., how to perform that which has been selected) is described in terms of manipulating the temporal, metrical, dynamical, and timbral levers that lie under drummer control, to add value to the music through expression and interpretation.

After the drummer has laid a firm foundation to the music, the second prerequisite of creative music performance is the construction of some combination of interpretive and expressive difference, the subject of chapter 5. It seems to me that the individual drummer's core function is the provision of appropriate performance, upon which individual strategies and processes for the construction of difference might be overlaid. These typically include the finding, recognizing, solving, resolving, or avoidance of problems, and the identification of factors that enable or disable creativity. They certainly involve the change or transformation of the music in order to "go further" in the production of "something better or cooler," as Mark Guiliana puts it in his interview. My argument is that creative difference is embodied in the way in which options are selected, constraints negotiated, and surprise occasioned at the effect of those selections. What counts is not at all where you got it from, but very much where you take it to, and the extent to which you communicate it in the process. Chapter 6 tackles this third dimension of the SDCA model—communication—but before it does so the narrative takes a necessary detour to explain how the cultural psychology attendant upon membership of the drum culture is a key determinant of the individual's experience of creativity and the way she or he communicates it to others.

We drummers have come to be positioned (and to position ourselves) as a breed apart and a breed below. Our activities are governed by a cultural tradition that regulates and shapes the experience of creative practice, and take place within a community that mediates and promotes the psychological behavior and meaning-making of the individual. This is the case in all community-based activities. Embracing a particularly corrosive ideology, however, the broader drum culture (that enfolds the community) is something of an extreme case. I highlight just three sets of issues: first is the extent of the impact of the Cartesian mind/body split; second is the degree to which intellect is downplayed in practice; third is a set of questions about performance on instruments of indefinite pitch. This rather negative worldview is countered, however, with a heightened sense of aligned feeling and shared purpose, allowing drummers to negotiate and communicate meaning with and among themselves, co-performers, and other listeners through collaboration and sharing. The notion of sharing, common to both culture and community, is described in this chapter in respect of groove, meaning, Flow,[61] and the problems of marginality, identity, and homogeneity arising in practice.

Am I creative? Who says I am or am not creative? Who counts? Chapter 7 addresses several issues surrounding the fourth and final dimension of the SDCA framework—the assessment of significant difference. Reflections on many years of high-level performance offer a useful window into the way people conceptualize their own creativity. Here the interviewees are asked to reflect upon and assess the actions and processes of self and self-selected others, in the expectation that such an approach might not only reveal fresh perspectives on their own endeavors but also provide a yardstick by which to assess significant difference. (A table of the self-selected examples of participants' creative performances is provided in appendix C.)

Emerging here is a domain-specific creativity that prefers to frame "everyday" drummer creativity in terms of a symbiotic collaboration with another or others, the principal goal of which is to make the music *work*. Then, something further is needed to make it *matter*. As suggested, the process by which this occurs appears to be, in part, cultural psychological. Drummers think not only as individuals and human beings, but as members of a particular community with distinctive cultural traditions that allow us to ascribe meaning to creative experience, and to circulate and exchange that meaning. In the context of a broader culture that avoids associating drummers with creativity it comes as no surprise that drummers do not prioritize its pursuit, preferring to see it not as an end in itself but as something to be pursued *as may be necessary to make the music work*. This is one of the ways in which we do things *because we are drummers*.[62]

Chapter 8 addresses the many ways in which drummers conceptualize creative music performance by asking our group of players (a) what it is and how it is experienced, and (b) what meanings they assign to that experience. Even though a performance may be captured in repeatable form, the experience of its creation is unrepeatable. This ephemerality is neatly captured in another of Mark's observations, "the experience that disappears." Creative performance is not merely the collaborative or interactive experience, it is the outcome of music action that is communicated and judged to be significant. It is also a set of social and music actions whose goal is to enable or assist others to be creative. Creativity is situated within and mediated by the performance context in the moment; such contexts are characterized in terms of the receiving, sharing, or giving of direction. While all music situations are construed as more or less supportive of creativity, playing *with* others rather than performing *for* others tends to afford both the greatest pleasure and the greatest exposure to creative possibility.

The consistent execution of the core function of "making the music work" is necessary and sufficient for a low-level attribution of creativity. For a higher-level attribution, something else is required to make the action *matter*, an alchemical component that transforms the mechanical into the musical and the functional into the compositional, often encountered by "going further" than others. These conceptions are somewhat at variance with the current discourse on creativity within classical music performance, which tends to focus on the perfect rendition of the highly prepared performance rather than the testing of its boundaries. I identify four subthemes that encapsulate participant perceptions of the meaning of creative performance: allowing, trusting, connecting, and surprising. Each is briefly addressed in turn.

The last chapter of the book offers a synthesis of the previously elaborated ideas and asks how far I have been able to satisfy the original aims and achieve the main objectives of the study. I propose that future studies in Western music performance distinguish between classical and other-than-classical performance traditions, the two having drifted sufficiently far apart as to warrant separate investigation. The extent to which unpitched practitioners in popular music differ in perception from their pitched-instrument classical colleagues with regard to the topics of creativity and meaning is substantial but poorly understood; the degree of transference of research from the latter to the former, and within both traditions, appear to be sufficiently low as to call for further work to be done in this area. I conclude, first, that drummers achieve creativity in music performance by the effective communication of significant difference, and second, that creativity is both experienced and assigned meaning through significant action in context. In other words, drummers find creative meaning in making it work and making it matter.

We begin, then, with a look at the philosophical and theoretical background that underpins the ensuing discussion. Its omission by the reader will not unduly disrupt the narrative flow. Those more interested in case studies and interviewee insights might wish to spin on to chapter 2. For the determined, however, chapter 1 builds upon approaches from cultural psychology to develop an original model whose purpose is to depict the relationship between the individual drummer, the drum culture, and the way action gives rise to meaning within the cultural context. I begin by problematizing traditional approaches to creativity and map out an alternative path to understanding based on the precepts of the pragmatist philosopher John Dewey. I draw on the analytical concepts of Boesch and Glăveanu to connect meaning to creativity through the construct of significant situated action. The key points are then used to construct and underpin an integrated model of the circulation of meaning (the IMCM).

1 • Action and Experience

The Foundational Dimensions of Creative Performance

It is difficult to detect much cohesion or convergence within the numerous approaches to creativity or their application within communicated music performance. Traditional "stage" models of creativity emerging from a background of science or mathematics, such as that of the mathematician Henri Poincaré's four-stage theory of creativity (1908; refined by Graham Wallas in 1926) or the writings of Hermann von Helmholtz (1896) seem to have limited use here.[1] The activity of performance is perhaps too fluid and unstable, and complicated in no small part by the co-occurrence of the process and product. Sender/channel/receiver models of post–Second World War communication theory provided another early framework within which to examine the way in which music is communicated.[2] The composer's musical idea, it was suggested, is brought into acoustic reality by a performer (who may or may not be the same person), travels along an information channel within the mind of the receiver, and is decoded with more or less efficiency. From the performer's viewpoint, the central flaw here is that such a model posits a minimum of two actors: sender and receiver. Both sending and receiving may of course be actions of the performer's single musical mind. Other accounts seek to go beyond the basic transmission model by incorporating the multiple personal, musical, and contextual variables in expanded models. David Hargreaves et al.'s work on reciprocal feedback, for instance, comprises two separate but complementary models depicting the feedback of, respectively, musical response and musical performance.[3] Neither, however, addresses the meaning-making of the single mind of the individual practitioner in culture.

More useful for our purposes, perhaps, are modern systemic approaches to creativity, which represent a step forward from the long-standing debate between psychological and sociocultural accounts of creativity. These perspectives represent "an attempt to go beyond binary choices toward a comprehensive and integrative perspective, where there is an 'and' rather than a 'versus' relationship between individual and social creativity."[4] If there is an orthodox position in creativity theory, it is surely to be found in the "environmental" or "evolving systems" approaches propagated most notably by Mihaly Csikszentmihalyi and Howard Gruber, respectively, and reflected in the work of Pamela Burnard.[5] The recent turn to the sociocultural in musicology has been prompted in no small part by Burnard's conceptual expansion of the nature of musical creativities, elucidated in her book *Musical Creativities in Practice* (2012). Her inclusive perspective, which sees a multiplicity of music creativities as within the grasp of many, acts as a powerful counterweight to the exclusive astringency of those systems theorists for whom creativity is by definition domain-changing and in the gift of few. The lone genius paradigm seems to have met its nemesis in Burnard's plurality of creativities drawn broadly and seemingly available to anyone by virtue of unique participation in the domain.

Focusing on Big-C creativity, Mihaly Csikszentmihalyi's systems model of creativity (1988) enfolds a tripartite interdependent system by which creative products are continually generated and integrated into our historical and cultural experience. Csikszentmihalyi is among those who see creativity as a judgment, bestowed in a post-hoc appraisal of the artistic endeavor by eminent practitioners in the field. At the risk of oversimplification, his model proposes three systems—the domain, the individual, and the field. First, a set of rules and practices must be transmitted from the domain, in this case the drum culture, to the individual. Second, the individual drummer must then produce a novel variation in some aspect of the content of the domain. Third, the variation or new artifact is analyzed by a group of intermediaries or gatekeepers who stand between the creative individual and the broader society. In the drum world, that group might include influential music critics, recognized drummers, teachers, and professional associations. The variation must then be selected by the field for inclusion in the domain in order for creativity to be attributed.

If this astringent, gold standard, exclusivist domain-changing level of creativity represents one polarity of the evaluation debate, the opposite polarity is represented perhaps in the everyday, inclusivist "little-c" level of creative action to which all may aspire. But if all are to be ascribed as creative by virtue of elementary music performance, we run the risk of devaluing the term to the point of redundancy. The extremes of these approaches thus appear unproductive in so far as they have been applied to the context of popular music performance. As will be shortly evident from a case study of drummer Max Roach, they seem to be drawn either too tightly, permitting creativity in only domain-changing action, or too loosely, seeing creativity in almost any musical engagement.

One solution to the dilemma is provided by Vlad Petre Glăveanu. Carrying Csikszentmihalyi's formulation forward, his cultural psychology of creativity draws upon theories of the extended mind and distributed cognition to focus on "the dynamic relation between the self and others," conceptualizing creativity as symbolic meaningful action.[6] A cultural psychological view such as this sees creativity less as a thing, more as action in and on the world. Glăveanu's Five A's framework of distributed creativity locates the phenomenon not *within* people or objects but *in-between* action, actor, artifact, affordance, and an audience.[7] This line of thinking extends and broadens the original systems perspective such as to offer a nuanced insight into the multiple ways in which creativity may be invoked as a form of action.[8] In this view, and in this context, the creativity is distributed between (rather than resides within) the action (the drumming) of an actor (the drummer) and the artifact (the performance). Exploiting the existing sociocultural affordances (for example, the street-drummer's reimagining of a set of buckets as a drum kit), this distribution exists in relation to an audience (listeners, non-performing colleagues, co-performers, promoters, and so forth) and results in music artifacts that are considered to be new, useful, and significant by that audience.

We now have some theoretical grounding from which to suggest those foundational dimensions without which creativity in popular music performance might be said not to exist. Neither composer, score, talent, virtuosity, nor newness appear to be absolute requirements for creative performance. Music may certainly exist without the composer: most of the world's music has been brought to fruition without the benefit of formal acts of composition. It may exist without the written score, and have only a tenuous connection to talent or virtuosity.[9] Glăveanu's extensions to the original systems model, at once systemic and distributed, highlight the temporal, material, and sociocultural dimensions that escape the high-level domain-changing view and offers a useful analytic lens through which to view the everyday collaborative creativity of, for example, the "originals band" drummer, the funk guitarist, the everyday studio musician, or our expert participants. Without claiming to cover the entire field, I draw four aspects of creativity informed from the discussion so far to represent a selective emphasis on a subset of dimensions that are necessary for the enact-

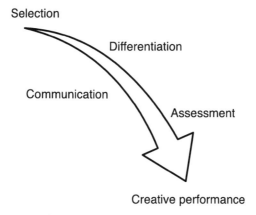

Fig. 1. The SDCA framework

ment of creative music performance. Taken together, the four strands of selection, differentiation, communication, and assessment (figure 1) frame and delimit the ensuing discussion, the many features of which might be distilled into a single overarching question: How do expert drummers construct, communicate, and assess significant difference?

First, something needs to be selected. In drummer practice, such selections tend to be made, at whatever level of consciousness, from a palette of temporal, metrical, timbral, and dynamical options available "in the moment" of performance. These options are selected within multiple constraints: of agency (the degree of control available), of style and genre (the projection or sublimation of stylistic preferences: if I do this it is grunge; if I do that it is gospel), of aesthetics (is it beautiful or ugly?), of technique (do I have sufficient technical ability to play what I want to hear?), of environment (is it concert hall or club, acoustic or electronic, analog or digital?), or of motivation (is it intrinsically or extrinsically motivated?).

Second, something needs to be differentiated. For any type of creative artifact to be original, there needs to be qualitative difference in some respect from any previously known instance of that type. For Glăveanu, "the creative quality of action, at all times, resides in how differences are negotiated, manipulated, widened or bridged by the person in concrete cultural settings."[10] What counts in drum performance is not where you got it from, but where you take it to (in other words, how it is differentiated) and how and with whom you communicate it in the process.

A third requirement is that something needs to be communicated. This SDCA framework requires consistency with a line of thinking that asserts the centrality of connection and communication; they are "part and parcel of what it means to create."[11] Music performance becomes connected to and interactive within a network of co-creators in several ways: for instance, audibly, through groove or feel; visually, through body language; culturally, through the sharing of meaning or ideology; or psychologically, through the engendering of feelings and emotions. Without communication, the putatively creative work is, at this point in its embryonic existence, on life support. Without communication there can be no assessment of significance—at least, by no one other than the creator. It has yet to connect with Csikszentmihalyi's field of gatekeepers, or Burnard's "field of struggles,"[12] or any outer world beyond the immediately supportive world of the creator. It has yet to find the oxygen of approval that will allow it to stand on its own two feet long enough to be deemed creative. Any divergent thinking or fresh ideas the creative agent may have remain merely as desirable traits if uncommunicated.

Finally, something needs to be assessed. But who is assessing what for whom? In the systems model, the assessors are held to be the gatekeepers in the field; all those who can affect the structure of the domain, or permit it to be affected. In the Five A's framework, the concept of the (individual or group) "audience" substantially broadens the idea of the gatekeeper to include, for example, novices, potential consumers of a product, parents evaluating a child's work, and persons from another domain who may "use" the product in unforeseen ways (for example, the use of recorded music as source material for sampling). Returning to Hope Mason, it seems to me that the crucial quality in the performance that is under evaluation is *the degree of significance*; not "Is it new?" but "Does it matter?" A performance may well be novel, useful, and appropriate, but its difference should qualify as significant to an audience. As yet, we have no single metric for knowing where or when variation becomes newness. In the sphere of music performance all variation is in some way new, but not all is significant, and it is precisely the significant variation that begets creativity. This observation gives us the key to unlock an operational definition of creative music performance: it is *the outcome of a set of choices and decisions, selected from possible options, communicated to and assessed by others for significant difference, in an interaction between at minimum an addresser and an addressee.*

This formulation is buttressed from three sides. First, the action-theoretical view I develop takes creative action as intentional, situated, and significant. Significance is produced by the articulation of certain ideas, beliefs, and aspirations within a "common network of assumptions and meanings." As Hope Mason continues, "New ideas can only become significant by engaging with that network in order to change it."[13] The performance of the student drummer who can knock out a passable beat on a drum kit in his or her bedroom thus remains unique rather than creative because, while only she or he will do it in that specific way, this particular performance fails to engage with the larger network of meaning. Second, a constructivist research design, embedded in phenomenology and guided by Glăveanu's work,[14] asks those who engage with the issue how they view the experience of creativity from their perspective. Our expert drummers identify multiple practices and experiences as important for creative participation in the music event, working within the constraints of tradition and culture but with sufficient room to strategically interpret and extend them.[15] Finally, a more pragmatic perception of creative music performance drawn from the philosophical orientation and fertile thinking of John Dewey provides a useful framework within which to view the crucial relationship between action, experience, and meaning.

The Philosophy of John Dewey

Three precepts of the philosophy of John Dewey, expounded in his influential book *Art as Experience*,[16] have particular salience to the developing argument. They address respectively the production, expression, and communication of experience. For Dewey, it is the cumulative experience of action over time, in a continuous cycle of doing and undergoing, that constitutes experience, which, in turn, may inform meaning for the creative music performer. The first precept addresses the production of experience. Beginning with the live organism in its environment, Dewey observed the interaction of the two from embryo to maturity, the crucial product of which is experience. Through his lens, culture is viewed as the outcome of a prolonged and cumulative interaction with environment, and experience is characterized as both a "doing" and an "undergoing" (a mirror to incoming and outgoing energy). As we listen (doing), so we hear (undergoing); as we touch (doing), so we feel (undergoing); as we look, so we see. As his model of human experience shows, action starts with an impulsion and is directed toward fulfillment (figure 2).

Second, and central to Dewey's thinking in this area, is the idea that creativity is the expression of experience, literally "ex-pressed" out of experience. If creativity is, in this way, a process that brings experience into meaning and significance,[17] so "the actual work of art is what the product does in and with experience."[18] To say something to us, Dewey contended, the art object needs to be expressive; by way of example he distinguished between Wordsworth's

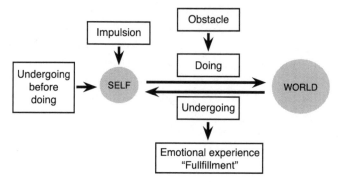

Fig. 2. A model of human experience, after John Dewey. Reproduced from Glăveanu et al. (2013). Used with permission.

1798 poem on the subject of Tintern Abbey and the factual, scientific statement of an antiquarian on the same topic.[19]

What gives the creative art object—"the juice expressed by the winepress"—its vitality, novelty, and distinctiveness is its connection to a prior (experienced) act or acts. If separated from the act of expressivity that brought it into existence, the art object becomes merely representational.[20] The self is characterized as assimilating "common-world" materials in a distinctive way to be reissued into the public world in a form that builds a new object, but, for that, experience is needed. The greater the experience, the greater the potential distance between scientific statement and artistic expressivity.[21]

Finally, the work of art does not work until it is communicated. Dewey argued that a work of art, "no matter how old and classic, is actually, not just potentially, a work of art *only when it lives in some individualized experience*."[22] In other words, a work of art is what the receiver makes of it. On his account, the several arts are placed on a spectrum. At one pole lies sculpture, expressing "the enduring, the stable and the universal." At the other pole is music, expressing "stirrings, agitation and movement [...]. The structure of things yields and alters, but it does so in rhythms that are secular, while the things that catch the ear are the sudden, abrupt, and speedy in change."[23] Following this, I develop an adapted and expanded model to throw the emphasis firmly on the stirrings and agitation of creative *action* as the means by which the individual (drummer) within the (drum) culture may be best understood.

The developing argument now has two strands. The first, sketched out at the beginning of the chapter, uses the SDCA construct to hypothesize that drummers achieve creativity in music performance by the effective communication of difference. In the next section, a second strand proposes that creativity, viewed through an action-theoretical lens, is both experienced and assigned meaning through significant *action* in context. The two are then combined to propose that drummers construct and experience creative meaning in the actions of making it work and making it matter.

Creative Performance as Significant Action

At approximately the same time as Dewey was conceptualizing art in terms of experience in the 1930s interwar years, three Russian psychologists—Lev Vygotsky, Aleksei Leont'ev, and Alexander Luria—were developing activity theory. One of the first postulates the Soviets agreed upon was the principle of unity and inseparability of consciousness (i.e., the human mind) and activity. To summarize, the essence of this principle is that the human mind comes to exist, develops, and can only be understood within the context of meaningful, goal-oriented, and socially determined interaction between human beings and their material environment.[24] Activity theory thus shifts the focus from the psychology of the individual to the interaction *between* the individual, a system of artifacts, and other individuals. Such an approach posits that activity is undertaken by a human agent (the subject: in this case a drummer) who is motivated toward a purpose or the solution of a problem (the object: creative music performance) mediated by tools and artifacts (the previous work of other drummers, technical aspects of the instrument) in collaboration with others (community and culture).

Activities are composed of goal-directed actions that must be undertaken to fulfil the object. The structure of the activity is constrained by rules, traditions, and conventions, and its meaning is constructed in action.[25] Actions are understood as consciously directed, and different actions may be undertaken to meet the same goal. Clearly, there is a good deal of overlap between the situated nature of action theory and the overarching meta-principles of activity theory, the precise details of which need not detain us here.[26] The focus here is on the former, not least because action theory asserts a common primacy of not only human action but also human experience and meaning.

Seen from this perspective, action is crucial to both the way music is experienced and the meaning that it is made to carry. The corporeality of this kind of meaning-making is emphasized in the developing field of embodied music cognition; the way music action is understood through the body. In his analysis of the "body at work" in the case of the singer Björk, Michael

Szekely describes the singer's facial convulsions and the unsettling reactions of the uninitiated listener on hearing the sound produced. One explanation for these reactions, he suggests, is because "the palpability of the body in Björk's singing seems to immediately register with/in our own bodies."[27] The body in my own drumming registers large quantities of sensory data that determine perception. I could purchase a sound reinforcement system allowing me to feel and experience the bass drum via a transducer system that delivers a powerful reproduction of the drum without any volume, transmitted through bone conduction.[28] The incoming sense data and my perception of them would be altered by this and other such mediational means, be they conceptual, physical, or symbolic. Cultural artifacts tend to reflect the experiences of other people who have attempted to solve similar problems at an earlier time and invented or modified the tool to make it more efficient. These are, then, "culturally impregnated resources," available for change in unpredictable ways.[29] One such artifact, for instance, is the expectation that drummers should keep time. The way that is done and the meaning ascribed to it may change unpredictably and at short notice.

It is through action, construed as artifact-mediated, goal-oriented, and intentional, that the individual thus transforms and is transformed.[30] The link between action and meaning binds the individual to the situational context in an unbreakable bond.[31] Drummers share learning, meaning, problems, and constraints within the context of culture and community, important notions further articulated in chapter 6. These correlates determine action, and action is always action in a situational context.[32] An action-theoretical approach such as this has the additional advantage of offering a firm theoretical basis from which to link significant action to creativity in drum performance. First, it provides the ideal lens to focus on individual action and experience in respect to actors' contributions to culture; ideas that crystallized in Boesch's symbolic action theory.[33] Drawing together the three elements of culture, individual, and action, all seen as inseparable from one another as well as mutually constitutive, action theory offers an appropriate way to understand the learning and negotiation of meaning that goes on between (music) actors. My approach thus converges with the contemporary line of thinking that interprets music creativity as a sociocultural, intersubjective, and interactive construct, as an action in between actors and their environment rather than "inside" individuals as a psychological phenomenon entirely located within the individual mind.

Second, an action-theoretical account takes one function of culture as defining the possibilities and conditions for action. The anthropologist Jean Lave's identification of the basic unit of analysis for situated action as "the activity of persons acting in a setting" is relational; the unit is neither the individual, nor the environment, but *the relationship* between the two.[34] The fundamental nature of music lies in action, in what people do. Through action, relationships are maintained and restored and humans may learn the patterns that connect.[35] It is through action that Lave and others have critiqued the shortcomings of the traditional cognitive science approaches to creativity, seeking to avoid the "cognitive straightjacket"[36] of the problem-solving frameworks of some creativity theorists.

Other like-minded thinkers have sought to link creativity to significant action, in support of John Hope Mason's observation that "to create is to act in the world, or on the world, in a new and significant way."[37] Some have directly or indirectly promoted the action-theory project within the music performance literature.[38] For example, recommending an examination of the behaviors involved in creative music-making and trying to account for them by identifying the processes involved, Irène Deliège and Marc Richelle argue persuasively for getting rid of creativity and examining instead the creative *act*.[39] Following this line of thinking, we can interpret music-making as creative action and drummers as potentially creative actors. If drumming is creative action, then drummers, I argue, are not only agents of change but also make meaning from their participation in change.

Several of the preceding ideas have been developed recently by Glăveanu in his action theory of creativity (ATC) (2013). Glăveanu weaves key tenets of Dewey's philosophy into a strand of thinking closely allied to Soviet activity theory, itself later modified by Boesch into symbolic action theory. Here, Glăveanu outlines the essential Deweyan elements upon which his theory is built and with which we are now familiar. Action starts with an impulsion

> and is directed towards fulfilment. In order for action to constitute experience though, obstacles or constraints are needed. Faced with these challenges, the person experiences emotion and gains awareness (of self, of the aim, of the path of action). Most importantly, action is structured as a continuous cycle of "doing" (actions directed at the environment) and "undergoing" (taking in the reaction of the environment). Undergoing always precedes doing and, at the same time, is continued by it. It is through these interconnected processes that action can be taken forward and become a "full experience."[40]

This key passage has been quoted in full because of its centrality to the ensuing argument. It is here that systems models of creativity on the one hand, and action theories of creativity on the other, overlap and find convergence.

It is here that the cultural psychology understanding of creative action as taking place "not 'inside' individual creators but 'in between' actors and their environment"[41] converges with the sociocultural leanings of those for whom music is less an object, more an activity done with other people in a community of practice. It is here that human experience brings action and creativity together, here that action informs and is informed by the broader drum culture, and here that action informs experience, which informs meaning for the individual music practitioner. Ultimately, it is here that creativity may beget significant action. As both a theoretical and methodological tool, the ATC not only helps integrate earlier cognitive models of creativity into a more contextual perspective, thus reuniting the psychological and behavioral aspects of creation with its material and social effects, but also advances the broader concept of creativity as action. Glăveanu is the most recent thinker to connect the pragmatism of Dewey to the action-theoretical approaches of Boesch and Lutz Eckensberger, the whole construct mediated by the cultural psychology understanding of Donald Polkinghorne and David Hiles. This book adopts and adapts this approach.

The ATC, however, does little to engage with issues surrounding the performance creativity typical of those whose functionality, usefulness, and validation tend to be construed as being "in the moment."[42] The reified product of solitary creative labor enacted away from public scrutiny may be easier to identify, isolate, and analyze, as in Glăveanu and his colleagues' work on designers, composers, scriptwriters, artists, and scientists, but tends to exist at one polarity of a creativity continuum whose opposite pole is occupied by the processual, publicly enacted, and predominantly collaborative creative labor of the actor, dancer, or musician. None of the five creative domains examined by Glăveanu and his colleagues in the construction of the ATC embodies the sort of messy entanglement with the (musical) obstacles and constraints from which the performer experiences emotion and gains awareness, and from which emerges the full experience that it is the work of art to communicate. All five domains permit revision of the creative product before its revelation to others.

To a significant extent, then, the crucial question remains unanswered. How do "in the moment" creators experience the phenomenon? Any new model seeking to illuminate the meaning-making of the drummer in culture will need to combine the reciprocal feedback of culture and mind that determines the musician-in-action. Building upon the same Deweyan foundations as Glăveanu's theory, I next introduce an original model of the circulation of meaning (the IMCM) to address some of the shortcomings of existing models. In its depiction of the circulating cogs of domain meaning and individual meaning, and their intersection at the point of action, the new model tries to illustrate the way in which culture and psyche are mutually dependent, and how, through action, drummers make meaning of their lived experience.

An Integrated Model of the Circulation of Meaning

The IMCM represents a framework for understanding the circulation of meaning within the drum culture. As previously outlined, Dewey posits that the organism interacts with the surrounding environment from embryo to maturity. In overcoming obstacles, that interaction produces experience. In the human experience, the product of prolonged and cumulative interaction with environment informs culture through action. The actor acts upon the cultural environment and undergoes feedback from it. Everywhere there is movement and perpetual change; like all cultures, the drum culture is a process in flux. The cultural psychology embedded within the culture shapes and partially determines individual goal-oriented action.

The IMCM is a situated action model that emphasizes the emergent, contingent nature of human activity, and the way that activity grows directly out of the particularities of a given situation. Its purpose is to model the relationship between the individual, the culture, and the way action gives rise to meaning within the cultural context. Such a model may prove useful because existing transmission and reciprocal feedback models of creativity are seen as problematic in the context of music performance, as noted above. Simply put, it shows how people make meaning from lived experience through action, itself shaped and partially determined by culture. The model attempts first to integrate two individual and collective (cultural) meaning systems, their development and interrelationship, and situate them within the same theoretical framework. Second, it seeks to bring culture in from the "outside" to the "inside" of creative action as a constitutive part. This is the objective of what Glăveanu calls the "cultural psychology of creativity."[43] Third, it complements Glăveanu's framework, which includes the Self, but "a Self that does not create alone but in dialogue with an Other, both embedded within existing socio-cultural systems,"[44] here construed as the localized system of the drum culture. The model shows us how, through action, drummers make meaning of their lived experience by integrating the cultural domain level and the individual level of meaning.

In figure 3, action informs meaning in the cultural domain in a clockwise circulation but only after communication and assessment of experience.

Fig. 3. The circulation of domain-level meaning. Goal-orientated action informs meaning in the domain, but only after communication and assessment of experience.

Domain-level variables such as the quality of collaborative relationships and expectations of creative worth inform both the action and its assessment for significance. Over time, the process generates lived experience, which, interpreted by Others, is assigned meaning, which in turn informs the drum culture and its psychology. The left side of the figure addresses the assessment of the action for creativity by the cultural gatekeepers or significant Others, a contested and poorly identified group to whom I shall return in chapter 7. The creative variation is then accepted or rejected by the (drum) culture, which in turn shapes the cultural psychology and future action.

At the individual level of Self, action connects the individual to the cultural context (figure 4). Action is seen as generating lived experience, which is interpreted, assigned meaning, and reflected upon, and that in turn instigates further action in a cyclical process. Meaning then forms a basis for possible change in practice.

For Dewey, lived experience, comprising factors such as learning orienta-

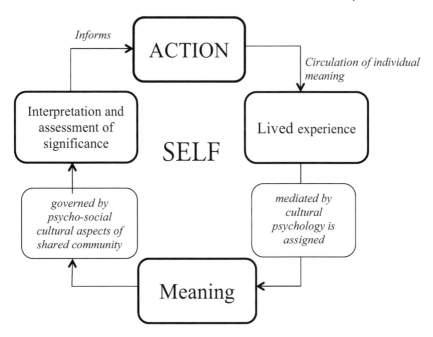

Fig. 4. The circulation of individual-level meaning. Over time, drummer action generates lived experience, which, interpreted by Self, informs meaning. Meaning forms a basis for possible change in practice.

tion, previous playing experiences, risk-taking propensity, and self-efficacy, is generated by the interaction with the domain in both a "doing" and an "undergoing," characterized as outgoing and incoming energy, respectively. Experience is necessarily cumulative and it gains expressiveness because of cumulative continuity.[45] Polkinghorne's assertion that "experience is meaningful and human behaviour is generated from and informed by this meaningfulness"[46] encapsulates the phenomenological undercurrent of this book, which concerns the structure of lived experience. An individual drummer engages with music through performance within a community of practice. Should the individual seek meaning in that engagement, to make sense of it, she or he must actively bring it into lived experience, here understood as the content of consciousness.[47] Individual interpretation of that experience assigns it meaning.

Figures 3 and 4 may now be integrated to give a fuller picture of the way drummers, through action, make meaning of their lived experience (figure 5).

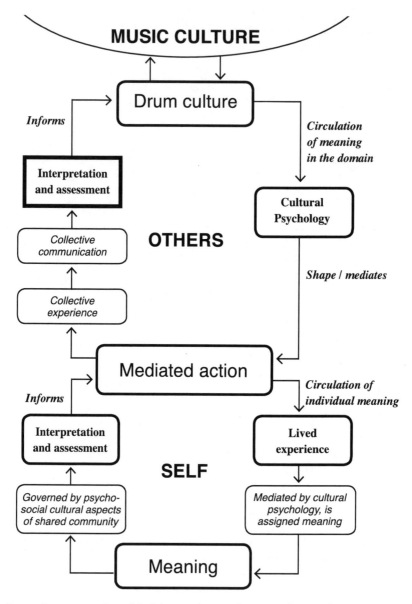

Fig. 5. An integrated model of the circulation of meaning (IMCM)

The clockwise circulation of the cog of the upper, domain-level meaning and the cog of the lower, individual-level meaning, and their intersection at the point of action, represent the mutual dependency of culture and individual mind. *Individual-level lived experience* intersects with *domain-level variables* (expectations of the drum culture, the assessment of creativity, and so forth) in action. Over time, drummer action generates lived experience, which, interpreted by Self (on the individual level) and Others (on the cultural level), assigns meaning to the experience (figure 5). Meaning is crucial because it forms the basis for reflection and possible change in practice or the domain.

The model shows how (a) through action, drummers make meaning of their lived experience; (b) the cultural psychology shapes and partially determines individual action, a precursor to meaning-making; and (c) drummer action is informed by and informs Self and Others in a fluid circulation of individual and domain meanings. Mediated action is then taken forward to become full experience, the communicative performance of which may be assigned creative significance by contributing to or changing the domain. The individual's interpretation of creativity is affected by individual-level lived experience intersecting with domain-level variables. Over time, mediated action, as the unit of analysis,[48] is interpreted and assessed by Others for evidence of creativity. Focusing on the interdependence of mediated action and cultural context as previously discussed, action may thus be seen as the link between the individual drummer and the drum culture, and accordingly is positioned at the heart of the model.

To understand how such a theoretical model might map onto the real-world actions and choices of the individual drummer, it is worth jumping ahead to the case study of jazz drummer Max Roach in chapter 2 and applying the model to his action-choices. In brief, Roach was faced with an obstacle: the action of playing four beats to the bar at 300 beats per minute for long periods of time, an increasingly typical requirement of the jazz drummer in the late 1940s, was unsustainable. The model suggests that the experience was interpreted and assigned meaning by Roach; presumably it was perceived as ineffectual and ultimately meaningless. After reflection, the action was altered significantly by his creative leap, which assigned the rhythmic continuum to the ride cymbal, thus permitting a complete reinterpretation of the bass drum function. This significant action generated further lived experience, which, interpreted by appropriate Others, was assigned creative meaningfulness. In sum, the experience, having been produced, expressed, and communicated by Roach, was attributed domain-level creative status in a process convergent with the systems model. There was Western kit drumming before Roach and there was Western kit drumming after him. The two were qualitatively different.

Two shortcomings of the IMCM will become apparent. First, assessments, judgments, and meanings as interpreted by individual and domain frequently diverge, and the model has little to say in this regard. For example, my own experience and anecdotal evidence support the frequently encountered disjunction in performance assessment by, on the one hand, the performer (or ensemble), and on the other, the listener (or audience) immediately after sharing an experience of the same event. So great might the disagreement be that performer and listener would seem to have attended different concerts. This syndrome was so prevalent in the rock group King Crimson's dressing rooms and the following day's press reviews as to pass mostly unremarked. It did, however, strongly reinforce the "them-versus-us" occupational culture identified by Howard Becker.[49] Second, there are temporal considerations that the model does not address. Clearly the circulation of meaning in the domain is much slower than circulation of individual meaning through performance action. The former may take months or years, as in the case of domain-changing creativity, identified as such in some cases only after the domain-changer's death. The latter may be nearly instantaneous with immediate localized change in the action, as may be the case of the jazz improviser. The implications of these discrepancies have yet to be examined and are not, as yet, reflected in the model. Further work may permit their subsequent integration.

Far from a global theoretical construct, the IMCM is a somewhat localized application of cultural psychology theory to the specific case of the drummer, drawing on the existing thinking of Dewey and Silvano Arieti. Arieti's schema illustrates the relationship between man and culture, which he viewed similarly as a dynamic circular process, in which man and culture are in a mutual dependency and in which the entire process begins and ends psychologically. Creativity is seen as an essential part of this relationship.[50] The new model presented here, however, both builds on and extends Arieti's approach. A similar dynamic circular process is elaborated, showing not only the reciprocal nature of the individual and cultural levels of meaning-making but also how the meaning systems depict the manner in which drummer agency is informed by and informs Self and Other. The model accords both with the idea that in a community of practice people are engaged with one another in action,[51] and the notion that musical creativity is a sociocultural, intersubjective, interactive construct, best seen as an action between actors and their environment rather than "inside" individuals.

To reassemble the bare bones of the argument so far, an action-theoretical perspective suggests that creativity and meaning may best be connected through significant situated action, here in the context of popular music performance. The IMCM shows how over time drummer action generates lived experience, which, interpreted by Self and Others, assigns meaning to the experience; meaning forms a basis for reflection and possible change at the individual or domain level. Action may be assessed as significant and hence creative. In the next chapter we return to the "real" world to investigate how drummers exert variable levels of control and choice over central aspects of their music performance.

2 • Sinta and Roach

Two Modes of Performance

One tool with which to make sense of what drummers do and the action-choices they make is the functional/compositional continuum (FCC), a construct that describes qualities of performance according to the degree of control available. If all art involves selection, it is difficult to attribute creativity to any musician if she doesn't have a measure of control over what she plays and how she plays it, or if, to borrow Lock's term, she can't "interfere."[1] A continuum of control may be helpful here. We can begin by introducing two artificial modes of "functional" and "compositional" performance (which should be viewed throughout as focal points on a continuum rather than as actualities), whose principal attributes are summarized in figure 6. These constructs are seen as embodied in the distinction between those who generally do, and those who generally do not, determine what they play and how they play it. Individual practitioners opt to locate themselves along a functional/compositional continuum of control. Action at one pole, we might say, intends to supply the expected; action at the other intends to supply the unexpected.

At the left hand (F) functional extreme of the FCC are those who play as directed by others with strictly governed license for interpretation. At the opposite (C) compositional pole, drummers determine and perform individual self-created parts, composed long before, just before, or in the moment of performance. The part may exist in text, in memory, or in the subconscious. It may be the result of prior consensual deliberation with colleagues, or it may be determined and framed in the moment by other musical events. The continuum depicts how drummers exert variable levels of control and choice over central aspects of their music performance. They do so through the manipulation of one or more "levers of control" (the foundation blocks of a drummer's expressive interpretation, to which I return in

F ⟵————————————————⟶ C	
FUNCTIONAL PERFORMANCE	COMPOSITIONAL PERFORMANCE

FUNCTIONAL PERFORMANCE	COMPOSITIONAL PERFORMANCE
• Extrinsically motivated, oriented toward the user	• Intrinsically motivated, oriented toward the creator
• Cedes control, choice, selection and thus decision making to others	• Exercises control, choice and selection from possible options in making decisions
• Neither contests nor defines genre or style borders	• Contests and defines genre and style borders
• Avoids imposition of character, personality, or self	• Seeks the imposition of character, personality, or self
• Intends to supply the expected	• Intends to supply the unexpected
• Craftsman-like; essentially recreative	• Artist-like; essentially creative
• Rearranges given materials to a preconceived end	• Rearranges found materials, concepts or ideas to an unknown outcome
• Economically disenfranchised, with no ownership of rights to the asset	• Economically enfranchised, retaining all or partial ownership of rights to the asset
• Passive/receptive	• Active/dominant
• Movement toward the functional pole represents movement toward the already known, thus decreasing the possibility of surprise	• Movement toward the compositional pole represents movement toward the unknown, thus increasing the possibility of surprise

Fig. 6. Principal attributes of functional and compositional performance. Functional practice is theorized as being at the left polarity (F) with compositional practice at the right polarity (C) of a Functional/Compositional Continuum of control (FCC).

chapter 4) and within the social, psychological, and cultural parameters of the *situation* within which the performance takes place.[2]

The continuum is relatively structured at the functional pole, and relatively unstructured at the compositional pole. Moving from the former to the latter generally involves "a shift from exercising deliberative rationality [. . .] to embodied involvement in performance where we move on the turning wing with what is being done";[3] in other words, a gradual surrendering of control, a shift from learning how to act to knowing how to respond. Elements of functional and compositional practice may both exist sequentially within the one performance. The absolute poles of the continuum tend to be inhabited only by those unable, unwilling, or unmotivated to adopt broader positions. Examples of extreme compositional practice might be that of the free-jazz practitioners of the late 1960s (such as Milford Graves or Sonny Murray) or the punk drummers of the 1980s; at the extreme functional end might lay the practice of a tribute band or that of circus or London West End show drummers. In these performance contexts, the self-identification may be so pronounced that the occupants of either extreme remain unmotivated to more flexible practice. In practice, most drummers tend to occupy a middle ground between the extremes, working from a variety of "scripts"[4] of varying degrees of precision provided by others or self-generated.

Supplying the Expected: Functional Practice

Functional practice seeks to push no boundaries in the recording studio or on stage, to question no understandings, to challenge no assumptions. It neither contests nor defines the stylistic or genre boundaries within which the drummer performs. Perhaps more accurately characterized as an attitudinal approach, functional drumming actively avoids the imposition of personality or individual character upon the music. Such practice is present in, quintessentially, a tribute band, for which the job specification is precisely circumscribed: namely, to reproduce exactly the sound, performance, and (sometimes) appearance of the original drummer. Functional practice supplies the expected and cedes control of musical materials and outcomes to others. Such ceding of control typically includes that of any economic ownership or share in the asset. Functional practice is disengaged (or disengages) from that part of the intellectual creation of the musical artifact that falls under copyright. Seeking no share in the principal business entity or group that creates the primary money-generating artifact, the functional performer generally plays no part as a stakeholder in the monetizing process. Milton Mermikides identifies an "asymmetrical currency of contribution" regarding the default economic status of the instrumentalist's contribution. Unlike those who provide the melody, lyrics, production, or possibly arrange, publish, manufacture, or distribute the product, the instrumentalist's performance has no necessary economic value.[5]

As an accompanist to musical theater, circus performer, studio vocalist, nightclub artist, or stadium rocker, the functional drummer's actions are typically determined by the appropriate idiomatic and stylistic conventions as translated through written text, verbal instruction, or prior knowledge of appropriateness. Such knowledge is usually derived from the practitioner's previous experience and adheres closely to the basic stylistic characteristics of the genre. Indeed, the style of the functional drummer is not so much the avoidance of style as it is the adoption of an appropriate style. The employer expects that the employee's performance will embody sufficient appropriate musical gestures to fulfil the necessary criteria for genre specificity. Such practice is adopted by the skilled, chameleon-like studio drummer, who can perform efficiently within disparate styles without attracting, or otherwise diverting, attention from the "true owner." His or her occupational understanding may be paralleled with that of the rank-and-file orchestral musician whose output is predominantly governed by the written text and the conductor. Functional practice assumes no responsibility for musical outcomes beyond the provision of a satisfactory performance, defined as the correct execution of the text in a manner that will as closely as possible satisfy the interpretive demands of employer, musical director, or producer.

As we have seen, considerations of creativity tend to entail some sort of post hoc evaluation in order to distinguish between the genuinely creative and the merely competent. Within music, those best positioned to do the evaluating, it is commonly suggested, are the listeners, upon whose recognition the attribution of "creative" depends. But which listener: the record company executive, the bass player, or the security guard? The individual instrumentalist's primary concern tends to be with the assessment of his or her performance by its "first-use" listenership. This comprises colleagues in the music-making process, chief among whom is the employer, be she or he the producer, an artist, a fellow instrumentalist, or, more indirectly, a record company. End-user assessment comes later and tends to be of secondary concern to the functional performer.

The art of the studio musician lies in problem-solving against a time constraint. Does the employer know what she or he wants and is she or he able to express it? Having located that, is the musician able to supply whatever is needed to make the music "work" (however that may be defined), and thus invite further employment? Interestingly, the definition, construction, and formulation of the problem is not of the drummer's own making; it usually comes ready-presented from the client or leader but it may be obfuscated in impenetrable language that the musician must disentangle and translate into meaningful, goal-oriented action.

These stages of problem-finding may not come sequentially and may have multiple aspects. There may be several problems simultaneously. The drummer's solution(s) may not work for his or her colleagues, whose active complicity is required to breathe life into any musical suggestion. On the other hand the drummer may well have "been here before" and thus be able to draw on her extensive experience to find a similar solution to that which worked well the last time she was in a similar situation, confronting similar variables. A creative environment is not always present in practice: mere competence may achieve a satisfactory outcome, and the genuinely creative may be unwelcome.[6]

Creativity in Functional Performance: Blair Sinta

These general comments on creativity in functional performance find specificity in the lateral thinking of Los Angeles studio drummer Blair Sinta, which he describes below. In this case, Blair finds one problem and is given another, along with a set of more or less favorable circumstances and a (short) time frame in which to solve them. Drummers frequently identify and solve problems while under personal, temporal, or peer group pressure. The sense of crisis, of having to do something in a hurry, is engendered in studio and live performance in which often-changeable audience and employer satisfaction is critical to job retention, yet counterintuitively may often be the locus of creativity. Drummers Max Roach and Jo Jones, active in a slower mid-20th-century world, had perhaps a little more time to arrive at their creative solutions.[7] Sinta's description of contemporary practice demonstrates the subtlety with which drummers can articulate and inflect the rhythmic feel of a piece to project aesthetic feeling across genre boundaries while under considerable pressure.[8]

Here, Blair describes the process of recording the track "4th Street Feeling" for singer Melissa Etheridge to a knowledgeable readership of drum community members in an industry magazine:[9]

> Capturing the vibe on this tune was all about restraint and holding
> back as long as possible without having it lack dynamics or energy.

It's definitely reminiscent of early 70s Motown, so we wanted to pay homage to that but modernize it at the same time. I used an 18″ bass drum with a goatskin head and a soft beater. In the rack tom position I put a DW 10″ x 2″ snare with a Keplinger tambourine taped on the head. On my left I placed a tambourine that I played with my left hand. In the first verse and chorus it is played on 2 and 4, but in the second verse the tambourine moves to quarter notes and the 10″ snare stays on the backbeat. At the second chorus I move to the main snare, which is a DW 10″ x 4″ snare tuned very low with the head loaded up with tape [i.e., heavily dampened]. This snare size tuned like this give a bit of an 808 feel and sound.[10] The 14″ floor tom with a towel on it becomes the driving rhythmic force here and picks up the energy. A ride cymbal enters at the bridge to give a more delicate feeling. The sound we created collectively on this tune was something that grew out of the three weeks we recorded together and something quite different for Melissa on any of her previous recordings.

In these sessions, Etheridge clearly depends upon and values Sinta's expert knowledge in a specialized area of the music: its rhythmic and timbral foundation. The drummer's understanding of how to "capture the vibe" of the tune is a sophisticated microanalysis that goes to the heart of the drummer's art: namely, how to "restrain" and "hold back" while still supplying forward momentum or "energy." It is also a problem that needs a quick solution: time is money in a recording studio. He is expected to be able to cross-refer widely to artists (Phil Collins) in other genres and styles (Motown) of music, and be fully conversant with their histories and current practice. In this case he wants to both "pay homage to" and "modernize" the Motown aesthetic simultaneously. His solution—"riding"[11] on the muted 14″ floor tom so that it becomes the driving force—kills two birds with one stone. First, it solves his restraint-with-energy issue; and second, for those in the same taste group,[12] such a gesture references Marvin Gaye's Motown hit "I Heard It through the Grapevine" in which just such a ploy is used to good effect. The use of the tambourines, both free-standing and taped to the smaller snare drum, further highlights and "modernizes" the Motown connection, while pointing to both the fluid nature and improvised approach to the mediational means, the drum kit.

From a wide variety of percussive possibilities, then, delineated and constrained only by these shared understandings, Blair seeks to produce exactly what Etheridge would have requested if (a) she knew it existed and (b) she knew how to get it. In this way he acts as the "invisible composer," offering creative input and problem-solving skills while remaining anonymous in terms of authorship. The disembodied nature of the description of the ride cymbal "entering at the bridge to give a more delicate feeling" further evidences Blair's composer-perspective and distances him from emotional connection to his performance (which in a very real sense is no longer his). Others may later decide, for example, that such delicacy is inappropriate, and remove, replace, or otherwise alter that part of the drum kit composition. Note also how the music dictates the components of the drum kit, rather than the other way around; the instrument itself is in permanent reconstruction in service of the music. Blair's reference to "the sound we created collectively on this tune" indicates that the sound is understood as being dedicated to this track only, and that the drum kit will be reconfigured for the next track. His generous and quick credit of others for the sound they created collectively both implicates others should it be found lacking further down the road and also underscores his persona as "a nice guy" with the subtext that this will increase his chances of being hired by the artist again, or by the producer for another artist.

The multiple levels of functional creativity embodied here reside in Blair's ability to first, function well in an ambiguous, abstract, and pressured situation; second, solve a preexisting problem within practice (how to "restrain" and "hold back" while still supplying forward momentum or "energy"); and third, solve the self-imposed problem of simultaneously paying homage to and modernizing the Motown aesthetic. Etheridge is conducting the sessions in a way that creativity theorists would understand,[13] providing "opportunities to experiment, negotiate, and make judgments within the social system in which specific works are created."[14] Having successfully identified, constructed, and solved problems, Blair evaluates his work as "something quite different for Melissa."

In practice, most drummers gravitate toward the functional paradigm, as Sinta does in the example just given, thereby avoiding much consideration of options. Performance tends to lie within the appropriate stylistic constraints that provide a rhythmic shorthand, with only certain approaches being permissible if the drumming wishes to remain within that style. Much of what drummers do is construed as re-creative rather than creative. They are typically seen as reconstituting the ideas of others from the written page (show, circus, theatrical drummers) or as interpolated from verbal descriptions or demonstration recordings, which is one reason why, as a community, they are not normally associated with creativity. Available options within a given style tend to be few. Boundaries that are surprisingly well defined, rigidly adhered to, and fiercely defended are circumscribed by notions of authenticity: "If I do this, I am a jazz drummer." "All hip-hop players do that." "A gospel drummer would never do that, so he can't be a gospel drummer."[15]

Appropriate selection from multiple options in the moment is generally interpreted as a foundational skill for satisfactory performance, be it functional or compositional. It may or may not be significantly different, but it should always be an appropriate performance, the core attributes of which I unpack in chapter 5. Degrees of instruction from others may vary considerably along the FCC and within any single text or performance, as will the extent of compliance with, interpretation of, and permissible variation from that instruction. All will have implications for notions of creativity. In so far as it is determined by another, functional performance provides less scope for creative action than its compositional counterpart, to which we now turn. Our interviewees may perform skillfully under the direction of others in the highly notated world of movie scores, studio dates, and big bands, but it is to their work as *composers of drum music* that it is necessary to turn for the clearest evidence of the expressive depth of their creative choices.

Supplying the Unexpected: Compositional Practice

If the core characteristics of functional practice are disengagement and disempowerment, the opposite is true of the localized imagining of "compositional" practice. In contrast to the former, the term "compositional" is deliberately selected to invoke Western art music notions of the "placing together" of musical materials by choice and with some measure of control over their production, subject perhaps to negotiation with others. Compositional practice seeks to push boundaries, question understandings, challenge assumptions, contest and define style, and elicit reaction through the imposition upon the music of a personalized interpretation. It exhibits a willingness to break with what Burnard calls "genre codes,"[16] and is subject to minimal editorial control. It offers greater latitude than its functional counterpart to juggle aesthetic and discriminative choice in a number of different areas simultaneously; compositionally (the actual notes played), temporally (when each note is to be played), metrically (where emphasis and accent is laid), timbrally (where upon which instrument and with what implement each note is played), and dynamically (what the relative amplitude of each note is to be). These elements are variously combined to produce a more or less expressive performance, one that may or may not have originated from, or come to be captured after the event within, notated music.

Compositional practice is typically adopted within improvising jazz, or some marginal forms of rock such as math-metal, punk, or progressive rock.[17] The occupational understanding here is more in keeping with that of the interpretive orchestral soloist, accepting of responsibility, identified and identifiable, exercising control through decision making, transforming the materials in his or her own image. The orchestral percussion soloist Evelyn Glennie neatly summarizes both her job and her locus of creativity. Her observation that "what I have to do as a musician is do everything that's not in the music" (by which is meant the written text) might serve equally for the jazz drummer, although her rock colleagues are seldom afforded such latitude.[18]

Contrary to Pierre Boulez's assertions above regarding classical instrumentalists,[19] compositional drummers in popular music do indeed possess invention in the definition and realization of their performances. In the sense in which Western art music composition became an "autobiographical statement" inseparable from the identity of the composer,[20] the composing drummer seeks identity through the adoption of a similar "compositional" approach. Like many artists, the composing drummer tends to seek change in herself or himself, in her or his co-performers and perhaps in the audience, but, above all, in the music. He may be afforded broader aesthetic horizons than that of his functional colleague; he may challenge, provoke, or unsettle either (or both) colleague and listener.

The components of a compositional performance tend to be devised either in real time as an improvising jazz musician, or (in the case of those forms of fringe rock in which the composing drummer is welcome) typically in advance of the performance, in the rehearsal room. What the drummer chooses to play may have its origins in the styles and vernaculars that she co-opts, mashes, bends, and blends, but just as likely in disciplines and domains outside those of music and drums. This accords with creativity thinkers such as Margaret Boden for whom combinational forms of creativity require rich stores of knowledge and experience outside the domain, and the ability to form links between them.[21] High-level composing drummers Terry Bozzio and Gavin Harrison have both spoken to me about juxtaposing ideas from art and design as creative wellsprings.

Such explorers tend to operate at the limit of the drummer's "known world," and strain to see what is over the horizon. How drums are played today is of interest, but of greater interest is how they may be played tomorrow. If functional practice is characterized by the approach of the craftsman, arranging given materials to a known end, then compositional practice requires the attitude of the artist, rearranging her or his own found materials to a yet-to-be-determined end. In so far as the compositional efforts of the drummer are realized within the asset-sharing framework of, for example, a royalty-sharing originals group, the compositional drummer is economically enfranchised, retaining partial ownership of rights.[22] In so far as he is obliged to bring his own works to fruition under his own auspices, the drummer will likely retain full rights to the musical "property," as almost all the expert drummers here have done on multiple occasions.

Whereas functional practice seeks to establish stylistic *competence*, compositional practice seeks to establish stylistic *individuation*, commonly manifested in choices surrounding the embodied constructs of "touch" and "feel." Both constructs are commonly applied to the expressive aspects of individual performance and tend to be interpreted as indicators of creativity. A drummer's "touch" may be understood as the aggregate of choice-selection in the timbral and dynamical aspects of how the instrument is to be played; broadly, which sounds to combine at what dynamics relative to each other and the musical context. A drummer's "feel" addresses the metrical and temporal dimensions of the performance, and may be understood as an aggregate of decisions concerning emphasis, timing, and placement of the note.

Jazz drummers are generally known and identified by their "swing," their unique touch on the commonly played ride cymbal beat. This cultural artifact is both measurable and understandable. Tony Williams's "feel," for example, is qualitatively and quantitatively different from that of Elvin Jones. All top players have, by definition, a unique touch and a unique feel, although not necessarily recognizably and significantly so. The systems model requires that, for creativity to be enacted, an aspect or aspects of these artifacts must be recognized by the field and selected back into the domain, as "Tony's swing" or "Elvin's thing." Neither "touch" nor "feel" is clearly bordered and understandings are subject to overlap; both, in combination, circumscribe and delimit a practitioner's individuated approach to style, which in turn may be interpreted as her or his "voice."

The functional practitioner adopts multiple touches and feels within differing music settings as the context may demand (be it a short phrase or passage of music, whole songs or compositions or collections thereof, or the demands and requirements of a particular producer or leader). Key skills here include the speed and flexibility to summon and reproduce the appropriate style at a moment's notice from a mental library of possibilities. In pursuit of the chameleon-like quality peculiar to operations of the functional practitioner, his or her style is, ultimately, no style. Conversely, the compositional practitioner tends to seek differentiation through the development of a singular, identifiable musical voice, recognizable in multiple settings, and far from which she or he is unwilling, incapable, or unlikely to depart. For an

example of a domain-changing level of creativity within compositional performance, we need only revisit in greater depth the work of Max Roach,
briefly outlined above in the context of the IMCM.

Creativity in Compositional Performance: Max Roach

Max Roach (1924–2007) has come to embody everything reasonably considered to be creative on the drum kit. In the short period from approximately 1944 to 1953 he redefined the role of the drummer in several areas,
opening up new vistas for subsequent practitioners. Jazz drumming underwent a particularly fertile period in New York City in the period after the
Second World War. The federal government was taxing any venue that was
offering singing and dancing, so instrumentalists were preferred to singers
when it came to hiring.[23] In front of a seated audience, the musicians were
able to fashion a tougher, less inclusive music, designed in part with eyes on
an African American ideal of high art, and in part to exclude other players
in displays of technical bravado known as "cutting competitions." Such
were the benign environmental conditions under which Roach spent much
of his career breaking musical barriers and defying listeners' expectations.[24]
He is acknowledged as the founder of a modern style of jazz drumming that
became standard procedure for players in the mid-20th century, and his
unaccompanied drum pieces are conventionally regarded as the gold standard of creative practice.

Roach's first variation was occasioned by both a problem and its solution.
The problem was unsustainable tempi. Until Roach's arrival, the bass drum
had conventionally been played four beats to the bar in 4/4 time, with peri-
odic accent, its primary function being to provide a steady pulse for dancing.
But marking out the steady four beats to the bar at tempi around 300 beats
per minute for long periods rapidly became unmusical and, in the absence of
dancing, unnecessary. The solution was to assign the timekeeping to the right
hand on a ride cymbal, allowing a wholesale reinterpretation of the bass
drum function in a process that became known as "dropping bombs."

Roach's choice of rhythmic placement echoed, underlined, or displaced
melodic motifs that lay implicit within the composition or any given solo.
With the rhythmic continuum now taken care of, his left hand on the snare
drum and right foot on the bass drum were free to prod, cajole, comment,
and support in an endless conversation with and between each other and the
top line melodic information. In discussions of Roach's work, the word "conversation" is in frequent use, specifically to describe the interaction between

his limbs, and more generally to describe jazz musicians' interaction within the ensemble.[25] Indeed, his own composition "Drum Conversation" is a cornerstone track on one of the most celebrated bebop albums of all time, *Jazz at Massey Hall*, by Charlie Parker's quintet (1953).

This first variation—removing the rhythmic continuum from bass drum to ride cymbal—appears to have prepared the ground quickly for a second, more conceptual innovation. Almost simultaneously, Roach underwent a subtle shift in perspective that went on to inform the essence of his playing, most notably in his ability as a drum soloist. Crucially, he now came to see the drum kit as one instrument rather than a set of several. The blocks, bells, and whistles of the "traps" set of the vaudeville and music hall era were performed upon by players with the approach of the symphonic percussionist, with a technique appropriate to each individual instrument, albeit handled by one performer. Even as the traps set was giving way to the trimmer standard drum set, Roach came to see the instrument as one whole. Like fingers on a piano, his four limbs on any combination of the seven (standard) instruments could produce chords, colors, and semidefinitely pitched melodies. Roach saw it architecturally:

> My first solo piece was called "Drum Conversation," and people would ask me, "Where are the chords? Where's the melody?" And I would say, "It's about design. It isn't about melody and harmony. It's about periods and question marks. Think of it as constructing a building with sound. It's architecture.[26]

These two key variations of (1) changing the locus of the rhythmic continuum from right foot to right hand and (2) reframing the drum solo in terms of structural design together repositioned the drummer as equal with others in the co-creation of the valid and durable new popular music style known as bebop. Roach's methods have become accepted techniques of the day; almost any drummer who sits down at the kit plays something of Roach. He came to be credited with raising the level of the drummer from the lowly functionary who kept time for the band to equal conversationalist within the whole band, when, for example, "trading fours" with the leader in Sonny Rollins's "Freedom Suite." His work was widely acknowledged within and outside the domain, with numerous honorary citations from the French and American academic communities in particular.[27] Viewed from the perspective of the systems model then, Roach seems to satisfy all the criteria of Big-C creativity. A set of rules and practices has been transmitted from the domain to the individual, two novel variations have been effected in some aspect of the content of the domain, and those variations have subsequently been selected by the field for inclusion in the domain.[28]

However, on the face of it, three issues surrounding Roach's creativity appear to run counter to the requirements of the systems model. First, and perhaps unsurprisingly, there seems to be an unresolved tension around the originality of the variation that the model requires. Definitions of originality coalesce around it being applicable to something that is not derived, copied, imitated, or translated from anything else. Music that could be so described, however, would be effectively unlistenable and probably go unrecognized as music. The great drumming "originals" like Buddy Rich, Max Roach, Roy Haynes, John Bonham, and Ringo Starr have clearly delineated antecedents in the work of their rhythmic forefathers, and it is precisely these connections that ensure their cultural value, relevance, and potency, if not their creativity. The minimum requirement is perhaps for an original or unique *approach* that results in the variation.

Second, if notions of originality also imply "being the first" to bring something about, there is evidence to suggest that Roach was neither the first nor the only drummer to make these changes. Drummer Shelley Manne, witness to events as they developed, is reported to have said: "Big Sid [Catlett] and Klook [Kenny Clarke's nickname] were the first ones to move away from your accepted traditional way of playing."[29] Finally, Roach's creativity may be seen as co-constructed, as much collaborative as individual. There is some anecdotal evidence to support the idea that the blueprint for the new drumming was as much initiated and nurtured by colleagues Charlie Parker and Dizzy Gillespie as by Roach.

The preceding exercise thus tells us almost as much about the efficacy of the systems model as it does about Roach's creativity. This sort of model appears to indicate that creativity among drummers is practically nonexistent. Since creativity is construed as the domain-changing activity of an *individual*, very few other drummers in many years of practice could be said to have fulfilled its requirements. From this perspective Roach may be seen as highly unusual—an extreme case, or outlier. "Evolutionary" paradigms like this go some way toward providing an understanding of how an observable effect (domain change) may be brought about but appear too coarse-grained in two further respects.

First, it might be argued that the systems model has difficulty digesting the more clouded, multiascriptive creativity that tends to emerge from collaboration. Musical creativity theorists, I have suggested, now tend to view the phenomenon as socioculturally constructed, an activity pursued with other people in a community of practice. The extent to which inwardly directed artifacts, such as Roach's unaccompanied drum compositions, were in fact created *socially* as a by-product of musical relationships with others, even if enacted individually and without accompaniment, is an interesting question that is not addressed by the systems model.

Second, temporal issues abound. Changing the way people live and think and act, the ultimate goal of domain change, takes time. Ascriptions of creativity are also notoriously fluid and changeable over time, as in, for example, the case of the 15th-century Italian painter Sandro Botticelli, or the Pre-Raphaelites, or anyone who played in progressive rock. The meaning of creativity is tied to ever-changing historical processes, technologies, and social conditions, and conceptions of the individual and society. The systems model can at best, it seems, ascribe creativity at only a frozen moment in time. The contention, then, is that Roach's work fulfils the criteria of the model, but is an exceptional case. Creativity in drumming cannot in most instances be understood in the terms set forth by Csikszentmihalyi. His systems model appears to be too coarse-grained, admitting only a few drummers in the last century of practice, and needs recalibrating in the context of the ordinary drummer. Big-C, domain-changing creativity, such as that of Roach, can only exist where the ecology permits.

Current sociocultural thinking is perhaps better accommodated by the idea of distributed creativity promulgated by Vlad Petre Glăveanu, among others (discussed in the previous chapter).[30] His solution to this dilemma involves reconceptualizing creativity as meaningful action, distributed between actor, action, artifact, affordances, and audience. His Five A's framework enables us to recast the subtle, nuanced ways in which creativity may be invoked. In Glăveanu's terms, Blair Sinta's functional creativity, for instance, is construed as distributed between his action (to self-impose a problem, that of simultaneously paying homage to and modernizing the Motown aesthetic) and his use of affordances and cultural resources (reconfiguring the drum kit) to generate a new artifact (the recorded outcome of his actions) for an audience (in the first instance, the leader, Melissa Etheridge) that considered Blair's action-choices to be useful and significant. They mattered. Viewed in this way, the creativity here is not a thing belonging to, or within the drummer; it is a quality of the relationship that connects two or more people in a common search for meaning, for understanding.

This analysis of Sinta's functional creativity brings me to an important final point. To the extent to which selection, difference, communication, and significance are present, creativity may be said to be accessible at any point on the FCC, subject to the constraints of genre. It is far from axiomatic that the rhythms of rock, pop, rap, hip-hop, and their multiple subgenres are propelled, for example, primarily by functional drummers (in so far as they are propelled by human agency at all) and those of jazz by composing drummers. As we have seen in Sinta's case, "simple and repetitive" (functional) rock drumming may be far from simple or repetitive. The tight constraints of tempo, meter, and dynamics characteristic of functional practice tend to focus thinking on the surface of the beat, or around the microlevel of its timbral and rhythmic delivery. Here, sonic and textural innovations are prized and promoted by drummers like Pat Mastelotto and Blair Sinta. Sinta certainly selected, differentiated, and communicated musical action, but evidently, and as yet, with a lower level of significance than that accorded to the illustrious Roach. (That assessment is, of course, subject to change.) A compositional practitioner would, however, find it difficult to avoid creativity altogether in a sphere in which the exercise of discriminative and aesthetic choice in the *origination of the performed part* is a necessity. One intention of the functional practitioner is to do things because other drummers do them (or to do the same things better); one intention of the compositional practitioner is to do things because other drummers do not do them (or to do them differently). The latter tends to generate that which lasts, and that which haunts, but both may embody varying degrees of creativity.

Different performance contexts mediate drummer action in multiple ways and afford multiple creative possibilities. In the next chapter, we go further in illuminating the thinking behind a drummer's creative action-choices by looking at how drummers navigate across the FCC according to a variety of scripts.

3 • A Variety of Scripts

Performance in Context

Ask a drummer about his current situation, and he will most likely describe it in terms of working (i.e., performing) for, with, as, or without a leader. The first two of these performance contexts may reasonably be grouped within the functional mode outlined in the previous chapter, the third and fourth within the compositional mode. Overarching both modes is a crucial distinction between two types of performance—"live" and "studio"—which I expand upon toward the end of the chapter. While in practice neither contexts nor modes are quite so clear-cut, as for example in the case of "recording live" (i.e., in front of a "civilian," non-professional audience), all our experts seemed to recognize their essential qualities, differences, and boundaries while acknowledging there are many shades of the ways in which people collaborate. The FCC is simply a useful thinking tool in the ordering of so disparate a collection of perceptions across such a wide range of practice.

Doing a Good Job: Performing for a Leader

The first performance context denotes minimal global control over the music, although much control over the individual's contribution may be retained. The for/with nomenclature represents a distinction that is not entirely trivial, and it continues to be used differently in U.S./UK parlance. Certainly UK drummers of my vintage played *with* people, not for them; one "played for" a soccer team like Manchester United. There was no coach in Led Zeppelin, the Who, or Yes, although at times in the latter one might have been useful. "Playing for" an organization comes with a whiff of subservience and a salaried position in the gift of an employer; "playing with" implies a level of collective collaboration that situates the performer and performance closer to the compositional pole of the FCC. Although the distinction may be fading, it is not too fanciful to suggest that U.S. groups continue to espouse the view of the drummer as employee with greater tenacity than their United Kingdom/European counterparts. Pushing the idea to its limit, one might argue that the for/with distinction was in this way embedded in the DNA of late 20th-century popular music-making on either side of the Atlantic, with an as yet unexamined impact on outcomes.

Functional performance is governed by a large degree of direction from others, and a successful outcome is typically seen as "doing a good job." One might be hired as an anonymous sideman ("just give me a [generic] bossa nova"), as someone else ("play it like John Bonham would"), or as yourself ("what would you do on this?"). Identifying which one of these is in play early on in the relationship with the leader/producer is paramount for a successful outcome to the performance event. Since the idea of leadership is fundamental to, and, in part, governs a drummer's collaborative action-choices, we can go no further without some elaboration.

•   Enlightened thinkers tend to view leadership not so much as influencing others to do what the leader wants, but rather in terms of helping a community to make meaning in its specific context.[1] It might be argued that the participants here have benefited from such enlightened thinkers: Frank Zappa, James Taylor, David Bowie, Robert Fripp, Van Morrison, Diana Krall, or Lenny Kravitz may have been difficult or confusing, even occasionally dictatorial, but seldom ineffective in their making of meaning. Our interviewees suggest there are multiple ways in which leadership is determined in collaborative performance. Structures of power within a given performance space tend to be fluid, contested, less straightforward than might be imagined and arising in unexpected ways that may require negotiation:

Chad Wackerman: We're playing with an orchestra; the drum set is right in front of the conductor, you know, the first violins are to my right, seconds and violas are behind me, I'm playing really quiet (*yeah, with sticks?*),[2] some; a lot of brushes. But Clifford Carter, the keyboard player, was saying "You know, basically you have to realize ... I know you've just started, but we're all following you, you've got to be the leader. Even though there's a conductor ... Look, actually James [Taylor] hired the conductor to follow the rhythm section," so that's how it's working because he wanted it to feel the way he's used to having it feel.

Chad Wackerman's telling anecdote about working for James Taylor reveals not only how such negotiations were moved forward by a third party (the keyboard player) but how conventional understandings (in this case, the role of the conductor) needed to be entirely inverted to accommodate the "feeling" of Taylor, the nominal leader. Part of Chad's expertise (and a necessary skill for drummers in general) resides in the accurate, speedy assessment of the locus of actual rather than nominal leadership in the music situation.[3] The leader with whom, for whom, or as which the drummer acts will likely have engagement with multiple communities of practice. This brings him or her into contact with a "multi-membership nexus of perspectives"[4] in the execution of his or her primary duty—the creation of a performance space. Etienne Wenger suggests using the notion of "brokering" to describe the way in which leaders can introduce elements of one practice into another: "What brokers press into service to connect practices is their experience of multi-membership and the possibilities for negotiation inherent in participation."[5]

A different situation might embrace the fringe experience of performance with others, none of whom assumes the leadership function (for example, free jazz or improvised performances). The extent to which any performance with others can be achieved without some degree of leadership, no matter how unstated, is debatable and perhaps beyond the scope of this book. We should note in passing, however, that while collective improvisation, for example, may purport to be leaderless, the music is furthered at any given moment by one actor or another. She who "gets to the next note first" may be described as exerting leadership, and is certainly, if involuntarily, exerting a temporal authority.

These general comments on leadership in music provide a contextual frame within which to examine how and to what extent creativity might subsist in the functional performances required of what Ralph Salmins calls the "lesser gigs." Participants adopt contrasting approaches to these, which are seen as somehow less supportive of creativity than compositional performances. Mark Guiliana has a straightforward conception of functional performance as embodying a "much more traditional role or model of drummer-sideman playing someone else's music (*finding the best thing for it, to make it work . . .*) yeah, exactly." For him, having the freedom to "interfere" in order to make the music work appears to distinguish a potentially creative performance space.

With his pejorative use of the term "pattern players," Chad identifies the salient characteristics of functional practitioners while preferring to distance himself from their practice:

I know people who are pattern players and they like to play what they know, and they sound good and they're comfortable, but that's not me at all.

In hard functional performance, all overt choice and control and "a level of responsibility" for the success of the project are ceded to the producer/leader and according to Ralph "I'm told exactly what to do." Asked how he feels about this, his reply is ambivalent: "I like it, I like it. Erm . . ." Perhaps unwilling to be seen as a "pattern player," he appears somewhat defensive about performing functionally. His repeated yet hesitant assertion that he likes being told exactly what to do belies the fact that, a little later on in the interview, he refers to the lesser gigs that "didn't warrant creativity." He ascribes his eventual creative burnout to "just doing so much music that required regurgitation of parts and it wasn't feeding my soul and it wasn't feeding my creativity." His remedy for this is to decline the lesser gigs and move further toward compositional practice: "*You started to decline less creative* (yes) *areas* (entirely) *to accept and encourage more creative areas?* 100 percent; that's exactly right." Despite his confirmation of my summary of his career path, there seems to be a sensitivity, as if he has taken it as mildly critical; he searches for reasons and justifications. He contrasts what he does with "creative" projects "where the music is central . . . it's got no commercial desire" and "I can do anything." On further reflection, he considers that "if something requires me to play in a certain style, as most of my gigs do, then I'm happy to do that and I don't feel it's stepping on my creativity."

• In fact, much popular music at the hard functional polarity on the continuum of control is performed without creativity as a goal. As I have touched upon, the creativity manifest in departure from the norm may not always be welcome. Several participants confirm this observation. The leader with whom Asaf Sirkis was working

was not comfortable because he felt that I was "improvising" too much quote unquote and it was not exactly like the album and he wanted things to be like the album.

Ralph Salmins concurs:

I played in a lot of [London] West End shows, played in a lot of bands that played very simple . . . well, parts that needed repeating; like if you were in a pop gig you've just got to repeat the part. If you go off that part then people complain.

Welcome or not, most saw the availability of choice and the exercise of control, and thus creative potential, in any genre or at any position on the FCC. Martin France's conception of creativity as being "sympathetic to any situation you might walk into; to be musically creative enough to be able to walk into a situation and play exactly the right thing for the music," allows him to perceive of creativity as potentially available in any situation. Peter Erskine agrees, reasoning that there are always more or less appropriate choices to be made:

> Every piece of music we play [. . .][6] however big or small that might be, or dramatic, or non-dramatic, it's filled with those possibilities . . . I mean, a 28.5 second breakfast cereal commercial doesn't give you a whole lot of elbow room but still there are some choices, albeit far less than a larger-form piece.

Martin agrees that elbow room is available even within the functional confines of doing a good job in musical theater or studio work. Creativity trickles down or "dribbles through" from the composer or musical director, the very looseness or vagueness of the musical direction itself being conducive to creative thinking:

> If you're working with a composer or a musical director, the creativity, if you'll pardon the expression, sort of dribbles through. He's got more of a creative idea that he then gives to you to create . . . because of the role of the instrument it's not like it's terribly defined, anyway. So even if you do a regular session for somebody, they might say something like "this is like a '60s soul thing like so-and-so and so-and-so; can you . . . maybe 16s on the hi-hat or something" there's still a lot of creativity, I find, in that.

Performance limitations may, of course, be imposed by a leader who *doesn't want* creativity from the drummer. Cindy Blackman Santana's distinction between "creative music . . . that's my favorite music," and what she sees as "non-creative" or "uncreative" pop music is characterized by the intentional or unintentional prohibition on interaction that she associates with the genre—"the oftentimes lack of letting and allowing." A related question asks how much creativity might be involved in fulfilling a tradition. Thomas

Strønen puts a generous spin on his critical assessment of the unchallenging functional performances of some modern stadium rock drummers as they "fit just into that tradition" and "fulfil that piece of musicianship," while acknowledging that he

> couldn't physically have played the whole concert like that, because I'm not like that, and I [would have] fucked it up, and at the end I would end up getting fired not because I'm not skilled enough to play it, but I haven't got the force to do that music.

Guiliana and Erskine adopt the most positive approaches to working *for* someone. Guiliana "exploits" it; he "enjoys the challenge." When he says "I really like the discipline that is required to execute that kind of precision," he speaks to the close relationship between creativity, discipline, and learning, and underpins the thread of developmental thinking that suggests that we learn by creating.[7]

Emerging here is the idea that these experts tend to see creativity as inherent in any music performance outside their comfort zone in part because of the potential for learning. A final instance will suffice. A potential employer has asked Salmins to play on his recording having heard him play some drum'n'bass: "I said, well, I'm not a drum'n'bass drummer. He said, 'I don't care.'" Ralph's eventual acceptance of the job is based on the possibility for learning and improved skill use in that genre. Referring to the functional demands of a different leader, he reports that, in the Waterboys, "Mike [Scott] in general tells me what to play. [. . .] But I'm being creative and I'm learning from it."

Peter Erskine characterizes functional performance as "enabling" others to do something[8] or accompanying them while they do it. He finds both activities entirely creative because

> in the role of accompaniment where it applies specifically to the drum set, the drummer is faced with an infinite number of choices that he or she can make. Ringo playing on a floor tom as opposed to playing on a hi-hat; Harvey Mason on "Chameleon" anticipating the snare backbeat with that 16th note syncopation as opposed to just playing on two and four; two examples that come to mind.

Using studio drummer John Robinson as an exemplar of creativity in this type of performance, Peter observes that Robinson didn't fall prey to the jazz drummer's thing of "I'm going to, or I must, play it differently every time." He would hone that part, perfect it, and craft what was not only a creative drum part but a very reliable drum part for the song and so that's a form of creativity that to my mind is very highly developed, yet at first glance may not fit our expectation of "oh, that's a creative part."

Thomas Strønen and Asaf Sirkis, however, both occupants of terrain close to the pole of high compositional performance, exhibit a pronounced antipathy toward some of the key dimensions of functional performance:

> *Asaf Sirkis:* Whenever people <u>insist</u> on really giving me . . . like, very, very strict directions about where the bass drum should be, how the hi-hat should be, you know, how I should tune my snare and so on and, and, all that kind of thing, I, I don't really feel comfortable and usually I would not stay in that situation for very long, you know, I would always respect my commitments if it's a gig, if it's a recording, but I would maybe discontinue that situation.

For Asaf, the idea of "functional" summons images of servitude, compliance, and loss of power that induce discomfort and are at odds with his existing self-identity. Although Robinson was not interviewed, it might not be too far a step to deduce that, for him, the notion of "compositional" summons different but equally negative images of performance excess, unreliability, and self-indulgence (and hence of ensuing unemployment) that induce an equally uncomfortable clash with *his* self-identity.

•   The degree of creativity in functional performance is often construed in terms of the production of comfort or discomfort for the leader or co-performers. Chad Wackerman shares drummer Steve Gadd's perception of the goal of the functional performer. He reports Gadd as saying: "I really want to give them whatever it is that they need and what's important, to make <u>them</u> feel comfortable." Bringing something fresh to the music, by which is meant offering suggestions as to how the music might be improved rhythmically or texturally by the removal or addition of elements, in a process that the leader has not (yet) conceived or realized, may be acceptable so long as she or he is "comfortable." According to Chad, some leaders like further input; some do not: "And James [Taylor] likes

that. He likes that . . . another personality type would not like that at all."
For example:

> *Chad Wackerman:* [Producer and composer] Steve [Wilson] is very
> structured in his thinking, but most of the guys in the band are play-
> ing parts and I have to play certain beats and parts that he wants to
> hear; he wrote them and he's not comfortable with anything else, so
> I'm fine with that; he wrote it, he's the composer.

The functional relationship between leader and sideman is frequently interpreted in terms of the locus of power: two interlinked perceptions warrant
mention. The first concerns the properties of the instrument itself: drums
can be powerful. Within the drum community, the drum kit is seen as having
a greater sonic facility to shape the music than other instruments common to
popular music ensembles. Second, partly as a consequence of the first perception, drummers see themselves as having the greatest power of all popular
music instrumentalists to affect outcomes. These perceptions indicate the
distance between the way drummers are seen and the way drummers see
themselves, between what is expected of them and what they expect of themselves, and underscore the oscillation between centrality and marginality. I
return to this theme in chapter 6.

According to our experts, the salient musical aspects of the relationship
between leader and sideman thus remain the prerogative of the drummer. In
Chad's view "we're hired by the leader, they have the final say on things (*yeah*)
but it's our band. It's the drummer's band, always." Martin France agrees that
somehow the power to "make it work" ultimately devolves to the drummer:

> I don't mind being told what to play. I'm quite happy. We've got a lot
> of power playing the drums, haven't we? [. . .] Even if you book me for
> something and you say "play that," then I'm still the drummer control-
> ling a certain amount, not that I'm a control freak or anything . . . it is
> very important that we get it right, put it that way.

These observations not only reflect the multiple evocations of the adage
about a band being only as good as its drummer, but also evoke a conspirato-
rial view of the covert nature of the power structure. From the practitioner's
point of view, the ball always remains in his or her court, *even though the client or leader may not know it.*

In the historical context of the advent of proto music technology in the
1980s, early drum programming frequently rendered the music stiff, awk-

ward, or otherwise uncomfortable, and the functionality of the performance lay in the drummer's ability to make it "feel like music" in contrast to "mechanical patterns":

> *Chad Wackerman:* In the '80s sometimes it was . . . just uncomfortable. If you were dealing with a producer who was a programmer, who came from a programming mind, and he thought of drumming as just levels, he thought of a bass drum part, a snare drum part, a hi-hat part, and he didn't see the thing as a whole. That would be sometimes odd. I could usually kind of figure it out, but the whole goal for me was always to make it feel like music and not like mechanical patterns.

In this first context of performance for a leader, "doing a good job" means "making it feel like music." In the broader thematic context, "doing a good job" tends to mean "making the leader sound good" and by extension "making it [the performance situation] work," an action imbued by participants with greater creative potential than might be expected.

Allowing Me to Be Me: Performing with a Leader

The second performance context is the next closest to the compositional pole but remains on the functional side of the FCC midpoint. There are degrees of functionality in any performance *with* a leader; varying degrees of input are required and expected. Here the constraints on selection and control are somewhat loosened, with those dimensions becoming increasingly available for negotiation between nominal equals, thus "allowing me to be me." In time, the expert sideman (for that is what he continues to be, for the time being) becomes known for a plethora of skills, preferences, and techniques for which he may be specifically hired because he will, it is hoped, suit the musical context.

> *Chad Wackerman:* People I guess after that . . . they'd like to hire me allowing me to be me, which is lucky, very lucky. Not all the time; I mean sometimes I'm a complete sideman, I'm paying the rent, you know . . . and happy to do so.

Most find this aspect of any employment "<u>very</u> encouraging," because according to Ralph Salmins "it's much more creative." Asked if one leader would accept creative input, Ralph replied:

He would if he liked it, which is a really nice way of working because if I've got something . . . he's the songwriter and he's got a good idea, but always obviously you don't go and see a doctor and then tell them what's wrong with you . . . that's the other thing with a drummer, if you let the drummer contribute to the music, if their ideas are good, and hopefully our ideas are good, then it's worth having.

This idea of letting the drummer contribute is picked up by Cindy Blackman Santana. Lamenting the lack of interplay in some genres of popular music, which she characterizes as the "lack of letting and allowing," Cindy emphasizes the benefits of both:

If you give in to the music and you allow the music to go where the energy is . . . the people creating it and what's coming in from the universe when you do create, if you allow those things, those energies, to fill up the music, and you let that happen, then music takes on shapes and forms before you've even said "okay, I want it to turn left here or turn right here" or do whatever.

In her view, for music to work it must be "allowed to go where the energy is" so it can take on "shapes and forms" even before the imposition of her desires. Even when she's playing "in a situation that is not creative, I still hear things going on in my head; I still hear things that could happen in the music . . . whether they are allowed to happen or not." She expands this idea a little later in the interview:

As my husband [guitarist Carlos Santana] says: "Willingness to allow, and allow willingness." Because you're absolutely right . . . everybody is creative in different ways. Everybody has creativity in different areas, different ways, different aspects. But do we have the willingness to allow that creativity? Are we allowing our willingness to bring about that creativity?

Cindy's own music, in fact, depends on "everybody's input to some degree. It needs everybody's heart; it needs everybody's openness and willingness to allow." The theme of "letting" and "allowing" is revisited and extended in chapter 8 as the first of four subthemes that encapsulate our participants' perceptions of the meaning of creative performance: allowing, trusting, connecting, and surprising.

•　　As skills and efficiencies develop, benefits accrue from close working relationships with talented and experienced leaders. Ralph Salmins with Van Morrison; Chad Wackerman with Frank Zappa or James Taylor; Peter Erskine with Joe Zawinul; Martin France with John Taylor or Kenny Wheeler; Mark Guiliana with David Bowie or Brad Mehldau; myself with Jon Anderson or Robert Fripp: these leaders provide both the space in which creative action is developed and the conditions under which it is nurtured and sustained. In connection with Zappa, Chad states simply that "to be honest, he gave me so much confidence." He explains that

> by working with Frank, again, I think it made me prepared kind of for anything, because we never knew what he was going to do on stage; you just had to trust that this is going to be really good. And we all have enough ability here where we can all make this really good, whatever he throws at us.

Reflecting on his time with Van Morrison, Ralph talks in terms of the classic master-pupil relationship:

> I just learnt a lot from him as a musician, and it taught me a lot about creativity . . . Some of the things he said about . . . not playing what's on the album, I want your stuff on this.

At this subtle, relatively underrepresented position on the FCC, where working *for* someone becomes working *with* someone, verbal instruction is minimized, although there may be some use of written music. The assumption is that the individual knows what to play, that his or her experience will guide the provision of an appropriate performance at the blurred midpoint between the functional and the compositional. For Martin France, there may be an emotional connection:

> I felt very proud to be not only in his [trumpet and flugelhorn player Kenny Wheeler's] company but in the company of the band, and to be able to present that music and play that music. Kenny is getting older; the music's becoming more refined, but yet more emotionally charged at the same time. So it's almost like it's becoming—not simpler—more refined, but more emotional.

Almost all participants spoke at length of the importance of one or more fruitful and sometimes intense musical relationships with these and other leaders. To some extent, their perceptions of rhythmic creativity are refracted through the leader's harmonic or song-based creativity. Martin, for example, enjoyed a high level of musical communication with pianist John Taylor, whose goal was the removal of "barriers, borders, and bar lines":

> What kind of frustrates me sometimes is when I hear jazz musicians go "As a jazz player, my goal is that I need to know where I am all the time, and I'll never lose the time, and I'll know where I am in the structure, and I'm going to nail it da da da . . ." Well, he [John] is the opposite. That's not what it's about for somebody like him because he's trying to remove all those barriers and those borders and those bar lines. Not in a superficial or obvious way; it's not like he sets out to do that, it's just how he feels the music.

Referencing Van Morrison's strategy, Ralph Salmins highlights the value of what he calls the "first take syndrome." This approach prioritizes a sense of immediacy with minimal repetition, and says "a lot about creativity in my opinion":

> *Ralph Salmins*: When you play a first take or you play a piece of music for the first time [. . .] you are going through a fresh creative process. When you play that piece of music a second time, back to back, that creative process has changed completely. (*It's changed into a re-creative process.*) Correct, and that is radically different, and Van doesn't like a second iteration of the tune in the studio or live even on the same day. So he doesn't like to play any of his songs even in a sound check. He likes to go on, or walk in the studio, and play them . . . once. (*That's called jazz.*) It is! It is! And that's basically sort of the crux of what I got from Van, more than anything . . . is to allow that creative process to happen.

Such an approach requires trust in the co-performers which, in this case, leads to successful outcomes. Additionally, working with people on a high level of performance can be transformative:

> *Thomas Strønen:* Some musicians you play with, you know, they make you a better musician. Some musicians do something to you that takes you to a different level.

Working for and with knowledgeable leaders is thus perceived as beneficial in multiple areas of performance practice: recording, rehearsing, composition, band-leading, and business skills. Such relationships provide the skill set and knowledge base upon which expert drummers sometimes build parallel "solo" careers, one necessary component of which is a musical identity, forged over the course of a working life. A performer's self-identification frames the creative experience and is one of the factors that interprets it and assigns it meaning. The development of an individual "voice" on the instrument is seen as one path to musical identity. Mapping the development and expression of identity along the FCC might offer insight into the point at which the expression of identity moves from suppression to projection, the point at which "doing a good job" becomes "allowing me to be me." A close working relationship with a leader, then, serves not only as a framework for individual performance creativity but also as a seedbed of identity construction.

Performing *with* someone rather than simply *for* someone evokes a hierarchical distinction, one that affords the possibility of a contribution beyond "mere" execution. Here, the drummer is caught awkwardly between two strands of oppositional thinking in regard to performance consistency. On the one hand, as Dewey insists, rhythm involves constant variation.[9] In so far as there is no variation there is no rhythm; to these ears much ineffectual music has been brought into existence on that premise.[10] On the other hand, the commercial imperative requires the consistency of functional performance. Understandings that deprecate rhythmic "inconsistency" and the "taking of liberties" while implying a degree of irresponsibility sit awkwardly with those that insist that artists have always taken liberties with music because those liberties "distinguish mechanical or purely objective construction from artistic production."[11] As we have noticed, expert drummers see creative variation as available in the smallest of gestures, in the tightest of corners. The idea of playing "out of time" consistently and with precision, for instance, is examined as one use of the temporal "lever of control" available to any drummer, and is further articulated in chapter 4. To play in such a way demonstrates a high skill level and is one point of reconciliation between the two concepts of rhythm. It is at their intersection that many, in the real world of the drummer, begin to develop a distinctive style or voice.

Special Chemistry: Performing as a Leader

We have seen how the musical and conceptual direction of the performance appears to be more freely shared when performing *with* a leader than in the context of performance *for* a leader. In the next context, that of performing *as* a leader, control tilts further in favor of the individual actor—in this case the compositional drummer. In this process, drummers tend to look for an empathetic relationship, a "special chemistry" with co-performers upon which to construct a situation that will support the compositional project. One difficulty identified by Dylan Howe is that "you only get those kind of combinations of that special chemistry like you [the author] had very rarely, don't you?"

Emphasizing the importance of the connection he has with the other musicians, Asaf Sirkis describes the early stages of this empathy: "it's when you feel firstly that you like the people who are playing . . . you like their playing, you like their sense of musicality and their musical sensitivity, and they like yours." This like-mindedness is discernible within the several modes of leadership identified by participants, ranging from the loose assembly of musically compatible individuals to "see what happens," through to the hiring of specific key individuals to realize the leader's more closely defined personal vision. Exemplifying the former, Cindy Blackman Santana instructs her musicians to

> bring in ideas; don't bring any songs . . . unless you have a song that you're completely confident it, don't bring in songs . . . just bring in ideas and open minds and open hearts and let's just play. We put a tape recorder on, and we just started playing different ideas and things and it was incredible because everybody put some ideas in.

At the other extreme, Martin France and his colleague "organized the whole thing, knew what we were going to do pretty much without necessarily talking about it, but knew the musical framework that we were going to shift in, and then built everything on top, and then we edited and organized afterwards." One doesn't have to have a full idea in mind before beginning to construct the circumstances from which a special chemistry might emerge. Martin felt that "I knew roughly what kind of feeling of sound I wanted to have." Crucial action as a leader is the creation of a "space" in which potentially creative music may occur, validating his or her position as bandleader at the top of a notional hierarchy. The leader tends to act principally as a catalyst for action, someone who puts a situation together and stands back. Further direction or control then may or may not be ceded to others, such as a musical director.

In the extract below, Mark Guiliana's perception of leadership requires "much more of the 'producer' mentality in the moment, thinking about the big picture and the ensemble sound and just trying to accommodate that." In a recording session with his own group the only direction I gave was, again, this idea of exploring all the different combinations of the four of us. So the only thing I went into the session with was a checklist of what are all the possible duos, and make sure we do a three- or four-minute improvisation with each duo. And then what are the different trios? And then, of course, let's do something with no time . . . and of course the main chunk of it was the four of us playing together. I wanted to make sure we had all the combinations. Other than that it was truly improvised.

Our interviewees adopt different strategic approaches within and between different projects that they lead. Having constructed a potentially creative situation, Martin's approach echoes that of Cindy. His generous inclusion of others in the ownership of the performance also allows him to delegate some responsibility for the outcome: "The music almost asks people to come in and bring their music with them, is really what's important. So it's not really my vision and my entire thing." We have already encountered this sort of creative ownership-sharing in the case of Blair Sinta and Melissa Etheridge.

Some find the process of shifting from functional practice to a more compositional practice difficult: "The whole idea of you being the 'presenter,' it being your thing, I struggled with," says Martin France. Dylan Howe similarly describes a hesitancy as he moved from the directed functional "sideman" to the directing compositional "leader." Chad Wackerman and Ralph Salmins both highlight change in their approaches to music performance over time that may be characterized broadly as a move from the functional to the compositional, interpreted by Ralph as the distinction between execution and creation:

> I mostly invent my own parts, I would say now. (*Even though it's in somebody else's context?*) Yeah. This is something that I've come into later on in my life . . . whereas before I would think about executing a part, now I think about creating a part.

Self-identified as the most functional of our corpus of experts, Ralph too is creeping toward the pole of the FCC that demands and rewards compositional creativity.

The onus of leadership is typically assumed only when sufficient status within the music scene affords promoter or record company attention. This course of action is variously seen as a way of (a) controlling the audio environment in which one's drumming is to be presented; (b) decreasing the chances of dilution of the creative intent; and (c) designing a vehicle for personal creative expression. For the intrepid practitioner, one undoubted benefit of running one's own group is that it may be possible to select colleagues from whom one can learn. As an older, less skilled, but more experienced musician I was able to offer an international platform to younger, more skilled, but less experienced colleagues.[12] The exchange was balanced and to mutual advantage, supporting the development of all parties and auguring well for a successful outcome.

Sometimes It's Enough with Yourself: Performing without a Leader

The three preceding performance contexts have all comprised some degree of giving or receiving direction. In this, the fully compositional performance context, the selection, choice, and control of all aspects of the performance devolve to the performer alone. This leaderless, "hard compositional" action is usually exhibited either in solo performance or performance with one other. Performance with three or more seems to incubate de facto some form of implicit or explicit leadership.

Professional drummers tend to perform alone-in-public (drum clinics, solo performance, installations) or alone-in-private (the stay-home drummer). We may also, of course, perform as a soloist while in the company of others. With its vaudevillian connotations of entertainment, juggling, and showmanship, few participants relish the idea of a drum solo outside of some framing musical context, either in concert or for demonstration purposes. As expert practitioners, however, we are frequently called upon to supply just that at drum festivals and workshops. Most dislike the process and do so only with backing tracks or accompanying players to provide a musical context, and with a sense of commercial obligation. It falls to Salmins to express the general view: "Put me on that drum set now and say 'play a solo,' I will do something just like you would or anyone else would, but that's not what I'd call the center of my working creativity in my musical life."

Thomas Strønen, on the other hand, is an internationally known exponent of solo performance in art spaces and galleries as much as clubs and concert halls. He emphasizes the potential for creativity in a context in which the direct relationship between performer and listener is unmediated by the actions of co-performers: "Sometimes it's enough with yourself—you can do a solo concert and it really works." Reflecting upon the resilience and longevity of an effectively communicated creative solo performance by another drummer, he describes the beautiful way in which it is "still alive inside me":

It was a solo concert, and after twenty minutes I left because it was still good. But I knew that he started repeating, looping, and this is what I want to take with me . . . it's still great, and I went. And now it's still alive inside me, because it was only good, what I heard.

Recently he is of the opinion, however, that the transition from the controlled performance space of the studio to the less controllable milieu of the solo concert might have an unfavorable impact on his music-making: "I released the record with solo electronics and percussion and I didn't really want to do solo concerts."

As a sentient organism, every musician is of course in perpetual interaction with the musical environment in the "doing" and "undergoing" highlighted by Dewey and discussed in chapter 1. Indeed, it is the outcome of this prolonged and cumulative interaction with the environment that informs culture through action. But to what degree, if any, is interaction with other performers or listeners required for creativity to be attributable? To what extent can I be creative on my own? It is generally the case that performance of any kind is to some degree collaborative and interaction hard to avoid, be it in the moment or postponed pending later dissemination of the (captured) performance of, for instance, the stay-home drummer. According to Ingrid Monson, the practice and experience of creative drumming requires the interactive shaping of networks and communities to facilitate the creative act and to develop the culturally variable meanings and ideologies that inform the interpretation of drumming in society.[13] This echoes the descriptions of the visual or plastic artists for whom the art-making process is an ongoing interaction between person, product, and environment.[14]

The idea that creativity might be experienced outside the demands of the SDCA framework in solitude, not "being seen," and uncommunicated to another, nevertheless has adherents among our drummers. Cindy Blackman Santana, for example, conceptualizes creativity as within her, and in need only of expression: "You know, we can create in a room by ourselves; I can create in a room by myself. So do I actually need anybody else, even another band member to do something creative? No, I don't . . . it's in me." An older Romantic view of creativity that posits the phenomenon as a divine or mysterious process in the gift of the gods and bestowed upon the lone individual, and which some thought long since debunked, thus continues to have traction. It is Asaf Sirkis's perception that creativity is an "expression of our human worthiness or divinity or whatever you call it." For Cindy, "my creativity is part of the way that God made me." Further explanation reveals a metaphysical slant on energy distribution:

Even if there was some decree that stated what you just stated, God forbid, and I were only able to play in my garage or in my bedroom, I would still indirectly be affecting people because I believe that when you put energy out . . . (*It doesn't go anywhere, it's there*) oh, it's definitely there and it affects people. We don't even know why certain energies affect us but they do and sometimes they're negative because not everybody is positive. But, for me, I love putting out good energies and positive energies, so I would still do that and I know that I would still be affecting people; it would just be more indirect.

Asaf finds it possible to be creative in any situation:

Whether you are playing, as you said, in the middle of the woods, where nobody is listening, or you're playing to an audience, you will have an experience of creativity, yes, definitely.

The experience of creativity when performing alone appears, however, to be diminished. Asaf and Cindy agree that the presence of others tends to "amplify" the experience. Asaf states that there is

an amplification when you are seen, when you express yourself and you are creative and you are <u>seen</u> by other people. So there's a high amplitude, so to speak!

A solo performance heard in the moment by no one other than the performer and thus, according to some, not creative, may of course *become* creative after the event if captured and embodied in an artifact for later dissemination:

Cindy Blackman Santana: If I'm creating something, and let's say I create something and I record it, then I have proof that I've created it. Whether I'm with somebody or not, I created it and it's there. Does it become more alive, does it become . . . bigger in terms of touching people where I share it? Yes, it does. But it doesn't mean I can't create it without people.

The extent to which creativity may be available and encouraged within private "deliberate practice"[15] "in a room by myself" as a type of leaderless performance is an interesting topic, in itself of some importance to educationalists and practitioners. Broadly, I've addressed the topic of creativity as embedded within music performance, an activity that generally takes place with others present, and one that assumes at a minimum an addresser and an addressee. Throughout this book I interpret popular music creativity as an *interactive* process, conducted in the public sphere, which brings experience into meaning and significance. The SDCA framework posits the *communication* of a performance that exhibits qualitative difference as an essential prerequisite for creative assessment. So this view would, on the surface at least, appear to rule out creativity as something that can be enacted within deliberate practice, subject only perhaps to its capture and later post hoc communication to another.

Clearly there is a tension here with the perceptions of drummers like Cindy and Asaf who see creativity as residing entirely within the person rather than the performance, and who characterize periods of idea incubation in deliberate practice most certainly as creative thinking, if not creative action. They might further situate the private/non-communicative stage as a part of the process that helps generate creative potential, which can contribute to—and make more likely—the realization of that potential in creative action. Moreover, when private practice exceeds mere repetition and strays into conceptual, interpretive, or technical territory hitherto unvisited or unknown to the individual, it would seem to fulfil the criterion for Boden's lower level "P" (psychological) creativity.[16] If we acknowledge the possibility of creativity in private practice, we row back from contemporary assertions that creativity is relational in nature and born of intersubjectivity, of explicit and implicit connections between an individual or collective creator and others, and in doing so converge strongly with thinking within the Western classical tradition, in which "by far the most significant creative activity takes place in the privacy of the practice studio when an artist first settles on a particular interpretation."[17]

One strand of thinking around dialogue offers a resolution to this divergence between theory and perception and is thus a way to rehabilitate the SDCA framework. Incorporating the conceptual and methodological framework of cultural psychology in his "We" paradigm of creativity, Vlad Petre Glăveanu adopts the view of the human mind as inherently dialogical—that is, it can communicate about the world and its realities in terms of the "Other," but the Other may be internalized.[18] When Cindy, or Asaf in the woods, or any musician is apparently creating in complete solitude, she or he is nevertheless engaged in mental dialogue with internalized parties such as her or his mentors, parents, or critics. Such interactive but *internal* dialogue, it might be argued, qualifies as the communication deemed crucial to the enactment and assessment of creativity.[19]

•   It is difficult to insert these observations of "leaderless" music performance into any investigation into the meaning of creativity for drummers because so little research exists. Opportunities to perform alone have only recently become sufficiently available as to attract attention, and "drummer performance" is itself a fluid concept in the postdigital environment. In one respect, performing alone may afford greater freedom of expression because the obligation to play a specific part so that others can play theirs is removed; no one else is impeded from doing their job by the performer going "off book." That freedom seems to be counteracted by our interviewees who strongly indicate that, when performing alone, the experience of creativity is diminished. The implication that the presence of co-performers or other listeners tends to facilitate, amplify, and heighten the experience further buttresses studies emphasizing the value of collaborative performance. Almost all interviewees had experience of leaderless "solo" performance, by which is meant performing alone and without external direction. Near-instant global communication renders external direction hard to avoid; the input of a producer/client may be no more than a computer click or two away. Solo work on previously recorded tracks, for example, might take place in a commercial studio or alone at home under any level of direction from a client/leader/ producer, be that person physically present or absent.

Performance combining a high level of autonomy with the benefits of leaderless collaboration is available in a duo, a format seen as highly satisfactory by those who had experienced it. Chad Wackerman has toured extensively in a drum duo with drummer Terry Bozzio, with highly satisfactory outcomes for himself and listeners. Mark Guiliana, Dylan Howe, and I have spent time in duos with keyboard players. Describing his work with his coperformer, a pianist, Dylan states that "there's something easy working with him . . . it doesn't really feel like work, we just mess around with ideas and stuff," an account that chimes nicely with descriptions of creative work in other domains. Mark's current (2016) duo with keyboardist Brad Mehldau is

> about as satisfying a musical situation that I've been a part of . . . as you said, because the template itself allows for lots of freedom and creativity, but also in my opinion he's one of the best musicians in the world.

Some shy away from leaderless performance, seeing it as both obscure in process and prone to excess and self-indulgence. If a participant's "job description" is one that "collaborates to build, you know, something that the sum of which is greater than the sum of the parts" and is "completely about collaboration," as Ralph Salmins suggests, she or he is unlikely to dwell long in the wilderness of the alone. If, like Ralph, you "feed off the collaboration with fellow musicians," then you inhabit the collaborative compositional space described earlier. With no guiding voice overseeing the development of the creative action, it might be difficult to discern direction and so guide a hard compositional project to a satisfactory completion. In this area, Martin France accedes to the editorial skills of an outside colleague who is "very good at shaping" but crucially "he's also very good at being able to work out when we've said what we needed to say."

"Being Seen" versus "Chipping Away": Attitudes to Live and Studio Performance

Attitudes to performance vary greatly depending on whether the individual drummer is performing publicly for a paying audience or client, or "privately," for example, in a home or studio. At the risk of being crudely reductive, but for the sake of brevity, the two performance types are identified henceforth as "live" and "studio." The latter may afford repetition in a process that may be reductive or additive, with minimal immediate assessment by arbiters of significance, but that is not to say it is without emotional intensity:

> *Martin France:* I mean you'll know what it's like when you record with people and you have a sort of rapport . . . it's quite an intense process for everybody.

Invoking the image of the sculptor, Ralph Salmins refers to the reductive studio process as "chipping away": "he sort of . . . worked on it and chipped away at it until he got a version he was happy with." He associates the live/studio dichotomy with extrovert/introvert, fluid/plastic, fun/serious. He ascribes equal creative potential to both domains, but the studio is

> much more introverted. [. . .] Making a recording is like making a sculpture or a painting. You have to chip away at things, you have to improve, you're making something of lasting value that's going to be listened to more than once and I think that's a heavy responsibility. In the live performance it can be more fun, flippant, off-the-cuff, spontaneous. (*Do you ascribe any more or less creativity to either of those two domains?*) No, not more or less. I think it's just there's more freedom . . . because you're not having to make necessarily such

an artistic statement, but being footloose and fancy free on a stage can make creativity.

There is something of a contradiction here. Privileging studio performance as "longer lasting," Ralph perceives it to be where his creativity is most likely to be assessed. Live performance, however, while more ephemeral, is also freer, more fun, and presented as more conducive to creativity. That which is most frequently assessed, then, is not necessarily the most creative.

An illuminating description of the more typical additive process is provided by Dylan Howe, in reference to a self-selected studio track that most embodies his creativity:

> That was the first track I'd built on my own at home with the synth and a bass part and then I did like a guide drums and then I took the track over to Ross's [pianist Ross Stanley's] house for him to overdub the piano on and then I redid the drums to his piano and then added all these extra kind of sound effects and other sounds . . . (*and other horn players?*) On that track it's just Ross and I and a bass player. [. . .] I did the keyboards, the synths, and the sound effects and everything, Ross is doing the live acoustic piano, and then there's an upright bass player. [. . .] So that in a way was the most creative for me, because I had to kind of create the track and then I was doing lots of overdubbing and then redoing stuff and reediting, so that had the most input from me . . . it wasn't just about what we played on that take.

In so far as the piece thus required no real-time performance from others, it may be characterized as a solo performance. Other performances were captured, but sequentially and with continual opportunity for review. Dylan's process exemplifies the postmodern blurring of composer into performer, composition into performance, product into process. The crucial importance to him as the "music inventor"[20] resides in the "adding something else," the going further: "it wasn't just about what we played on that take."

Framing "liveness" as a "distinct musical value," Sarah Thornton points to a particular music place (the live gig) and time (from roughly the mid-'50s to the mid-'80s) as the "main site" of authenticity. She writes that "[t]he essence or truth of music was located in its performance by musicians in front of an audience."[21] Her choice of end date coincides with the watershed moment of the arrival of the computer in music creation, and it must be remembered that our interviewees, like all creators, have a temporal dimension of experience in straddling the schism between the old world and the new, in surviving and flourishing in the postdigital ecology. In Salmins's perception, live performance is ultimately "a different beast" from the studio, with a life of its own and potentially harder to control than the studio equivalent. France likes performing live "sometimes, sometimes not [laughs]. Sometimes it doesn't feel quite right." He takes succor in the invisibility of his position in the pit of a London West End show because "everybody would know if you made a mistake, particularly for the drums because you're having to come in really loudly. [. . .] But also nobody knows who you are."

By contrast, visible authorship in live performance—the "being seen"—is crucial to Sirkis as a source of additional energy: "There's more energy when you are creative and being seen as creative." Strønen highlights the pleasures of live performance and his ease in its realization: "I like it a lot, and . . . I'm never uncomfortable. I've had times when I've been nervous walking across the stage, but when I'm behind the drums everything is fine [. . .] I love it." If for any reason he was unable or not permitted to perform in public again "that would be a disaster."

Those who prefer the studio environment sometimes see touring as a distraction, with the additional nervousness that client relationships built over many years may be jeopardized if the drummer is out of town for too long. Conversely, those who perform most easily in front of the public tend to find the studio environment less free, less fun, and, *as a consequence*, less conducive to creativity. Both these observations, however, should be seen in the light of the music business's current (2016) turn to live performance, with the studio variety in long decline from a perceived peak in the 1960s to 1980s.[22]

The predominant environmental change in the performing lives I am describing here is uniformly considered to be the digitization of the domain. Almost all interviewees describe some sort of engagement with a music technology that affords the facility to compose and capture their performances in private, with no further need, necessarily, to seek the input of others. Music technology is generally seen as a helpful tool, albeit with several accompanying drawbacks. For instance, it is inherently unable to distinguish the musical from the unmusical. Some ascribe to it mechanistic properties that need to be guarded against. Furthermore, it is held responsible in part for a diminution of collaborative interaction in performance, lamented by some of our experts. Technology is seen as disconnecting the younger player from the cultural ways of learning that transfer skills and deliver a cultural context for their appropriate use. It is thus a principal agent underlying the decline of cultural connectedness identified earlier.

Three further observations in particular reveal something of the meanings expert drummers make of their relationship with music technology. The first outlines some of the complexities of "pretending" to perform for an unknown and unseen virtual customer:

> *Chad Wackerman:* Because you're working alone and in that situation you do start to question things, "Well, if this sounds good to me . . ." and of course as soon as you put the drums on any track that's had a drum machine or a loop or something, it makes it completely different. The dynamics of the band sound different, because the way we play makes them sound like they're playing quieter or louder or more intense or more laid back, and of course there are so many ways to shape this tune I wonder if the guy's going to like it? I wonder if he has any idea (*what he wants?*). So I'm playing and I'm kind of in essence producing it by the way I'm approaching the tune, because it's very cold sounding when I get it. And often they'll put their solos on later so you're playing "pretend there's a solo going on" (*"pretend solo" gig*) so you just hear the chords . . . but it's being an actor.

The superimposition of the qualities of human performance on the unbending nonnegotiable aural space of the automated track alters perceptions. What is quiet, what is loud? What rushes, what drags? As an "actor," Chad also has to play the part of "producer by default" because the nature of any contribution by the agency of a human drummer in the electronic domain will have such a powerful effect upon all aspects of the finished product.

A second description is also in the context of overdubbing or layering on to prerecorded tracks, typical of the performance of the stay-home drummer who adopts and adapts the skills of both recording engineer and producer. It is worth remembering here that "solo" performance is not synonymous with undirected performance. Work on previously recorded tracks might take place in a commercial studio under tight direction. In Ralph's next example, other musicians were previously involved

> but not at the same time. I did drums on their own. (*So it's sequentially recorded?*) Yeah. So he had like a demo track, I put the drums on and then he built a lot on that. He had a pretty specific idea of what he wanted [. . .] Drum'n'bass in three.

A final vignette illustrating technological mediation within the context of an improvising electronic keyboard-and-drums duo exhibits an unusual set of constraints and opportunities. Mark Guiliana describes how, working with keyboardist Brad Mehldau, the duo's methodology is to a large extent governed by "the world of pre-sets." Creativity inheres in "in the moment" selections between available sound combinations:

> So our first set lists were just those sonic combinations and it's like "okay, we just kind of completed an idea . . . maybe we stopped and people clapped, okay, now let's start a new idea, so okay I'll go to this bass sound and this accompanying sound and now we're in a new place." So the world of pre-sets and being able to recall sounds helped shape where we would go at each moment. And actually I like that for chunks of time throughout the set we're in a box of these sounds . . . and in a healthy way, because if he [Mehldau] was just spinning that knob every 30 seconds and going to new sounds . . . "Whoa, where are we, where are we going?" It's kind of nice that even if we're improvising it's kind of a song right now with this template, you know.

Once the contents of the "box of sounds" have been selected and the box opened, the direction and quality of the music emanate from what comes out of the box. The sonic selections determine both the new starting point for each fresh piece and, as Mark puts it, "where we would go at each moment."

Expert drummers continue to understand performance as either "studio" or "live," even as distinctions between the two are becoming increasingly slippery and contested. From inception to the adoption of editing techniques, recordings of performances have tended to be characterized as permanent and immutable. To the performer, they used to permit a relatively objective scrutiny of performance. Currently, however, the invasive surgery into the body of the recorded performance afforded by music software offers impermanence and mutability in a perpetual reimagining of the original performance by remixers and remodelers, constrained only by the will of rights holders. The audio recording is now more typically seen as capturing a performance that can be revisited and reworked, while both live performance and *the experience* of any kind of performance tend to be characterized as unrepeatable.

Live performance is generally seen as freer and less constrained but with potentially less controllable outcomes than the studio equivalent. An imperfect connection with a live audience seems to be marginally more conducive to creativity than the potentially more controllable connection achieved by "chipping away" at a studio performance. This view adds a certain weight to Alexandra Lamont's observation that performers' strongest experiences of music (as characterized by engagement and a search for meaning) are in front of an audience. In her view, these experiences provide valuable and positive memories of performing that performers can draw on to sustain their motivation for music.[23] Performance expectation in the popular music recording studio lies somewhere between the relaxed live concert and the potentially inhibiting expectation of perfection that some writers now identify as the norm in classical music recording sessions.[24]

No clear preference emerged from the interviewees as between studio and live, between the type of controlled performance embodied within a recorded artifact available for repeated listening with no immediate response from others, or the messy, largely uncontrollable, unrepeatable, live performance with immediate audience feedback. Both tended to be seen as two sides of a performance coin, each with its meanings and mediations of creative action. The presence of feedback in an evolving live performance versus its absence in listening to a recording may be an important part of why the two are valued in different ways, and why their creativity is situated differently.

Summary

In this chapter I've focused on five contexts in which our experts perform, as follows:

1. "Doing a good job": performing for a leader
2. "Allowing me to be me": performing with a leader
3. "Special chemistry": performing as a leader
4. "Sometimes it's enough with yourself": performing without a leader
5. "Being seen" versus "chipping away": performing live and in the studio

Boundaries between working for, with, as, or without a client/leader/producer are not as clear-cut as might be imagined. Music is a domain in which power and differentials of power are significant factors. The structure of power within music collaborations is fluid, negotiated and renegotiated, and often more covert than overt. In a robust subtheme that speaks to drummers' strong sense of cultural identity, the salient musical aspects of the relationship between leader and drummer are seen as always remaining the prerogative of the drummer. Of all actors it is the drummer, interviewees suggest, who retains the power to make the music work or not work.

The first two drummer narratives distinguished between functional performance *for* a leader and *with* a leader. While all agreed that creativity may subsist in functional performance, there was less agreement as to how and to what extent that might be so. The central dilemma here is how the individual drummer might creatively participate in the event while, on the one hand, remaining within the constraints of tradition and culture, and, on the other, strategically interpreting and extending them. To what extent is creative performance achievable for those who play only as directed by others with strictly governed license for interpretation?

Broadly, reports here suggested that being able to play on demand, to supply an appropriate performance in any genre in any situation at any time, constitutes one aspect of creative action. In specific musical instances (for example, transforming the demonstration recording of a track into a finished master, or breathing life into a poorly programmed version of a recording), "doing a good job" means "making it feel like music." In the broader thematic context, "doing a good job" tends to mean "making the leader sound good" and by extension "making it [the music] work." Even though functional performance is perceived as less directly supportive of creativity than compositional performance of the type explored in contexts three and four, creative expression is nevertheless available in the "little corners" of even the most tightly constrained of functional situations. Almost all performance is perceived as permissive of creativity, notwithstanding that creativity is not always an "unmitigated good," to use Richard Florida's phrase.[25] The notion that the creativity manifest in departure from the norm may not be helpful in making the music work is borne out in the responses. While our participants insist they can see creative potential in almost any musical situation, they are judicious in their unlocking of that potential in functional performance, lest it prevent the music from working to the leader/client/producer's satisfaction.

The third and fourth performance contexts focused on narratives of compositional performance *as* a leader and *without* a leader, respectively. Here, assumption of the leadership role was seen first as a catalyst for action, and second as a way of designing and controlling a vehicle for creative expression, thereby decreasing the chances of expressive dilution. A spectrum of leadership models emerged. Different models might be adopted for different, sometimes simultaneous, projects, ranging from the loose assembly of musically compatible individuals to the complete control of all aspects of the collective performance. Common to all is the creation of a musical space in which music may occur.

Having created a space and possibly, but not necessarily, a text or composition, the leader may or may not cede further direction or control to others. In this process, many looked for an empathetic relationship, a "special chemistry" with co-performers upon which to construct the situation that would support the compositional project. The drum culture imbues a primacy to "making it work," that is, the music must work functionally before it can be said to work compositionally. The forming of participants' own bands (or "situations") tended to be informed by prior experience of successes, failures, and inhibitions undergone in other peoples' bands or situations. The benefits and drawbacks of group "brainstorming" have long since been identified in the literature and continue to be debated.[26]

The perspective on creativity as social and interactionist has been propagated particularly within organizational and management fields.[27] Both are concerned with team creative processes, and often use the improvisational nature of the jazz ensemble as metaphor or exploratory focus.[28] David Bastien and Todd Hostager characterize jazz as a social process of coordinated innovation with a collective outcome, as an activity in which inventiveness is to be expected. Our experts supported these ideas. They considered that the purpose in assuming leadership is to offer something perceived of as new or original (cf. "originals bands") and to produce what Burnard calls "new modes of discourse and new means of presentation."[29] Interestingly, they tended to consider the experience of creativity in either functional or compositional performance as equally valid. In this sense, they achieved and experienced similar dimensions of creativity, albeit in different ways and to different degrees, in the propulsion of their own musical vehicles as in the propulsion of someone else's.

• Experts offered the following insights:

(A) Narratives of functional performance *for* and *with* a leader:

- Creative performance is contingent in part upon an ability to control or affect outcomes, as mediated by the performance context.
- Functional performance is less directly supportive of creativity than compositional performance. Nevertheless, creative expression is available in even the most tightly constrained of functional situations.
- The creativity manifest in departure from the norm is not always welcome in music performance.
- A close, symbiotic relationship with an experienced leader enables, nurtures, and sustains creative collaboration. Benefits tend to accrue from such relationships with leaders.

(B) Narratives of compositional performance *as* and *without* a leader:

- The music should work functionally before it can be said to work compositionally. Compositional performance thus has an element of functional performance already embedded.
- As performance moves increasingly to the compositional, individual co-performers will need less overt direction.
- When performing alone, the experience of creativity is diminished. The presence of co-performers or other listeners tends to facilitate, amplify, and heighten the experience.
- Drummers achieve and experience similar dimensions of creativity, albeit in different ways and to different degrees, in both performance modes.
- All performance contexts are construed as affording more or less creativity.

(C) Attitudes to studio and live performance:

- Live performance is seen as freer, less constrained, and with potentially less controllable outcomes than studio performance.
- An imperfect connection with a live audience is seen as more conducive to creativity than a potentially more controllable connection through studio performance.

When Ralph Salmins distinguishes between executing and creating a part, he identifies a key distinction between the functional and compositional modes of performance. The former, associated with carrying out the directions of another, backgrounds creativity and focuses on "doing a good job" even up to the extent of "allowing me to be me." The latter mode suggests "playing with no nets," searching for that elusive "special chemistry" between co-performers, and the bringing of something extra in the search for Mark Guiliana's "unclaimed territory." Participants tend to occupy a given position on the FCC between the two polarities until changing circumstances, ideologies, or self-conceptions (for example, Ralph's creative burnout) precipitate a move. Broadly, we can think of compositional performance as functional performance *plus* something, rather than as an "either/or" binary. That "plus something" is now examined more closely in the context of selecting what to play and how to play it.

4 • The Biggest Challenge

Selecting Content

Choosing What to Play

What is the drummer doing back there, tinkering around in the engine room of the popular song? How do drummers choose to play what they play? What factors impact upon their choices? One artist manager I knew was sure he had the answers to these questions. On one occasion he was watching a drummer in action. Asked his opinion of the musician's efforts, it transpired that he was unable to detect any pattern, any temporal coordination, any dynamic or metrical emphasis, any selection from among possible options. He concluded that the individual *hit anything* she wanted to at *any* time she fancied, mostly as hard as she liked. On one level, the stratospheric degree of ignorance implicit in this analysis is breathtaking—incomprehensible even, especially if you are a drummer. On another level, he was right. That's exactly what we do: except drummers *play*, they *never* "hit."

Selection and decision making in drum performance are under varying degrees of autonomous control, assigned varying degrees of importance, and constrained from multiple perspectives. Reflecting on his position as the "decision maker" in respect of his compositional big-band performances, Ralph Salmins considers that in such a context the big problem is deciding upon the appropriate musical choice on the drum kit for the music and the ensemble. Given that he more generally inhabits the functional sphere of practice, where he is on occasion told "exactly what to play," possession of a full range of choices in *every* musical situation is, however, "not important." Asked how he decides what to play, Chad Wackerman gets to the heart of the issue when he responds:

Well, that's the creative part, isn't it? (*Both laugh*)

The first dimension of the SDCA framework proposes that for creativity to be enacted there needs to be selection. Creativity is seen as enabled by choice and control over possible courses of action, and disabled in their absence. If, as Dewey suggests, all art involves selection,[1] then an inability to choose or to select from possible options certainly impinges upon, and may preclude, creative action. Even John Cage *selected* to relinquish control over sound for his composition " 4'33." Contemporary compositional drummers may wish to co-opt Cage's alleged admonition that it is the composer's job to come up with "something better than silence" into their own performance practices.

In privileging an appropriate performance over a creative one, drummers seek to reduce the available choices and components to those that will make the performance work. One way to do this is to use preexisting rhythmic templates: a "standard shuffle," some "16th-note funk," or "straight-ahead swing." In this vein, Allan Moore formulated the notion of the "standard rock beat," by which he means a bar or measure of four beats distributed around the kit with certain emphases. This drum kit pattern, found throughout Western popular music, he takes to be normative.[2] The extent to which any drummer's engagement with this model permits, constrains, or enables the effective communication of experience that might come to be assessed as "significant" (and hence potentially creative) is an important question. In practice, our experts seldom engage with the standard rock beat, from which it might be deduced that they find that particular formulation an overworked seam when it comes to the search for significant difference.

Agency and Control

The extent to which individuals perceive that they have control over situations, what psychologists identify as an "internal locus of control," mediates thoughts about and perceptions of events.[3] In both individual and collective music performance the possession, surrender, loss, requirement for, or absence of control of musical materials has profound implications. Perceived of as either soloist or functionary,[4] the classical music performer's ability to select may be highly constrained by the dictates of the text. A similar demand is in play in the pop recording studio: the score or text may be literally immaterial, but composition, construed as the strict putting into play of an explicit will, may be very much present.

Selection, choice, and control require some level of individual empowerment, a conception of oneself as agentive. I interpret "agency" here as the intentionality and control an individual feels that she has over her circumstances in a particular situation. The ability to determine key aspects of performance both distinguishes and enables lower and higher levels of music practice. From an atomistic viewpoint, the creative act is embodied at the microlevel within the agentive striking of the drum. From the striking emerges sound, to have brief life before decay, death, and silence. Whether that sound leads an eventful life of change, collision, merger, and elision with other sounds or exists in anechoic near-silence, it is nevertheless in perpetual timbral and dynamic mutation within itself. It was given life by the agentive creator, who decided upon action determining the temporal length and dynamic and timbral qualities of the sound.

Control in performance may be degraded, surrendered, or lost altogether. Many musicians have spoken of a loss of control, in being "taken over" by the process of acting creatively.[5] Popular music instrumentalists sometimes describe the surrendering of control at the moment of peak performance.[6] Drummer Ian Wallace reported feelings of being "borne along at a tremendous rate by something you only just have control of. It's almost like it's controlling you."[7] There is a paradox here between the exertion of control over musical materials and aspects of their realization and transmission (with which creativity might be enabled), and the loosening or surrendering of control that Wallace and others might deem essential to achieve peak performance. The experiential feeling of loss or surrender is explained within cognitive psychology as the change from *controlled* processing to *automatic* processing.[8]

Historically, the "lone genius" paradigm within music saw the abandonment or surrendering of control to the ancient muses at the "Eureka!" moment of creativity. Igor Stravinsky was "just the vessel through which *Le Sacré* passed."[9] The art of music improvisation has traditionally been much associated with a "mystique" connecting it to a surrendering of control. Creativity is conspicuously evident in this ancient and modern form of music-making, with implications of change, surprise, unpredictability, and dealing with the unforeseen, qualities not universally approved of.[10] These perspectives suggest that if the outcome of the musical act is already known, the creativity involved in its enactment is already compromised. If it is explicable, it is already known; if it is already known, it is not creative. In this view, the individual enacts creativity *because he or she wants to know what happens*.

From a more general psychological perspective some catalysts for creativity may be *beyond* individual control.[11] Serendipity was very much present in the seemingly haphazard compositional methods of British progressive rock groups of the 1970s, in which trial and error, vague hunches, playful exploration, and a sense of what could be "got away with" all played their part. In practice, most drummers move instinctively between an exertion and loosening of control of the text, on a spectrum of precise execution, interpretation, and improvisation, sometimes within a single musical rendition. At the functional pole of the FCC, a precisely defined part indicates the dominance of the composer; at the other pole, composer functions devolve to the performer, now charged with responsibility for what he plays and so partially determining that which is played by those around him.

Individual empowerment in creative performance may be engendered through the negotiation of constraints upon selection. A highly commoditized Western popular music culture requires a uniform product and its near-identical reproduction on a nightly basis. Such a product tends to emerge from the sort of standardized performance in which the groove or swing expected from drummers is generated under increasingly rigid constraints, and which is now viewed through the "oscilloscopic prurience" of the ever-dominant computer.[12] Drummers are further constrained by the relationship between patterns, which have to be understood, recognized, and appreciated before departing from them.[13] What counts as rhythmic coordination within an ensemble is thus defined and constrained by generic, stylistic, technical, environmental, and ethical considerations, and the cultural norms of the individuals within it. Here we refer again to the perceptions of our interviewees.

Genre and Style Constraints

Expert drummers generally understand creativity as both constrained by and achievable within any genre or style of music, contingent only upon its appropriateness in the given situation. Cindy Blackman Santana, for example, selects from differing perceptions of stylistic appropriateness: "You're going to play with [bandleader] Jay McShann differently than you're going to play with [Rolling Stone] Mick Jagger. You're going to play with Mick Jagger differently than you are going to play with [saxophonist] Wayne Shorter." Even though she loves "freedom of choice," her choice selection is constrained by the desired outcome: "Playing whatever I choose at any moment and making any situation into a creative situation is a fantastic choice, but it depends on what you want out of the situation." Thomas Strønen points out (and "finds it quite funny") that contrary to their much-vaunted "freedom," jazz musicians are more constrained than might be imagined: "so many jazz musicians feel they cannot repeat themselves." In an effort to transcend constraints of style and genre, musicians joining King Crimson were asked to develop both a fresh instrumental vocabulary and a way of doing things specifically for that ensemble, which, it was to be expected, would be of little use outside it.

Blurring distinctions between notions of style and genre, Chad Wackerman reports that he does not think "style matters. I think you can have a creative head space and it can fit into any genre; I really do." As an example, he references the highly imaginative work of an internationally known colleague (drummer Steve Gadd) whom Chad is temporarily replacing on tour with James Taylor. Chad is shocked:

> I can't believe he [Steve] is doing that! It's odd; it's so odd! I would never think of that. I wouldn't have the bravery! But you listen to it and it's . . . poised. [. . .] So you can do that in reggae, you can do that in country music, you can do it in . . .

There was some confusion within the interviewees as to which genres are more or less conducive to allowing the communication of creative difference. Cindy interprets the "goal of pop music" as being "for people to keep within a certain box in terms of their thinking. They are thinking inside of a box and it's a control weapon and it's a conformity weapon, where creative music is not that." Her analysis, however, goes on to exhibit a degree of inconsistency. On the one hand, she is clear that there is something called "creative music," which she loves to play and is not, unlike pop music, a "conformity weapon." In pop music

> the impetus is on conformity; it's not on individuality, and that's a problem for me. It's an issue for me because I love individual thinkers. [. . .] You know, I love innovation and I think that pop music doesn't make room for that, because that's not the goal of pop music.

On the other hand, she asserts that "rock music is not a music that is uncreative; it's the interpretation of the music that is sometimes uncreative. It's all what we do with it." In this book, the verb "to interpret" has hitherto encompassed the idea of assigning meaning and the subsequent making sense of that meaning. Musical interpretation of the sort that Cindy is addressing here, however, has a more specific usage implying the reframing of the composer's intention, or the adding of value to the material at hand. That idea is embodied in two further extracts from her interview:

If you have a rhythm that goes [sings to demonstrate] that's a cool rhythm, you know, and you can put it somewhere, and it can feel great and whatever . . . it's the interpretation or the usage of that rhythm that could be bad or good or better used or less better used. [. . .] So to me the definition of rock music in pop is typically not creative, but to me rock music can be creative and it depends on interpretation and taking it further.

By this reckoning, the two central agentive actions (interpreting it and "taking it further") that might ignite a creative spark are the very actions least likely to be found in (generally functional) rock performance. While it might be argued that the scope for interpretation—and therefore the potential for creativity—is defined to a large extent by the genre, most interviewees insist that they can find creative corners in practically any situation.

Jazz performance tends to be seen as an ongoing interaction between person, product, and environment, one which an audience is invited to observe. It is expected that the product (the performed outcomes of these interactions) will change frequently and in response to multiple environmental conditions. The emphasis in that genre is on the process, not the product. By contrast, the pop or rock process is de-emphasized in favor of the highly polished product, which is offered for admiration, enjoyment, and purchase. The pop product requires a high level of consistency and is generally expected to be identical when exhibited in different locations. To what extent might the constant repetition of well-prepared material on, for example, a stadium-rock tour, encourage or constrain creativity? Peter Erskine's response to this question reveals that one reason he sought performative difference in the "minor aspects" of his highly constrained nightly renditions with Steely Dan was to "amuse himself":

> When I was doing it there would always be something just slightly different in the contour leading up to maybe an ensemble thing . . . I'm one of those guys that easily amuses himself, so I can get pretty interested in some minor aspect.

This is not, however, entirely convincing. The functional nature of performance in "heritage" rock acts such as Steely Dan is perilously close to that required in tribute bands. As a revered and well-known jazz musician who recommends that "we compose every time we play," Peter may well feel expectation to "interfere" with those aspects of the music over which he has control and re-present them in a fresh light.[14]

In the case of Mark Guiliana, the issues surrounding what to play and when to play it are sufficiently substantial as to intimidate him: "Sometimes even just that way of looking at it scares me, you know." His solution is bipartite and sophisticated:

> I selected the ensemble and have a hand in the way it sounds mostly by selecting that personnel but also selecting the music through editing and very casually Tim would say, "Hey, what should I bring?" . . . "Make sure you have this pedal, that pedal . . ." (*Yeah, that's the producer function right there*) Yeah . . . I guess producing and creating the environment.

By virtue of having determined the performance situation, Mark perceives that he has the right to "make any decision I want at any moment and it's right because it's mine, which sounds very ignorant [laughs]." Personnel and instrumentation thus selected, and retaining editorial control, he interprets the creative action here as residing, in part, in his "producing and creating the environment" conducive to creative performance. His final decision is to relinquish all further decision making to the improvised moment, for which preparation is crucial:

> The music is making all the decisions for me, and am I connected enough to the moment and am I prepared with the proper tools to be able . . . ? I'm not making any decisions, I'm just trying to accommodate the decisions the music is making, and am I prepared to do so? Can I play with the appropriate dynamics, can I play in time, can I produce the proper sound for that situation, and so on and so forth.

In a similar process of delegating responsibility Asaf Sirkis describes how he internalizes the melody "and then I just let my hands decide what they want to do."[15] How long the internalization process takes before action is required of his hands is a question that went unanswered, but these extracts evidence imaginative ways in which participants delegate responsibility as a way of negotiating constraints.

Technical and Environmental Constraints

Generally, the greater the variety (and the better the quality) of tools (such as technical control) at the drummer's disposal, the greater the number of options from which to select. Responses to the question "how important to you is it to have choice and control over what you play?" are framed by a majority within the context of control of the sticks, the principal skill that permits fine control of performance-level microparameters (dynamics, timbre, touch, feel). For Cindy and Peter, greater stick control affords greater choice of phrasing options, or, more accurately, generates phrasing options from which a choice becomes available to be made. Cindy reckons that "to have choice is the most important thing . . . and to have control . . . is the right hand or left hand of your choice. Because if you are able to control what you do then you are able to make choices." Achieving a high level of instrumental control is, on Dylan Howe's account, not only the focus of practice but also a tool to render "multilayered options at all times," so his performance feels "like a natural thing and it isn't so intellectual."

Asaf Sirkis's case is instructive. Rare among drummers, his highly developed finger technique is a key determinant in the way he plays, affording him the ability to play softly with great articulation. It has "conditioned" the way he plays so that "I can play softer maybe better than I can play louder." However, he sees the internal balance of the ensemble as important, it being crucial that "the energy of the soloist is backed up by the drums." Even though the power of the drum set has been noted by many participants, in this instance Asaf's saxophonist co-performer—"a bomb of energy"—outguns the drummer to the point where Asaf assesses his control at the higher dynamic level to be insufficient, and different instruments are required:

> It was always important for me to create in my playing and especially in my music a big dynamic range, so I would play really soft with brushes, even without the hi-hat, just the swishing, and to really heavy metal kind of double bass drum and cymbals.

Here, Asaf's two mediational means—his instruments and his technique—both need adaptation to sustain creative action in the particular situation of the saxophonist's group.

A further technical constraint lies in the different conceptual and physical approaches to the "natural" acoustic kit and its electronic counterpart, paralleled for example in the different approaches necessary for transitions to and from the Steinway Grand and Rhodes electric pianos. In the early days (1980s) of electronic percussion, that transition could cause havoc with wrists, fingers, and touch.[16] Mark Guiliana talks about his difficulties in using a "prepared" or "treated" drum set (that is, one that has been tuned beyond the respective components' natural ranges, for special effect): "I need to hit them mezzo-forte and up to achieve a certain sound . . . You know, the floor tom is wrinkly and it just won't speak at a quiet volume." Audible differentiation may come at a price.

In addition to issues of genre, style, and technique, action-choices are further mediated by the social and sonic environment. Asaf explains how environmental variables (room acoustics, the physical and emotional health of the performer and co-performers, audience disposition, lighting, instrument quality, sound monitoring, and so forth) mediate not only the performance itself, but its effective communication: "Everything changes how I play. The room, the audience, the musicians, the musicians' mood that same day, you know." Mark, too, observes how environment affects content:

> The music I've been making lately is heavily reliant on gear. . . . Ideally, for the Mehliana [current group with Brad Mehldau] set to come across well, we're reliant on a nice room, maybe a dead room, with a big P.A. with "subs" and the whole thing, so, it's amazing how in that context the environment can really affect the content.

In the excellent vignette below, he elaborates this idea in the context of performances at two London venues:

> We played at the Village Underground [. . .], it's maybe 800 standing, is kind of like rock . . . DJs play there . . . it was loud, and people standing the whole time and it was really inspiring, it really felt good. And then last November we were at the Barbican for the jazz festival (*yeah, concert hall . . . different thing*) beautiful room and it's an honor, but man . . . (*Cold*) yeah . . . (*Cold*) . . . The sound is just everywhere, flying around . . . the snare drum is at the back of the room. It was cool; we did it, but a very different experience. So this acoustic repertoire and ensemble . . . you know, saxophone, piano, bass, drums, that was the template I was using . . . and I feel like we can set up in a park outdoors and just play; we can be in the corner of a library and play; we can be in the Barbican, we can be at Ronnie Scott's [a small jazz club], we can be in a subway station and deliver this and express ourselves.

Here, one set of environmental conditions promotes the successful communication of the intended performance and its potential assessment as creative; another set militates against it. One solution might be to offer content appropriate to each room, but the artist might reasonably argue that while the environment necessarily affects the content of the performance, it should not dictate it. Mark's solution is characteristic of exemplary problem solving.

For him, the remedy is to be found in the creation of a parallel situation based on the traditional jazz quartet lineup, which both sidesteps the "room acoustics" problem and opens up fresh compositional horizons.

The number of people involved in any music situation is a crucial determinant of drummer action. It is axiomatic within the community that the greater the number of co-performers, the tighter the performance constraints; in other words, the more functional the drummer's performance must become, or remain, in order to glue the music together. In Peter's view, an orchestral or big band situation is like

> marching a legion somewhere, you've got a lot of people; you've got to deal with it. [. . .] If there's an M.D. or a conductor we are like the outrider for the conductor . . . we have to flag up that there is a bend coming up, or there are Indians over that hill. We're them; because other people are looking at the music or doing other things. We are the guy who keeps it all together.

Dynamic and other considerations constrain Peter in his performances in the large orchestral setting: "It's a very large boat and I've just got to paddle. I can't do the usual [snaps fingers and sings to demonstrate] kind of ensemble things that I might enjoy with a big band or a very fleet-footed small group." However, when performing alone or in duet with another drummer, or when the performance is embodied in his original compositions, creativity is increasingly prioritized. The greater the number of performers, the greater the attention the drummer will need to pay to Guiliana's "checklist" of foundational concerns: the fewer the players, the sooner one can proceed to those compositional areas in which creativity may appear. This is an interesting instance of how collaborative performance can sometimes impede rather than facilitate greater creativity.

Having recently gravitated to larger venues as the coheadline star of an improvisational duo, Mark expresses both irritation at and acceptance of the more predictable constraints associated with the daily logistics of touring. This should be seen in the context of his enjoyment and the effectiveness of his studio performances, against which he frames touring as both "a blessing and a curse." The ability to surmount or incorporate environmental variables is a key skill of the performing artist who aspires to creativity. Ultimately, certain hardships appear to be unavoidable in the patient search for special combinations of people and places that, given helpful environmental conditions, might deliver a situation supportive of creativity.

Asked about the importance to him and to his creativity of having choice and control over what he plays, Peter chooses to interpret the question rather as one of control over others in determining outcomes:

> In my case there is a definite want of some measure of control. When I play very open, just as you played by not playing, by being *tacit*, the general obvious response would be "how selfless that is; why, you're so generous to the music," but in reality I see that as we're being completely manipulative, or we're the string-pullers because we're determining the outcome with far greater results than if we just play in parallel.

The paradox of choice in performance is that it both enables creative achievement and complicates it. For Dylan, the creative waters are thus muddied: "It's complicated because you're in a situation where you can kind of do anything, so then therefore what do you do?" Options demand choices, to which attach notions of responsibility, obligation, and appropriate behavior, topics to which we now turn.

Ethical and Motivational Constraints

Within an emerging hierarchical distinction that associates compositional performance with greater creativity than functional performance, the interviewees are motivated both intrinsically and extrinsically to seek out significant difference in their performances.[17] Martin France, for example, sees the composition of original music that might facilitate creativity in terms of an obligation: "It's something you have to do, isn't it?" A wide range of intrinsic and extrinsic motivations enabled change at various times in participants' careers. As beginners, Asaf Sirkis and Mark Guiliana were both motivated by a need to escape from the expectations of significant others, parents, and family. Asaf, and to some degree Thomas Strønen, were further motivated by the fear of embarrassment or humiliation. In the late afternoon of my career I was strongly motivated by a desire for personal change to be effected from within.

Almost all of the drummers under discussion are motivated to develop an individual musical identity or "voice," to contribute and determine outcomes, and to communicate significant difference in our performances—in other words, to inhabit the compositional sphere of practice. "Artistic hunger" and "a definite want of some measure of control" were given as drivers toward a compositional approach to creativity by, respectively, Ralph and Peter. Thomas now requires no further motivation ("it's what I do"), and Mark's creativity is contingent upon a strong social component. Frustration, discontent, and a desire to "prove" something surface in Dylan's interview, while Asaf is always compelled to take the road less traveled: "when I see a lot of people going in one direction I <u>have</u> to go the other way."

Two participants spoke of the motivating strength of the need to solve problems. Asaf referenced my experience:

> I remember in one of your interviews you said about your particular snare stroke, yeah, that everybody kind of yeah said, oh, this is Bill's stroke, and you spoke about the <u>necessity</u> of having to be heard while the other guys were so loud (*no mics!*), exactly, so you know all these things are very important, you know, necessity will give you a lot of opportunity.

Peter, too, highlights his tenacity in the context of creative problem solving when he says: "I feel like a person who is compelled to find the solution to any given challenge or problem. I don't like to give up." None reported being motivated toward the *exclusively* functional or the *exclusively* compositional; approaches to those constructs continued to be pragmatic and flexible. Interestingly, the subject of remuneration was seldom raised as a motivational dimension of achieving the experience of creativity, although it was generally and implicitly understood that functional performance tends to bring greater pecuniary reward than the compositional variety.

Individuals revealed a keen sense of responsibility and obligation, not only to those with whom they share performance but also, variously, to themselves, to music commissioning bodies, to the wider music community, or simply to "the music." With the creative urge comes an attendant obligation to express and communicate it. On Salmins's account, "You do have to allow things to come out. [. . .] I do support my own creative urges and I try to be as creative as I can." Viewing composition as a chore, France seeks excuses to avoid having to live up to these perceived responsibilities: "I don't have a band"; "I don't have any tunes." On another occasion he "had to make sure [the music] was very good, but not from a personal perspective, but for the sake of the music and the ensemble as a whole." Here, "the music" is characterized as having a personal benefit or interest: "we had to . . . live up to the music. (*To reach the standard that it deserved?*) Yeah."

Responsibilities to co-performers include taking a great deal of care before one "interjects" or otherwise imposes oneself on a collaborative performance because, as Blackman Santana maintains, "it takes taste, it takes intellect, it takes heart to . . . do that and keep the music swingin'." As Guiliana has previously noted in the context of performing as a leader, interjection is a right to be earned only after his checklist of moment-by-moment drummer obligations has been attended to. Like me, Erskine feels a responsibility to produce some "written" ideas (i.e., predetermined ideas transmitted by any means, not exclusively graphic) for an initial rehearsal at the outset of a project. The thoughts of many are expressed by Salmins for whom "making something of lasting value that's going to be listened to more than once" is a "heavy responsibility." The responsibilities being described here are thus not simply to the leader/producer/client but to more abstract and ephemeral ideas. Creativity is not simply a self-serving expression of self; rather, it brings with it a sense of responsibility to something larger—to persist with the creative action not until it is perfect, but until it *feels just right*, "for the sake of the music."

•   There are plenty of psychological and methodological minefields there, then, for drummers to tiptoe through in the search for creative outcomes. How do they avoid, transform, or circumnavigate these and other constraints in their pursuit of difference? Constraints seem to be self-imposed internally or imposed externally by or upon others, and are in some way inherent to the genre or situation. They may potentially have either positive or negative effects on the creative process. Internal negative constraints arise most commonly, and with greatest affect, from a surprisingly rich vein of perceived limitations: Peter Erskine's shortage of "mechanical skills," Dylan Howe's "self-consciousness," and Thomas Strønen's decision to stop writing music because he "didn't know the rules well enough" all come to mind.

Constraints are also self-imposed as creative strategies, voluntarily and deliberately, in several ways and with more positive outcomes. For example, in discussing his recording process, Dylan on one occasion gave himself "complete freedom but also only allowed myself to do two takes. So that one [song] called 'Unitune' is just essentially me completely improvising over me improvising." Thomas is governed by a strict protocol in his use of music technology: "it has to be organic." As a compositional aid, Mark sets parameters for himself: "Okay, I want to write lead-sheet songs. They have to fit on one page and it has to be a melody with chord symbols." In the extract below, he traces "some of the creativity" back to the extraction of as many sound combinations as possible within an orchestrationally "limited world":

Even with the sound of the drums, you know, I kind of limit myself orchestrationally to maybe more of an "okay, now I'm here, and I'm playing this character, and he's . . . ," trying to really extract or pull out as many different possibilities as we can within this seemingly limited world as you know and I feel like that's where some of the creativity lies.

In as much as addition or extension ("going further") are identified as transformative strategies that promote the construction of difference, so equally might be removal, restriction, or omission. Describing the actions of a colleague, Thomas put it like this: "He played much more open and loose, but you could tell he could play everything. He just . . . didn't; he held back instead." Similar strategies are echoed in Thomas's report of the performances of another provocative drummer who delighted in the unexpected. In my experience, a radical restructuring of the mediational means (the reordering or removal of some of the drum kit's constituent parts, most notably the hihat and ride cymbal) is yet another way to disrupt habitual practice and encourage fresh thinking.

Some, such as Cindy Blackman Santana, construe whole genres as so constrained as to be essentially inimical to rhythmic creativity. Others see performance within constraints as a challenge, allowing them to both demonstrate their creativity and gain useful experience. In Ralph Salmins's opinion, for example, a big band can be

> a bit of a millstone round one's neck, but I like it. It's got certain boundaries, but it does allow you a lot of freedom. (*Are those stylistic boundaries?*) They are stylistic boundaries mainly, and the most creative I've felt in a band apart from just swinging a straight big band like the Count Basie band, have been playing in this band The Guy Barker Jazz Orchestra, which is a very creative orchestra.

In the context of his orchestral and studio work, Peter is "energized" by the constraints of the arrangement:

> So my most creative expression, just by these two examples at least, is completely in the context of an arrangement or, in a more academic sense, a constrained structure. So I think my most creative work is within a framework.

Preparing for a rare drum kit performance in an orchestral setting, Peter changes his process to accommodate the constraints of a cadenza he has been asked to perform. He develops a strategy that operates between a predetermined "mapping out" associated with composition and the going off on what he calls a "whatever," which he associates with jazz performance. He tends to hear creativity in small things rather than the brash gestures afforded by Thomas's or Mark's abrupt changes in conceptual direction. Peter's conception of the process embodies an element of stealth, the art being to conceal the art. It is useful in relation to deconstructing traditional notions of what creativity is to note that the phenomenon does not necessarily draw attention to itself, especially if it is in service of something like a piece of music. So it may not appear to be "creative" to someone who was not involved in the process. While classical music promotes the notion of the "informed listener," democratized popular music acknowledges no such person. The expectation that if I, the performer, think it is creative everyone will recognize it as such appears unreasonable and will likely be unfulfilled.

Experiential evidence within the literature supports formal structural constraints like some of the above as conducive to ingenuity. Observing one interviewee's choice of engagement with the rules of a particular poetic form, Matthew Peacock notes: "These rules are arbitrary but also self-chosen. Her statement that 'the appeal of poetry is that it's not just words . . . it's words in a framework' implies that the presence of the framework adds something to the poem because it necessitates ingenuity on the poet's part. Essentially, it forces her to be more creative." The evidence here supports Peacock's conclusion that "contrary to common assumptions, restriction and creativity are not inversely related."[18] Our drummers' experiences of constraint found substantial fit with existing creativity models that see "pre-inventive" or preliminary ideas frequently interpreted during an exploratory phase (in the domain of music, in practice, and in rehearsal) and then expanded conceptually through modification and the imposition of such constraints.[19] Real or perceived constraints are not "merely" conducive to creative achievement in the course of performance but they are a *necessary aspect* of the creative process.[20] As we have seen, drummers devise a multiplicity of imaginative ways to circumnavigate or co-opt them. Our interviewees confirm that interaction with these constraints through multiple interlinked strategies and processes, far from being restrictive, tends to fuel creative action.

Choosing How to Play It

Having decided what to play, the manner in which it is expressed becomes crucial. Within music, expression might most simply be thought of as the "added value of a performance" and as "part of the reason that music is interesting to listen to and sounds alive."[21] To communicate experience, I argue, it must first be expressed. As discussed in chapter 1, it is the production, expression, and communication of experience that may, in turn, be assigned significance. Music performers blend instrumental, interpretive, and expressive skills with their "expressive intentions" to determine specific performances.[22]

The idea of "playing expressively" is often defined in terms of "communicating emotions" and "playing with feeling,"[23] but our participants' perspectives appear to diverge from this. In so far as drummers' expressive intentions were specifically broached within the interviews, they were characterized less in terms of an intention to express emotion to a non-performing listener, more in terms of an intention to express experience to a co-performing listener, and receive recognition and acknowledgment for it. This may in part explain an orientation toward the conveyance of meaning to co-performers rather than non-performing listeners, an observation shortly to emerge from the experts' testimony in relation to the audience.

In practice, it is through the exercise of choice and skill over when and what to play, and the manner in which to play it, that the individual drummer exerts expressive control as a starting point for creative practice. The extent to which she or he does so is the extent to which the practice may be characterized as "compositional" within the terms of the FCC. As the drummer is afforded greater control of the levers of expressive performance—tempo, meter, dynamics, and timbre—she or he appears to exhibit a rising level of aesthetic awareness and increasing proximity to creativity. While the several points of intersection and interrelation of pulse and meter, metric dissonance, swing, and beat, tempo, and groove[24] have attracted much analytical attention on the understanding that these musical notions are sufficiently stable to permit useful analysis, the focus in this section is on how drummers actually define, constitute, hear, and ascribe meaning to them.

Drummers "add value" to the music through creative expression. This tends to be interpreted in reference to a broader set of what Patrik Juslin identifies as "perceptual qualities (e.g., structural, emotional, motional) that reflect psycho-physical relationships between 'objective' properties of the music, and 'subjective' . . . impressions of the listener."[25] Here these include, for Cindy Blackman Santana, touching, sharing, and being able to take the music to "unbridled heights." Cindy refers repeatedly to her love of "touching people" and how much she wants to "touch their hearts."

For Asaf Sirkis, they include connecting and communicating. Asaf sees the communicative moment as "the moment where everything that's about you comes out." Unlike myself, he finds it easier to express himself in music than in words: "I felt that music held something for me that I could express myself... in a way I couldn't express myself in words. That was a big, big thing for me. It still is, yeah." Expression is tied up with "developing your own sound, your own style of playing, your own way of expressing yourself." On his account, an audience is an essential component of successful expression:

> I started music because I wanted to express something, but you cannot just express it for yourself. You really do need an audience [laughs], you really need to be, I would say, to be <u>seen</u>. <u>To be seen</u> is a very important thing. You want to be yourself and you want other people to say, "Yes, I see you. I can see you. I hear you."

Here the expressive intention is recognition and acknowledgment, both important goals of the drummer in compositional performance. Asaf communicates in order "to be seen," in sharp contrast to the musical chameleon in functional performance, for whom a crucial aim (unless otherwise directed) is to *avoid* "being seen."

The ability to be expressive may be constrained by the performance context. Any drummer might reasonably say that freedom of expression presupposes that (a) he or she has some degree of agency over what is performed, and (b) there is perceptible change as a result of his or her playing such as to permit evaluation of any creative input. In a discussion of creative expression in his own recorded performances, Ralph Salmins quantifies his degree of creativity in terms of the FCC:

> If somebody says "go and play this really simple part on a pop track," I'm being creative, but much less so. If somebody gives me one of these pieces of music or these musical situations, I'm being <u>very</u> creative in what I do.

Difference, too, may be constructed from reinterpretation, in a form of recombinational creativity. Describing a performance of one of her songs by drummer Tony Williams, Cindy Blackman Santana claims that "his interpretation made that song be a whole different thing." Elsewhere, she reflects on the meaning of expression:

> You can express at any level. I'm talking about a certain degree of expressibility; I'm talking about a level of expressibility. If you can play

one note and you can play it convincingly, you can express with that one note. But I'm talking about a level of innovation . . . I'm talking about being able to take the music to unbridled heights. [. . .] That means that anything coming into you, any energies that you're thinking, anything you're feeling, you're able to express through actually playing it.

In the above extract, she characterizes the "unbridled heights" as the highest level of performance capability, as the ability to express "anything coming in to you" (through a process of letting and allowing) by rendering it audible. She expresses melody and harmony through her compositions: "I love to write. [. . .] I love harmony and I love melody, and as a drummer it's so beautiful to be able to express those things through composition." Creative expression is one way to add value through change or transformation. Expression of experience is the "something else" that both adds value to the functional performance and embodies the significant difference between the functional and the compositional; it's the alchemical component to be communicated prior to creative assessment. That component is typically found by "going further," an action drawn out in chapter 5.

Four Levers of Control

While Gareth Dylan Smith's drum teacher may have constantly reminded his student that "it's all about time,"[26] I would suggest that he was only one quarter correct. Earlier I briefly described the foundational mechanism of a drummer's expressive interpretation as comprising four levers of control: temporal, metrical, dynamical, and timbral. These performance parameters are typically manipulated to provide her or him with a different-sounding voice and an identifiable style, and each deserves a closer look.

THE TEMPORAL

A drummer's primary function is generally construed, from within practice and without, as keeping time. The revered community elder most frequently named by participants, Elvin Jones, allegedly said that "the role of the drummer is primarily to keep time."[27] At the highly constrained, somewhat homogenized end of the FCC, proficiency is evidenced by the ability to maintain Moore's standard rock beat with minimal deviation and maximal consistency within tight stylistic boundaries. Summarizing the emotional effects of discrete musical factors, Alf Gabrielsson considered tempo to be the most decisive.[28] In short, keeping time is seen as important.

There are, however, many ways in which time may be kept and many people who may keep it. Personalized notions of tempo have long spoken to the Western drummer's sense of self-identity, and continue to form one of the loci of creativity in drummer performance. Punk drummers like Rat Scabies and jazz drummers like Tony Williams, for example, tended to increase the tempo, as did Buddy Rich.[29] Blair Sinta spoke earlier about his studio work in terms of "restraint and holding back as long as possible without having it [the music] lack dynamics or energy," a difficult feat of balance over "negotiated" time.[30] Gareth Smith, a practitioner himself, spoke eloquently of the drummer being expected to both lead and follow, and to drive while accompanying.[31] Elsewhere I have described my precomputer experiences in progressive rock as calling for an "orchestral" approach to time, whereby the drummer saw himself as the conductor of the ensemble, at liberty to approach the tempo with the fluidity he thought appropriate.[32] I suspect that the rather sudden and arbitrary removal of governance of tempo in recording studios since the mid-1970s may have been responsible, in part, for a seismic shock to the body percussive, lowering its status and questioning its purpose, with the important ramifications outlined shortly in chapter 6.

Any interagentive rhythmic creativity between music technology and human performance lies in the relationship between the click and the human. (References to the "click" or "click track" identify any type of automated metronome, typically played to the drummer through headphones and designed to keep him or her in time.) Much discussed within practice, this has tended to be analyzed in the literature from the perspective of measurable deviance between one and the other, and the implications any such deviance might have for swing or groove.[33] Only recently has this relationship been addressed from the perspective of the psychology of performance and any real or imagined impact on creativity.[34]

The immediate beneficiary of the arrival of the automated click track in the mid-1970s was the producer, now afforded a greater ease of tape editing in the surety that edited sections would at least be consistently in time.[35] One early consequence was to discourage the personalized attitudes to tempo already illustrated. Consistent tempo was now something scientifically measurable, no longer under the subjective control of the drummer or open to discussion. The use of click tracks became established as normal practice in the recording of commercial genres such as rock, pop, film, TV, and advertising music. The ascending power of the record producer/technologist over the practitioner/drummer in the latter half of the 20th century was clearly signaled in terms of the (respectively) expanding and contracting space afforded to each in the recording studio.[36]

Despite anecdotal evidence of recent accommodations between practitioner and technology, a tension remains between conflicting understandings of consistency and its relationship to the individual expression of musical identity.[37] Drummers live in an awkward world between what the drum culture expects of them, what the public expects, and what they themselves expect.[38] On the one hand, the producer expects performance consistency (a notion that is frequently interpreted by practitioners as limiting expressive possibilities) to facilitate cutting, pasting, looping, editing, and beat matching, and to fulfil a real or imagined commercial imperative.[39] On the other, the drummer may expect, through control and choice of musical materials, to use his own "voice" to express his self-identity. The jazz musician in particular spends much time developing a voice that eventually may speak clearly and expressively with its own "vocabulary," that stock of timbral and sonic preferences and habitual tendencies to approach the music in a personalized, idiosyncratic (and thus recognizable) manner. For him or her, "consistency" may be interpreted as the consistent use of the personalized language.[40]

This tension tends to be resolved in practice through the sublimation of self-identity in the interest of successful performance. Functional practice expects such sublimation on demand; compositional practice requires the projection of the drummer's identity as a component of the playable performance being assessed.[41] The extent to which (and the ease with which) the drummer is able to oscillate between sublimation and projection of an expressive identity is mirrored in the ongoing "identity work" of advanced classical piano students in their struggle to bring forward, on the one hand, personally meaningful, creative interpretations, and, on the other, interpretations deemed acceptable within the canon.[42]

Identity may further be expressed in the "playing out of time with precision." Among pitched instrumentalists, the playing or singing in tune, the adhering to a pitch standard in performance, is generally considered to be a normative standard of practice in Western music. Playing out of tune "with precision," however, has been conceptualized as a distinguishing mark of musicianship.[43] This exerting of tension and release between the "being out of" and the "being in" is paralleled in the unpitched rhythmic sphere in playing out of time with precision.[44] Within the constraint of stylistic convention, the drummer becomes subtly adept at playing with time—that is, playing marginally behind or ahead of the beat to create and release tension. The ability to play ahead of, with, or behind the computer's clock-time to engender feel and groove has become a highly sought-after skill among exemplary practitioners such as Steve Gadd, the late Jeff Porcaro, or Ahmir "Questlove" Thompson, all key exponents of the second of the core areas of drummer expression to which the discussion turns—the metrical.

THE METRICAL

It is not my intention to offer a full musicological analysis of the notion of meter and its relationship to groove. I interpret the term "metrical" rather loosely to comprise the notion of musical emphasis as it relates to groove. It is sufficient for my purpose to take meter in the general sense as a recurring pattern of stresses or accents that generate the music's beat or pulse. The location, consistency, and variation of such accents have an intimate correlation with the construction of musical identity and together represent the second lever of expressive control available to the drummer.

Philip Tagg's adroit characterization of the groove as consisting of "one or more rhythm patterns, lasting, as single units, no longer than the extended present [...], but those patterns have to be repeated several times before they constitute grooves" serves here as a working definition of the phenomenon.[45] The groove has been conceptualized in several different ways within the literature: as external objects and embodied processes, as emerging from forms of sharedness and entrainment, as shared knowledge, as an engagement of experiences, as an expression of empathetic creativity through attunement, in terms of cellular groove patterns, and as, in LeRoi Jones's beautifully concise phrase, "the changing same."[46] We would be detained unnecessarily were we to engage individually with each of these interesting approaches; rather, I want to pull together some aspects of them in order to refocus the groove within a humanist/technological binary as the most useful way to think about the topic in the context of the discussion at hand.

One line of thinking interprets the groove (and grooving) as an essential, expressive component of popular music, characterized by human agency. From this viewpoint, the groove is something that has to be "found" before it can be enacted between people. It is understood to be mutually constituted through human interaction arising from the timing behaviors of the players,[47] and as denoting "something negotiated between musicians that is larger than themselves."[48] Charles Keil's often cited theory of "participatory discrepancies" has done much to evaluate the importance of these small and continuous negotiations; they not only help avoid the dehumanizing feel of absolute metronomic coordination but permit the participatory interaction between people that is at the essence of groove.[49]

Such views coalesce within a humanist perspective that posits groove as a framework for drummer creativity.

Approaching from a phenomenological perspective, Harris Berger sees groove as an "engagement of experiences." For him, "the sense of what has been called groove in music (that the rhythm of a particular piece is stiff or flowing, mechanical, graceful, danceable or static) isn't a product of the structure of a musical text and performance but of the engagement among the experiences of the musicians and listeners that the performance mediates."[50] My own experience at a 1975 Tower of Power concert confirms this. When 3,000 seated people in a theater stand as one to applaud a critical combination of tempo, key, lighting changes, and a new groove, this critical audience feedback confirms that the groove is good, and the band grooves even harder. This and similar situation-specific interpretive behaviors on behalf of the audience are necessary to the constitution of musical creativity.

The "polyphonic streams"[51] that comprise the groove as constituted and manipulated by several performers in a group are, in solo drummer performance, collapsed into the four-limb coordinated independence of the single practitioner, as in, for example, the work of Max Roach. Street drummer and jazz soloist alike may perform alone, but never in a vacuum. In so far as their efforts, shaped by the cultural psychology, are distributed and communicated within the community of practice, meaning may be constructed, significance assessed, and creativity attributed.

An oppositional "technological" paradigm of groove asserts that no such human agency is necessary to its constituency. The proponents of electronic dance music or music for gaming, for example, assert that machines can groove effectively on their own.[52] In light of the digital age redefinitions that see the computer as a musical instrument and the inputting of data as performance, both musico-humanist and musico-technological creators function as composers, performers, and producers in collaborative acts of grooving (collaborative by nature of the musical environment in which both are agents).

The groove that both powers the humanist artifact and gives it meaning is *intra-performer* in nature, generated in real time in a collaborative act with, typically, an audience present. The technologist's groove tends to be embodied in audience co-construction of a groove already part-composed in nonlinear time, real or virtual, away from public scrutiny and with no, or minimal, intra-performer dimension.[53] The central commonality between both humanist and technological perspectives is that groove is something constructed with, or in the presence of, others. One important difference lies in interpretation of "others"; the former sees the groove as co-

constructed between performers, or performers and listener/audience, while the latter understands the groove as a co-creative experience between DJ/producer and crowd.

Ever since the early 19th-century introduction of the metronome, the practitioner's role has been on a slow shift from one of interpreter to "repro-ducer of an ideal with exact specifications,"[54] from "being human" to "being mechanical." It is worth noting the ontological tension here—it is impossible for a human to be mechanical:

> He cannot give back unaltered what he gets, as the parrot does. He is not a repeating machine. His mental creations are much more vital and transforming. Try as he will he cannot exactly reproduce; and when he comes near to it his self-love protests and claims its right to do its own thinking.[55]

The hardest thing to do, should the drummer wish to do it, is to be mechanical in drumming. The very absurdity of such an enterprise is matched only by the tenacity with which it is pursued, most notably in the twilight world of the tribute band. It remains a project doomed to failure because the individual persists in thinking and imagining in his or her own way. The drummer's spiritual home continues to be found, at least primarily, within the humanist paradigm of groove.

THE DYNAMICAL

Recent analysis tends to support anecdotal and empirical evidence that much popular music is performed loud and getting louder, and is becoming more repetitive.[56] I was once working with a powerful drummer-colleague in a two-drummer group. His "pocket" was deep, his time steady, but he was so loud that the floor shook. I went over and told him how much I loved what he was doing, not to change the part, but if he could do it all a little quieter, it might work better in the overall sound of the ensemble. This he seemed to take on board. The next time we tried the song, however, he played exactly the same dynamic with three of the four limbs that previously played the part, but simply omitted whatever he had been playing with the fourth limb. His idea of dynamics, it transpired, was *to leave something out* if he wanted it "quieter," and to *add something* if he wanted it "louder." My original suggestion had falsely presumed he would play exactly the same notes that he had been playing, with no additions or omissions, at a lower, but still balanced, overall dynamic.

This anecdote speaks to a homogenization of dynamics in popular music drum performance, arguably in support of the demand for consistency. Dynamic compression on both the recording itself and the broadcast output of FM commercial radio may be deemed necessary in the attraction and retention of a listening audience,[57] but it tends to render performer expression through dynamic control largely redundant. Such minor dynamics as may remain in the original performance tend be smoothed out on broadcast. The effective absence of a requirement for dynamic control leaves the functional drummer tightly constrained in any pursuit of creative expression.

Moreover, the "loud and getting louder" paradigm impinges on what is physically playable on a drum kit and for how long it is playable. If carpal tunnel syndrome, hearing loss, tinnitus, and blistered hands are the physical manifestations of the paradigm, the musical consequences for the art of the drummer are equally evident in the abandonment of finesse, restraint, seduction, metrical ambiguity, and timbral control—in short, many of the aspects of drumming that embody its musicality. It is a commonplace that all percussion instruments have a maximum volume at which they sound well, after which, if struck harder, the timbral quality deteriorates and either the instrument or the striking implement simply breaks. Optimum maximal volume is reached quite quickly. The Herculean quantities of performance effort evident on the arena circuit are thus sonically unnecessary, serving more theatrical than musical ends.

The Timbral

Manipulation of three of the four levers of control, then, appears circumscribed by some combination of the engagement with music technology, the requirements of performance consistency, and the flattening of dynamics. The timbral dimension, however, fares better in two respects. First, multiple timbral options and variables are increasingly available to the drummer in matters of strikers (hands, sticks, mallets, reed-like Blasticks, brushes and shakers of all description, held butt-end or orthodox, matched or unmatched) and instruments struck (choice of drumheads, shells, dampening), the whole attenuated by the immediate audio environment (room reverberation, choice of mics and their placement) and subject to the whim of sonic fashion. This is the area brought forward in the Blair Sinta case study. Experimenting with boundaries of timbral color established by guardians of the canon, within and outside the community, may however attract approbation in the musical arts similar to that in the visual arts. My efforts to extend the sonic possibilities of the drum kit by developing a hybrid electroacoustic kit in the mid-1990s led to a somewhat checkered intercourse with both technology and the commentariat.

Second, it is worth briefly considering the timbral implications of the drummer's "chords," evidenced particularly in the work of Terry Bozzio and Max Roach.[58] Assuming a four limbed-drummer is playing a standard seven-piece drum set of bass drum, snare drum, hi-hat, high tom, low tom, ride, and crash cymbals, she or he may strike any combination of seven instruments with any combination of up to four limbs. Conceptualizing each of these combinations in terms of unpitched "chords," they may be likened to the 60-chord family of the jazz pianist, the five qualities of seventh chords available on each of the 12 degrees of the chromatic scale.[59] For instance, the timbral implications of a drummer striking a chord of her or his three highest-pitched instruments (all metallophones: hi-hat, crash, and ride cymbals) are quite different from those arising when three lowest-pitched instruments (all membranophones: bass drum, low tom, and high tom) are played.

The sforzando attack of the bass drum and crash cymbal in unison, a direct import from the symphony orchestra, is now so ingrained in practice that many drummers avoid using a crash cymbal without a bass drum in support. While providing a good example of the timbral homogenization within performance practice, this two-note chord has become so common that the seeker after a different musical identity may wish to avoid it altogether. The drummer's chord family comes to life with (a) the timbre (tone color) occasioned by the position of the strike; (b) its volume (amplitude) caused by the velocity of the strike; (c) its placement in the measure; (d) its placement relative to the preceding and following "chords" or blocks of sound, and (e) the implements with which it is struck. Within that schema, the possible variables affecting timbre appear to be infinitely gradable.

Summary

In this chapter I have highlighted some of the constraints and considerations that impact upon performance as the drummer selects what to play and the manner in which it is to be played. We have come some way since the concert at which my artist-manager acquaintance was unable to detect any selection of rhythmic components whatsoever in the performance of a rock drummer. Effecting significant audible difference of the kind that might attract creative attribution within the constraints of the performance environment appears to be becoming increasingly difficult as the available levers of control begin to seize up under the weight of conflicting expectations.

Almost all drummers, however, have some choice in what they play and how they play it. A clear demand for an unwavering rendition of the standard rock beat will seldom stipulate the timbre and precise dynamic relative to the other instruments. The adventurous creator at even the hard functional extreme of the FCC is sensitive to the ways in which navigation of the multiple constraints surrounding such a performance can add an expressive dimension that may, more or less covertly, engender significant difference. She has selected what to play and has pulled some levers. Now she has to make it sound different, and significantly so. The manner in which that is achieved is the subject of the next chapter.

- The expert perspective suggests that:

    - The first action-goal is to decide what to play and how to play it. Experts problematize selection, choice, and decision-making.
    - Creativity is understood as both constrained by and achievable within any genre or style, although different genres and styles may be more or less conducive to the communication of creative difference.
    - Goal-orientated action is mediated as much by the sociocultural as by the sonic environment.
    - The paradox of choice in performance is that it both enables creative action and constrains it.
    - Most locate creativity in the recombination of existing elements rather than in the pursuit of newness for its own sake.
    - Creativity does not necessarily draw attention to itself.
    - Notions of constraint may be categorized as (a) negative and internally imposed, (b) positive and internally imposed, (c) negative and externally imposed, and (d) positive and externally imposed.
    - Multiple interlinked creative strategies are deployed to negotiate these constraints, the construction of which in itself represents creative action.

5 • It's All What We Do with It

Constructing Difference

The purpose of the SDCA framework, introduced earlier, is to depict the essential dimensions of creative performance (figure 1). The second dimension, addressed in this chapter, insists that some aspect of the performance needs to be different. This has much in common with Glăveanu's Five A's framework. While Glăveanu acknowledges that difference is a central component of creative expression, he prefers the notion of differentiation, which finds its expression within action. The creative quality of action, he argues, always resides in "how differences are negotiated, manipulated, widened or bridged" by the individual in "concrete cultural settings."[1]

For any type of creative artifact to be original, there needs to be qualitative difference in some respect from any previously known instance of that type. But we should be careful to avoid conflating the two distinct notions of originality and uniqueness. Every performance is unique in the sense that it takes place at a different time and place, and every composition is unique in that it uses different notes in a different order, but to ascribe originality to either artifact is to render the term useless. If the analysis is sufficiently fine grained, every drum performance will necessarily differ from every other in some way.[2] What, then, is "difference" to an expert drummer? Those interviewed tend to interpret the idea as "not sounding like anybody else." Construction of difference is governed to a large extent by reference to what the "other guys" do (by which is meant "other drummers"): "that's not something I've heard other guys do," says Peter Erskine. Citing one of his own self-selected works, Chad Wackerman feels able to attribute it as creative because

> it does sound really different and it doesn't sound like anybody else and I thought I'm proud that it doesn't sound like anybody else.

In the previous chapter we saw how Tony Williams's reinterpretation of one of Cindy Blackman Santana's compositions met with her approval because it "made that song be a whole different thing."

To the extent to which they want to construct it at all, there are many ways by which drummers might construct difference in performance. The use and manipulation of the timbral palette and metric dissonance;[3] the aleatoric unpredictability of improvisation; compositional or band-leading skills involving a collaborative creativity of the kind invoked by Pamela Burnard; stylistic individuation through touch, feel, or technical virtuosity[4]—all may, on their own or in combination, engender difference as a catalyst of the creative process. Difference may further be sought through personalized interpretation and expression, two components that many consider essential for creative music performance. The latter has been discussed as a "value additive" in the previous chapter. Two further observations are important in any consideration of the former and its relationship to the creation of difference.

Understandings of "interpretation" within music have migrated from the classical tradition that sees it as an aspect of performance that is highly prepared in advance.[5] This might be contrasted with the popular music conception of interpretation as unprepared, spontaneous, and aleatoric, such as might be found in jazz and other contemporary idioms. The individualistic modeling of a piece of music according to the performer's own ideas or musical intentions has at some times and in some places been denigrated in both music traditions. In the sphere of the contemporary drummer, for example, such interpretive modeling may be deprecated as rhythmic inconsistency, as the "taking of liberties" so reviled within record production, as noted earlier. By way of neutralizing this unfortunate tendency, Simon Zagorski-Thomas highlights the "specific contemporary approach to performance for recording which might be characterized as 'getting a good eight bars' which can then be copied throughout the song arrangement."[6] In the ever-more determined pursuit of "consistency," contemporary producers remain untroubled by the consequent homogenization of the rhythmic culture. Anecdotally, many practitioners warm to the contrasting Deweyan view that rhythm involves constant variation and those liberties differentiate mechanical construction from artistic production.

From another perspective, the spontaneous microadjustment of a highly prepared interpretation is what makes each performance a creative activity.[7] Each performance exists somewhere on a continuum of interpretative preparedness with, for instance, a tribute band performance positioned as the polar opposite to a free jazz performance. However, if small spontaneous adjustments define each performance as a creative activity, then almost all drum performance would seem to be identifiable as creative, and thus a long way from the Csikszentmihalyian modeling of the work of a domain-changer such as Max Roach, described in chapter 2. Everyone seems to agree that ambiguities in musical notation in either tradition, however, allow a performer considerable freedom in deciding how to interpret the music's content.

Gluing the Music Together: The Core Functions of Appropriate Performance

Even in compositional performance, the mode in which I think drummer creativity is most available or accessible, the construction of significant difference is seldom pursued remorselessly. Core functions of performance have to be attended to first, earning the drummer the "right" to "interfere." Mark Guiliana has a list of these functions:

> My subconscious checklist of my responsibilities at every moment . . . you know, time, or groove, dynamics (*form has got to be big*) yeah, form, dynamics, sound . . . So long as I'm accommodating these responsibilities, then not only do I feel like I've earned the right to either inject my own personality or inject new musical ideas into the moment, but I feel like I've also built my confidence to a place that will even allow me to make those kind of statements. If I'm in a situation where I feel like the time's a little funny, I feel incapable of really making creative decisions until that settles.

The developing theme here is that creativity tends to be seen not as a foundational concern, but as a secondary issue to be attended to after foundational concerns have been addressed. The issues that Mark feels it is his responsibility to accommodate usually cohere around the establishment of some sort of stability in the music. The music must first be made to work through "appropriate performance," the provision of which expert drummers take as a key function. The notion of appropriateness is much in evidence in creativity studies as a "crucial birthmark" of the phenomenon.[8] Appropriate work has been described as that which "satisfies the problem constraints, is useful or fulfils a need"[9]—by that token and in this context, appropriate performance fulfils a musical need. Referencing the work of a colleague, Peter Erskine describes the man's choices as "almost never outrageous but they were always perfect." Although not explicitly stated, the sense here is of choices that were *perfectly appropriate* to the musical situation.

Peter speaks for many drummers when he characterizes appropriate drum performance as providing the "right thing . . . what's best for the music." "Providing the right thing" tends to be informed first, by listening, and second, in Ralph Salmins's illuminating metaphor, by "working out the glue that will glue the music together":

> You play what's appropriate, and that I think is one of the central tenets of what a drummer does creatively, is to understand, listen to the music, and then . . . almost create some alchemy whereby you work out the glue that will glue the music together, by creating parts that work. So if, for instance, a band is maybe in danger of falling apart, the first thing a drummer will do is pull it together because it needs to be done. [. . .] It can be on as simple a level as that.

The glue needed here is to prevent the band "falling apart." Although Ralph doesn't specify within which domain, music or social, the band may be falling apart, drummers become adept at applying adhesive in both, generally perceiving themselves to be there to serve and shape the music in ways both musical and nonmusical. Ralph maintains that "we've got a job as much as anything. It's not just being in charge of the time; everyone's responsible for the time" and we provide "that alchemy to try and make a musical ensemble work." Mark, meanwhile, is "just trying to serve the music as much as possible." Chad Wackerman articulates yet another view of the core function in terms of "building it" and "making it go":

> Usually as drummers—as leaders—we're always shaping the dynamics of the band and the transition points to the second verse, the chorus, the bridge. We are the ones who are building it or making it go dynamically. There is a certain weight or density you get by playing sparse to dense, making it more exciting, obviously, or do the reverse, bring the band down with the nano notes with the transitions.

Dylan Howe interprets his role and that of drummers in general as being "support and foundation and then occasional prodding or reacting . . . But it's very much a supportive role to the lead actors." That supportiveness recurs in the previously identified subtheme of making the lead actors comfortable enough to perform creatively, with such action itself being interpreted by some as creative. This "prodding and reacting" evokes the actions of the driver of a four-in-hand horse carriage; the four horses have their reins rigged in such a way that the vehicle can be driven by a single person. In races, an iota of excess speed from the lead horse can tip a carriage in an instant. Although I have never tried driving such a vehicle, I suspect there are parallels here with the drummer in a thoroughbred, listening jazz group. Seated behind and sometimes above his or her standing charges, the drummer nudges, accelerates, lays back, or drives forward at critical moments. A scintilla of slippery syncopation from an overenthusiastic co-performer that goes uncontained by a dithering drummer can undermine Flow and mess with groove. All four horses must run as one to develop maximum horsepower. The carriage driver instantly feels a dragging, malingering, or overenthusiastic animal through the reins and can communicate his commands back with delicacy or firmness as may be necessary. The drummer feels it through the sticks; something is wrong, lumpy, or not running smoothly. While the touch of the whip and the vocal instructions of the four-in-hand driver are, metaphorically speaking, rare in music performance, both were nevertheless dispensed with considerable enthusiasm by drummer Buddy Rich in his orchestra.[10]

Most of the drummers I cite in this book continue to refine an individual performance style in the development of a personal voice, the production of a sonic identity that cannot be usurped by another player. This is both a means to differentiation and individuation and a useful if not essential component for the development of a solo career. I shall shortly develop the notion of sonic identity further in the context of expressive consistency; the key point here is that individual performance style seems to be interpreted always as subject to behavior appropriate to the *broader* musical style in which the performance is embedded. While drum styles may be unstable and somewhat contested, there remain sufficient typical examples to permit broad agreement as to the main features of, for example, "funk," "grime," "metal," "gospel," or "hip-hop" drumming. Drum action then becomes more or less appropriate for that style. Experts are highly attuned to shifting stylistic borders and sufficiently confident as to mix, match, appropriate, challenge, or transgress them at will by means of individual strategies and processes, governed only but always by the constraints of the immediate performance situation.

Appropriate performance, then, is foundational; creativity is something that may be attended to after foundational concerns have been addressed. It may be possible, or even essential, to be appropriate without being creative, in, for example, the highly constrained world of the tribute band or the circus drummer. On the other side of the coin, unconstrained solo performance is the only context that would seem to entertain creativity without appropriateness. If one function of art is to shock, it may be appropriate to be inappropriate.

Avoiding Demons: Individual Strategies and Processes

What are some of the individual strategies and processes that drummers deploy to engender difference, the second dimension of the SDCA model, after the core functions have been attended to? Our experts reveal the exotic, the unlikely, the functional, and the imaginative: a brief sample conveys some idea of the breadth of thinking. Asaf, for instance, constructs a situation in which he hopes creativity will beget creativity: "I try to surround myself with people I like, their playing, and they like my playing as well and . . . hope that, you know, this thing will <u>attract</u> more of itself to it." He puts his long car journeys to gigs to good use internalizing the principal components of the music—chord sequences, rhythmic motifs, riffs, and melodies—by learning them by heart. He needs nothing external to the music.

Ever since he attended a particularly influential drum clinic, Chad has been avoiding "demons": "I've been trying to be exactly in the moment and not having these kind of demons that say I'm not playing creative, or I missed that one, or . . ." As a "spontaneous composer" his creative strategy is to focus on immediate selection between options, fully aware of the implications his decisions will have for affecting the course and sound of the music:

> So what I'm thinking about is, I guess, the choices I have at that moment. So if the guitar player plays something, do I want to reinforce that or do I want to give him a bed of something so he stands out, or do I want to play some flurry when he stops, or stop? . . . All the tons and tons of choices you have as a spontaneous composer—and try to be in that head space.

This reads as an interesting combination of partly responding spontaneously to what the other players are doing while simultaneously considering the available options, mirroring a dimension of creative performance found also in dance and theater.

Mark Guiliana and Thomas Strønen are astute conceptual thinkers. Both describe using a fluid, aleatoric creative process, expressed in terms of making something out of nothing, or not much, with predictably unpredictable outcomes. As Mark puts it:

> Sometimes I've found just saying "hey, let's play this" and that could be 18 minutes of music, and it could end up in a completely new place, but having allowed it to become that, maybe just kind of having a bit

of ignorance and saying "this is the bass line" . . . even though I'm handing it to a virtuosic bass player who of course would come up with something better or cooler or whatever. . . . Just say "here, this is it" knowing that in a moment it will become something different.

This transformative process allows for early motifs to be abandoned as the music gets rolling, to be replaced with "something better or cooler" such that the music might end up in a "completely new place." A related process leads Thomas to a profound moment of awareness. He describes a rehearsal bogged down with overwritten scores. A co-performer mentions to the leader that he also had something prepared:

He took out a piece of paper with three bars, and that was it. And we started playing, and that piece ended up on the record, [. . .], and it lasted for ten minutes! [. . .] And then I thought: I can do that.

Echoing Chad's strategy of avoidance, Thomas adopts a degree of naïveté as a protective wall "in order to keep my perception of music alive." He strives to avoid what he hears as the most offensive popular music of the day: "I try not to think of all the shit music that comes out and how it's being made."

Mark has much to say with regard to the use of multiple interlinked creative strategies. His psychological toolbox and checklist of responsibilities that allow him to defer them to the music; his artificial limitation of sonic options; his "arranger-type" view of performance that aims to extract "as many different possibilities as we can within this seemingly limited world"; his efforts to try to show up to the gig psychologically "empty," without pre-planning: "therefore I have all this room for new ideas, to take them in, and then it's what I do to them in that moment that becomes its own vocabulary" — all these reveal a creative mind at work. He likes to think in sizeable conceptual blocks that may then be conjoined and transformed into fresh tintinnabulations. He takes some "Jim influence" (Jim Black, highly influential drummer) or "some of that programmed stuff," steals "some influences from the underground or less highlighted places," and manipulates the whole into something unlikely or unusual. As a bandleader, he finds creativity in the imaginative exploitation of all the possibilities of his ensemble: "For me I'm investing more in those other ways of thinking to try to exploit all of our possibilities . . . and I think it takes a creative mind to (a) find them, and (b) to try to pull them off."

Constructing the completely new appears to Thomas to be not so much impossible as irrelevant: "I can't make something totally new, it doesn't work like that. But I can make a different mixture" and the music could end up in Mark's "completely new place." The new mixture might be combustible:

> *Thomas:* Before the tour I went to the studio for three days and I ended up trashing everything, like hours and hours of recorded material, just threw everything away.

> *Mark:* For the first time in a while I didn't feel those expectations because I was just doing a 180, and the reaction was "Whoa, I've never heard you play the ride cymbal before," so . . . cool! Okay!

Reflecting upon the effect of his own dramatic volte-face, Mark's actions strongly mirror Thomas's violent destruction of a substantial body of work and subsequent decision to learn to write for stringed instruments. In both processes, an abrupt schism from existing thought patterns unlocks fresh pathways. Mark is pleased with listener reaction ("so . . . cool! Okay!") because it confirms the validity of the strategy.

Left to their own devices in fully compositional performance with freedom of selection, what precepts govern individuals' action-choices? Thomas sees it as his responsibility both to get a reaction from his co-performer and to look for solutions through divergent thinking: "I force myself to think outside the box. I like thinking outside the box." For example, he might "play things on the hi-hat that you would never play on the hi-hat, but still force yourself to do it just because you never do it." Again: "If I learn to place beats where I normally don't place beats, then I'm sort of walking up a new road, you know, and making possibilities." Rare among drummers, Thomas seeks to do less:

> And then with this music, which is very melodic, very colorful, I'm thinking all the texture can lie in the strings and in the piano . . . some pieces with tempered piano . . . and they can do that, and I can do less.

Allowing creativity to flourish through deliberate self-restraint—knowing when not to try to impose one's creativity upon something—is an interesting topic in itself, and one that echoes Cindy's emphasis on getting out of the way, of "letting and allowing" things to happen.

Peter similarly wants to avoid the "typical" by composing when he plays, and suggests that the drummer should simply "play what you would like to hear next"[11] without fear or favor:

> You can't play what I would like to hear, or you think I might want to hear next, you don't know that, and I can't presuppose or waste my time worrying about what Steve Gadd might want to hear next when he walks into the club that I'm playing. I don't know.

Some of our experts, then, focus on getting a reaction, on unusual beat placement, on making sonic or textural possibilities, on conscious decision making in the moment. Others favor the avoidance of the typical, the avoidance of conscious decision making, the making something out of nothing, and the restriction of sonic or textural options. Two subthemes are helpful in teasing out structure from this multivariance. The first collates a set of issues around problem recognition and solution, and the second addresses the circumstances enabling or disabling creativity.

The finding, avoiding, solving, or resolving of problems associated with the performance mode (functional or compositional), the performance context (for, with, as, or without a leader; live or studio), the social context (producers, co-performers, listeners), and the mediational means (for example, drum hardware and software) underlies many of the strategies and processes that drummers adopt to achieve creative experience. All the interviewees problematize selection and decision-making. Mature experts like these tend to have an encyclopedic knowledge and a wealth of experience of performance across all genres and styles, and, as Ralph Salmins points out below, "the biggest challenge" is making the right choice from multiple options:

> And I suppose the creative process, relative to what you're asking me, in a big band is interesting because you have to be the decision maker about what you're going to play, and I think the biggest challenge is finding the right musical choice on the drum set for the music and the ensemble. And that's a big thing in a big band; that's why a lot of people struggle with it.

Technical problems arise frequently. Earlier, we briefly noted Mark's difficulties arising from his association with electronics. For a series of reasons he began to miss a touch on the instrument that he remembered once having:

> My musical path has been taking me down a more electronic music inspired path. . . . The sound of my drums has been going that way and my vocabulary has been leaning that way, and I felt like my touch was suffering a little bit due to the way the drums are tuned. They are very low, so I need to hit them mezzo-forte and up to achieve a certain

sound . . . You know, the floor tom is wrinkly and it just won't speak at a quiet volume so I kind of was remembering when I was younger—I was probably practicing more—but I was missing a touch that I remembered.

While his solution to the problem has technical and aesthetic benefits, it also has two further dimensions commonly associated with creativity—it is "fun" and it is "bringing out new ideas":

I got my hands on a bebop kit and cranked it way up, and left them wide open and I would go to my rehearsal space and just play along to Art Blakey records. It was the most fun I had in a long time, actually, at the drums . . . and it was bringing out new ideas, and I was able to play more fluently and more quietly.

A related problem for Mark lies in how best to remain emotionally connected to "that earthy thing" in the visceral power of the instrument, especially in an age of heavy product-marketing of "nice new heads" and "shiny hardware":

I think it's difficult sometimes to find that earthy thing, and it sounds ironic—it's the <u>drums</u>, you know—(*You'd imagine so, wouldn't you?*) but you know you put those nice new heads on and you get your shiny hardware and even just sometimes emotionally you're already in a very distant place from that.

Peter's perennial problem, as mine in King Crimson, is how to avoid the obvious. He offers an example of one solution at the microperformance level: "So I played everything <u>but</u> the downbeat, the three 16ths after the downbeat. That always seemed . . . that's kind of cool, like my one contribution to the drum beat lexicon! [laughs]." At the macroperformance level, Dylan seeks change from the problems of maintaining a working ensemble, which he sees as impeding his delivery of creative performance:

So what I've learned is that in the future I'm not going to do things in the ways that I did, I suppose . . . I'm going to make it easier on myself in some ways. Maybe it was to do with a little bit of understanding the kind of practicalities of how to make everything a little easier so creativity is more immediate.

Having learned from his previous creative endeavor, Dylan's intention is to make a "thing" (a situation) that, by focusing on the better or best rather than the different or new, will offer more immediate access to the creativity afforded by "a constant evolution of yourself."

Ultimately, creative drum performance lies less in the solving of problems than in their resolving, in the balancing of seeming incongruities. Several writers and drummers have observed this and characterized it, for example, as changing while remaining the same, as playing out of time while in time, as leaning back while maintaining forward momentum, as simultaneously leading and following, or driving while accompanying, or, as Blair Sinta put it earlier, "restraining and holding back as long as possible without having [the music] lack dynamics or energy." Drummers regularly negotiate the balance between seeming incongruities to make the music or the performance work, between being "fluid as a stream and steady as a rock."[12]

• The action-theoretical perspective I have adopted sees action as goal-oriented. Those dimensions of music performance subject to some degree of control may be manipulated toward the goal of creative achievement as strategies that seek to allow, invite, or encourage creative performance—as *enablers* of action that may be creative. Conversely, participants cite hectic schedules, mental pressure, and multiple vexatious issues surrounding everything from health, family, and personal relationships to visas, transport, and equipment as inhibitors or *disablers* of creative action. Cindy insists that the prospective creator must ignore those elements and allow life to happen

> because creative music, or jazz, as a friend once told me, is part "street" . . . and "street" means what's happening in life . . . what's happening in your life . . . what's happening in the life that you look out of your window and you see, you see on the street.

According to Asaf, creativity can be invited but only "when you're relaxed and when you're ready for it, you know, when everything . . . when you are at peace." When the stresses of his domestic relationship lift, he experiences a "a sudden release, sudden explosion of things that really wanted to come out for a long time, and everything just 'BAM' . . . in one year I made two albums":

> Tunes started to come in and I started to feel better about my playing, and when you feel better about your playing you affect the people in

the band that's playing with you so everybody's, you know, feeling better, playing better, being more creative.

In his view, the experience of creative performance is fluid, connected to mood, changeable, and subject to personal "conditioning." The only reason "we're not creative <u>all</u> the time, 100 percent of the time, is because our conditioning, the way we condition ourselves."

In the context of his studio work, Ralph finds functional performance more likely to be enhanced if producers hire him for his personal approach. He likes "a track that contains a lot of different things and that keeps me stimulated compositionally, musically. It's fun, lots to do." Creativity may be encouraged by a drummer being "offered" the musical space in which to be creative, to play, to experiment in a forgiving environment. In such a "good situation," Martin France finds that personality and the ego are minimized or removed, "so it's about the music; it's not about me or anyone else that is playing it." This perspective flies in the face of many genius- or vision-focused traditional ideas of creativity that very much are "about me."

This supportive or forgiving environment may be built into the foundations of the drummer's own "situation" or group. Mark's group, for example, offers him maximum creative space

because it's my conception and therefore I feel I have the most confidence in the decisions I'm making because I can do no wrong, basically . . . there are no consequences.

This approach allows him varying degrees of latitude in making his own decisions, a perspective that supports the construct of the continuum of control: "the more open the environment, the more creative I feel."

In brief, little commonality with regard to the multiple individual strategies and processes in the bringing about of creative difference emerges from our drummers' reflections. Emphasis is given to things avoided: the avoidance of the typical, of the obvious, of "demons." The two most common pathways to individuation seem to be (a) the avoidance of what others are doing and (b) the development of an individual voice, a topic first addressed in connection with identity construction in chapter 4 and shortly to be revisited in the context of boundary testing and "going further." Other strategies include the artificial imposition of constraints, abrupt severance from existing patterns of thought and action, the adoption of a faux naïveté, the "showing up empty," and the doing of less—all framed within a broad precept that sees the construction of the completely new to be not so much impossible as irrelevant. As mature individuals long enculturated within the drum culture, these experts tend to select and adapt cultural contents to create the idiosyncratic meaning of the action for them.

These ways in which participants engage with the finding, solving, or resolving of problems underpin much of the existing thinking about performance creativity. While Irène Deliège and Marc Richelle find little support for the hypothesis of creative acts in music as problem solving, the conflation of the two continues to be widely accepted in the dominant cognitivist paradigm.[13] Our expert drummers invoke the notion more frequently than might be expected. Problem finding, particularly the decision to deliberately seek out a problem and the ability to select a really useful and stimulating one, is a well-documented strategy in creativity studies that does not have quite the traction in music performance that it does in, say, scientific invention. Only Mark and Thomas, the most highly conceptual thinkers, deliberately look for or construct problems at the gig to promote creativity. Problem finding is used in order to think, and to develop new attitudes or approaches to the instrument and its practice from which "new problems are seen and old ones seen in a new light."[14]

Other problems pertain to the circumstances surrounding the creative performance rather than to the performance itself, encircling the creation of a "good situation" in which creative action might take place. Overcoming these peripheral issues "allows" one to "invite" creativity into performance, thus permitting engagement with Csikszentmihalyi's "Flow" state, an idea developed in the next chapter. One frequently deployed strategy for the realization of creative performance is for the individual to control the social, musical, and audio environment in which the drumming might be heard. One way of achieving that is to form and lead your own band. All interviewees but one pursue this in parallel careers in which the nurturing of creativity is seen, implicitly or explicitly, as the primary action-goal. Those who seek to control the performance space in this way tend to find that, on occasion, they have replaced one set of problems with another.

Knowing It Will Become Something Different: Change and Transformation

If choice and selection are precursors to creative action, change and transformation have long been generally understood as indicators and consequences of it. The IMCM depicts the co-construction of a particular structure—drummer action—to show how it generates lived experience, which, interpreted by self, informs meaning. In turn, interpreted meaning forms a basis for possible change in practice at the individual or domain level. Popular music instrumentalists seem concerned less with the origin of an idea than with its change or transformation. Jazz musicians frequently transform standard tunes into novel versions, and the degree of skill and novelty involved in doing so is commonly taken as a yardstick of creativity.[15] The drummers here understand their practice to take place in the context of perpetual change in the ecological, technological, sociological, and psychological dimensions of drum performance within the greater domain of music invention. Accordingly, they change or transform that which has been selected by adapting their practice, absorbing new impetuses, acknowledging and reviewing their obligations and responsibilities to cocreators, and adding value through creative expression.

The cohort's status as expert suggests that individuals generally have been (and continue to be) good adaptors, deriving benefit from change. Cindy Blackman Santana finds creative impetus in life itself: "And all those things—street, heart, and intellect—if you're a living, breathing person, they are always changing . . . those things change all the time. There's always some new impetus." If the action-goal is transformation, what counts is not where you take it from but where you take it to. According to Mark Guiliana, it's *all* "fair game." Referencing Jim Black again, he admires him because

> he was one of the first guys I saw in the flesh truly blurring the lines . . . he gave me the confidence to start thinking like . . . everything is fair game, really breaking down the walls of genres. You know, I heard some Dave Grohl in his playing and I heard some Elvin Jones and I heard some Jeff "Tain" Watts and so on and so forth, so that was really encouraging.

Approaching from another direction, he feels that:

> If I steal this Tony Williams phrase, you know, and it inspires me . . . if I'm technically taking someone else's source material or creative seed, and it inspires me to do X, Y, or Z, then it's more about where it goes than where it comes from.

The two powerful extracts above illustrate the way in which the "breaking down of walls" has significant creative meaning for Mark. Significant meaning here is constructed less in terms of novelty and more in the way in which it *mattered* to him; he is, in this case, the arbiter of his own significance.

Change or transformation in the choice of the selected material might be involuntary and enforced externally, in reaction, for example, to a surprising or unpredictable situation. Even seasoned performers like Chad occasionally have "to come up with something" to avoid potential musical disaster. It might also be involuntary and enforced from within by personal perception of circumstances and conditions or by personal dissatisfaction with the status quo. For example, having dwelt in (and observed others in) the functional sphere of practice, Dylan feels he might be able to do things better or differently by moving along the FCC toward the compositional sphere:

> You want to get out of the thing you have to do to make a living, maybe . . . and you want to make a thing which is your own thing because you've done so many things with other people and you've seen how they do it and generally . . . unfortunately I suppose I felt quite dissatisfied in those settings or have thought "if I was doing it I wouldn't do it like that" or that kind of thing. And so you want to make a change.

Going Further

A final theme to emerge from the notion of the construction of difference is that of boundary testing. Expert drummers characterize creative action as the deployment of a suite of music abilities. They are able to "hit the right thing at the right point" (Strønen), to "come up with something . . . that always works musically" (Wackerman), to "explore all corners of the music at the drop of a hat" and to "get inside the sound that's being created with what they're involved in right at that specific moment . . . being able to change and create with sympathetic sounds" (France). These abilities and others enable the fulfilment of another criterion of creative action, namely, as Blackman Santana puts it, to "go further" or "take it farther" by means of the deployment of a series of creative strategies. Whence does one go when one goes further? One goes close to the edge and looks over, risking the possibility of going too far. As T. S. Eliot noted, "of course one can 'go too far,' and except in directions in which we can go too far there is no interest in going at all; and only those who will risk going 'too far' can possibly find out just how far one can go."[16]

While the traditional function of the drummer as the "timekeeper supportive guy" (Guiliana's description) who provides the glue remains, a significant subtheme emerges from within the interviews to expand that understanding. It characterizes contemporary drumming as having become freer, looser, broader, less constrained:

> *Thomas Strønen:* I think it's opening up in a way. [...] Whereas it was timekeeper in the beginning, even with Gene Krupa in an advanced way, still it was a lot of timekeeping into the late '60s as far as I know and history tells us. ... I think one thing is that the drummer has a freer role today; people don't get surprised if the drummer is a leader, if he's playing out of time while the band's playing time or vice-versa.

It is in the "job description" of many to exploit this reorientation, to go further, to see where it leads. None of the participants appears to doubt that she or he has the power or authority to do so. The essential nature of the instrument and its high visibility combine to not only engage attention but also to establish the instrument as the dominant force within the ensemble: "The power we have as drummers is that people will listen," says Wackerman. Peter Erskine attributes the drum kit's uniqueness to several key dimensions of its essential nature, and explains how those aspects shape performance:

> A drummer does not have the means at his or her disposal of melodic expression, excepting of course we have implied melodic ... we don't have harmonic functionality in the traditional sense. [...] Therefore we function in a very different manner of shaping harmonic movement, of implying melodic content, of inferring things which we do not expressly play on our instrument because it's not in the traditional sense a tonal instrument, you know. [...] So I think the drums are unique and it gives the drummer an interesting form of power or influence with the other instruments in that regard, because we don't meddle in those areas.

"Going further" is interpreted by Asaf Sirkis as "creating more intensely," enabled by the quality of the musical relationships he has with his co-performers. Echoing Glăveanu's conception of distributed creativity, he insists that the "the connection you have with the musician you're playing with is also extremely important; again it's coming back to another thing that will allow you to create more intensely." In his experience, playing with strong co-performers pushes him to bring something equally strong to the table, to raise his game: "(*So they are creative drivers?*) Absolutely, yeah. (*And they make you dig deeper, work harder*) Exactly, exactly."

Many of Cindy Blackman Santana's perceptions are founded on and conditioned by the cultural legacy of her African American rhythmic forebears. She frames her own creativity within the preservation and continuation of this legacy: "Tony [Williams] was the continuation of that force of nature, that propulsion, and that drive that those gentlemen and others before him had, so for me he took that torch and just took it even further . . . and completely creative." She interprets "going further" as a personal desire to know and do more than she already knows and does: "I love pushing myself beyond what I've learned, and beyond what I've previously done." From Cindy's perspective, the ideal relationship with the audience is built around a shared energy and a feedback loop that encourages and supports exploration:

> You know, I really love, as I was saying before, energy and feedback from people. So when we get that, it's inspiring and encouraging to go further, to do more, and to take things farther than I or we imagined we could do.

Pushing boundaries may require the deliberate placing of oneself in a situation where something might occur in a particular way in order to have an unusual experience. In a lengthy anecdote already excerpted, Thomas Strønen revealed his violent destruction of a body of recorded work, creating a tabula rasa that invited a fresh approach. An abrupt change of milieu, namely a tour of Japan, informed a new, effortless process: "the pieces fell together." This sequence of events itself provoked or necessitated a further lurch into an unfamiliar area of music invention, that of writing for string quartet.

Such extreme behavior exemplifies a trope commonly associated with the creative process. The motivation to "go further" (with implications of going too far and thus into savagery or madness) in the search for difference has long been a part of the artistic personality.[17] One aim of this book is to tease out commonalities as to what the alchemical component that transforms functional into compositional, mechanical into magical, uncreative into creative might or could be. Creative drummers thirst to go further than others in the search for it. One of Thomas's self-selected practitioners, for example, is "provoking; he's not playing what you expect all the time, he's adding a different color, he's not being just behind." That characteristic resurfaces in the compositional qualities of Thomas's own practice: "I'm not just a timekeeper. I want to add something else":

> I started adding some things to my drum set, some different colors and textures, and also the fact that I didn't normally want to play

short notes. […] I wanted to make longer … (*Long sounds, something with decay?*) … yeah, and that's also one of the reasons I started with some electronics. That enabled me to do different textural things.

The hunt for the alchemical component is the "drug" that keeps Mark Guiliana "coming back," like a moth to a flame:

> For me my most exciting experiences have been in a heavily impro-
> vised situation and those are the uber-creative and uber-open-minded
> moments [that] have led to some of those pinnacle moments … for
> me, tasting those moments, that's the drug, that's what keeps me com-
> ing back, tasting and experiencing those moments and, you know, be-
> ing on the pursuit to live there as often as possible and with the goal of
> finding those places more frequently. But still they may be—depending
> on how you define that moment—could be once a night, once a tour,
> once a year.

One might, of course, always go further by developing an individual sonic identity or "voice," to rise above the clamor, to be identified, to be heard. It is also a way to contribute to and determine outcomes, and thereby to commu- nicate potentially significant difference. Any recombination[18] or synthesis of past or current stylistic approaches of others is fair game in the pursuit of this type of identity construction.[19] Participants tend to frame individuation as a sonic composite of what is said (content), the way it is said (expression), and the tone of the voice in which it is said (touch, feel, and timbre). In the previ- ous chapter we observed how some or all of these might be projected or sub- limated in performance, not least in accordance with the performer's per- ceived position on the FCC.

One recurring consideration is whether to settle for one's voice as cur- rently constituted—after all, people may not recognize you if you keep changing—or continue to find progressively unusual approaches to enable ever greater creative expression. It is axiomatic of functional performance that individuals avoid imposing a personal approach or voice on the music unless otherwise directed. The question then arises as to how the functional practitioner may be considered creative if effectively unidentifiable. A cur- sory functional/compositional reading would suggest that only composi- tional performers are creative, that one has to have a voice before one can be "heard" and assessed as creative. The issue is revealed, however, as being more nuanced, with creativity in functional performance framed in the collabora- tive "making it work," or in, as Ralph puts it, the being creative enough to be able to walk into a situation and play exactly the right thing for the music.

The action of "going further" thus has powerful implications on two levels. It not only challenges boundaries and alter borders, but it also is identified by many participants as *required to make a difference*. It may have one source or many. In a youthful and evolving discipline like kit drumming, not yet old enough to have decided upon the most effective way to hold a pair of drumsticks, everything is, to use Mark's phrase, fair game.

Summary

This chapter has focused on the hunt for the something extra that is required to establish significant communicable difference. What is it that matters? While under certain circumstances creativity may inhere in functional practice, our group made bold statements about their performance practice along the lines of "it's not just . . ." It is not just building it up; it is making it work. It is not just keeping time; it is making it go. It is not just keeping some of it together; it is keeping all of it together. It is not just interfering; the right to interfere has to be earned first. These drummers' reports provide a fascinating insight into a constellation of ideas around what they do being "more than" just keeping time, or other "menial" functions. The fact that such an essential custodial function is seen as menial may be another manifestation of the pitched-instrument prejudice that, running deep in the culture, informs the attribution of creative meaning.

- How the experts see it:

  - Most take their primary function to be the provision of appropriate performance.
  - Constructing difference tends to be seen not as a foundational concern, but rather something that may be attended to after such concerns have been addressed.
  - The degree of attention paid to foundational concerns is contingent upon the number of performers in the space.
  - The drummer perceives himself or herself as having the greatest power to affect outcomes.
  - The origin of an idea is less important than its transformation.

- Expression of experience is the "something else" that adds value to the functional and embodies the significant difference between functional and compositional performance.
- Most thirst to go further than others in the search for the "something else," challenging boundaries and altering borders in the process of constructing difference.
- Individuation is most commonly achieved through (a) the avoidance of what others are doing and (b) the development of an individual voice.

6 • Reaching Others

Communicating Experience

Creativity in music performance has thus far been characterized as a set of choices and decisions, selected from possible options, with the purpose of producing a work or an event that exists for a reason. For the individual drummer, those selections tend to be made, at whatever level of consciousness, from a palette of temporal, metrical, timbral, and dynamical options available "in the moment" of performance. The freedom to make those selections, however, may be constrained by his or her perceived position on a continuum of control (the FCC). Creative difference is embodied in the options selected, the constraints negotiated, and the surprise occasioned at the effect of those selections. It must also, I contend, be communicated to someone for assessment of significance.

We drummers communicate with and among ourselves, co-performers, and listeners through collaboration and sharing. Our actions are regulated and shaped by cultural tradition, and take place within a community that mediates and promotes the psychological behavior and meaning-making of the individual. The cultural psychology attendant upon membership of these collectives is the primary determinant of the individual's experience of creativity and the way she or he communicates it to others.

However, before venturing further into the third dimension of the SDCA model—communication—it might be helpful to step back somewhat to show how drummers are positioned (and position themselves) in the music culture as a breed apart and a breed below. In this chapter I want to situate the drummer in both culture and community and consider the negative cultural ideology surrounding three sets of issues. First is the extent of the impact of the Cartesian mind/body split upon performance perceptions; second is the degree to which intellect is downplayed in practice; and third is a set of questions about performance on instruments of indefinite pitch. Having brought these ideological components into the light, I develop a view as to how aligned feeling and shared purpose allow drummers to negotiate, widen, and bridge these things successfully in performance. The notion of sharing is common to both culture and community; the topic is examined here with respect to groove, meaning, Flow,[1] and the several problems surrounding marginality, identity, and homogeneity in practice.

A Breed Apart and a Breed Below: Drummers in Culture

At the risk of oversimplification but in the interest of brevity, we may interpret "culture" very broadly as the totality of what a group of people think, how they behave, and what they produce that is passed on to future generations. Brian Wilshere's understanding of a "drum culture" as the "totality of the musical paradigms and cultural preferences of drummers as a group" will serve as a working definition.[2] The Deweyan view of culture as a prolonged and cumulative interaction with environment[3] underpins the discussion and echoes the thinking of both the systems theorists like Gruber and Csikszentmihalyi and the action theorists such as Boesch.

The importance of culture to drummers is crucial as a framework for meaning-making; it guides and governs the individual's development. The idea that the act of music performance might both possess and create meaning is a new one, largely arising from the educational or developmental perspectives of those such as Margaret Barrett. In her view, we begin, as children, to make sense of our place in the world through participation in the sociocultural context that surrounds us.[4] Culture is more than a mere causal factor; rather, it is "formed by and formative of human thought and action, and inseparable from human development."[5] Seen in this light, music does not work effectively until and unless participants belong to a shared culture that gives it meaning.[6] These views converge with "Darwinian" creativity models such as that of Csikszentmihalyi that posit an individual's variation on existing domain knowledge being accepted back into the domain as a creative improvement, and suggest how meaning might arise as much for adult drummers as children in the construction of new performative artifacts.

Cultural influences on drummer practice and meaning-making are many and varied, and ebb and flow over time. Initially they might include parents, siblings, friends, peers, teachers, and other music-makers in school or college; then audio-visual-mediated sources found on television, audio files, films, DVDs, videos, the radio and the Internet. Later on in a career they may include experiences of teaching, of success and failure, and of other cultures through international travel. The results of these multiple influences are mediated through practice and appear to be offered back to the music community. This is what Wenger means when he suggests that a community of practice "produces its own practice."[7]

Several important dimensions of drum culture might fruitfully be examined from the perspective of cultural psychology's phenomenological approach to the process of interpreting lived experience. This field of study is both central to the meaning-exchange and the meaning-circulation process and a useful tool for an examination of human behavior and experience.[8] Its insights give rise locally to the IMCM but also, more generally, to implications for any study of creativity. The meaning drummers make of their experience(s) affects the way they carry out that experience in their actions as musicians.

The cultural psychologists David Hiles and Donald Polkinghorne are both interested in meaning-making, but Polkinghorne's approach is through narrative discourse, which he foregrounds as the primary scheme by means of which human existence is rendered meaningful.[9] Becoming a cultural being and arranging for others to become cultural beings are closely linked parts of the single process of enculturation.[10] In Polkinghorne's view, preexisting cultural traditions from within a community offer a store of "plotlines" that can be used to configure events into stories.[11] A plot narrative, for example, that says that to live an authentic life as a jazz drummer in the bebop business one had to endure an unhappy existence around substance abuse, racial harassment, and indifference to one's music was a powerful driver in my teenage experience, despite the obvious disconnection with my comfortable, white, middle-class background and my uncertainty about exactly which substances to abuse.

Narrative discourse is a complex form of meaning-making that "recognises the meaningfulness of individual experiences by noting how they function as parts in a whole."[12] Over time, drummer action generates lived experience, which, interpreted by self, informs meaning. Meaning may then form a basis for possible change in practice at the individual level. This idea forms the basis of the IMCM and was echoed in my own experience: "Personally, I see music as a path to change. It works much like a mirror: music will show you your reflection, but if you don't much like what you see, you can change through music. You can become a different person through your striving, possibly a better person."[13] The personal narrative thus formed partially explains a drummer's past and directs her or his future. In this way too, the practitioner may assign more or less importance to attributions of creativity as part of her identity construction, as mediated through her cultural narrative plotline. The manner in which she makes meaning of the drumming process is determined by, and determines, the drum culture. Narration and description are value-laden and culturally contingent; even in telling one's personal story it is the voice of the culture surrounding the action that is heard in the description.[14]

Having arrived from a variety of different routes, cultural psychology theorists have tended to converge around several generally stable core precepts, of which two have particular salience to the discussion at hand. The first precept holds mind and culture as fundamentally interdependent. When Carl Ratner insists that culture be construed not as an external independent variable but rather as "a system of relationships and processes which organize psychological phenomena in a particular manner,"[15] he underlines the discipline's core contention that culture is embedded within the mind rather than outside as a set of rules and descriptors; culture and psyche should be regarded as inseparable. Unfortunately, academia separated them when the human sciences split into the social sciences and the humanities. When psychology became institutionalized as a social/behavioral science, the constituent parts of mind were divided among several other sciences. The history of cultural psychology has thus been to put back together again something that was torn apart.[16] Arguing that change in the pattern of an individual's activities can only be effected by addressing the surrounding situations in which those activities live,[17] Michael Cole's insistence on discussing the "act in context" accords with the action-theoretical approach of Boesch, and, in the context of music creativities, the thinking of Burnard.

In Lutz Eckensberger's view, the way human beings think, feel, and act cannot easily be explained by "natural laws" alone; cultural "rules" have also to be taken into consideration.[18] A cultural psychology approach acknowledges that we think not only as individuals and human beings, but as members of particular communities with distinctive *cultural* traditions that allow humans (and, in this case, drummers) to ascribe meaning to creative experience, and to circulate and exchange that meaning. Precisely because, as Michael Cole reminds us, "we fail (like fish in water) to see culture because it is the medium within which we exist,"[19] it does not mean that the medium is any less a life source of crucial importance to drummers and the meanings we make.

The second precept has already been touched upon in the context of action theory—namely, that the way to the human mind is through its cultural products and artifacts. These products, material and immaterial, inform drummers' collective worldview and open a window onto individual experience and behavior. In this view, culture is the entire pool of artifacts accumulated by the social group in the course of its historical experience.[20] This might include, for example, the culture's mythology (of, quintessentially, the drum "hero");[21] its technological language ("batter heads," "triple-flanged hoops," or the language associated with the grading and classification of drums and cymbals); its pedagogical language ("ratamacues," "paradiddles," "flammed mills," and "ruffs"); its particular narrative; and its own literature, embodied in the blogs, webzines, chat rooms, and monthly magazines that dominate and border the culture, connect its far-flung members, circulate meaning, and attempt to impose a "satisfactory graspable, humanizing shape on experience."[22]

To these artifacts may be added the culture's icons (for example, Max Roach, Buddy Rich, Ringo Starr, John Bonham); its iconoclasts (Keith Moon, Rat Scabies, Andrew Cyrille); and in particular the multiple potential identities—drummer as guru-teacher (Freddie Gruber), movie star (Gene Krupa), drum hero (John Bonham, Buddy Rich, Carl Palmer), and hell-raiser[23] (Keith Moon, Ginger Baker); and the drummer-as-animal[24] or intellectual (Max Roach, Terry Bozzio). In this regard, how are we to think of the drummer, and how do we wish to be thought about: as bricklayer to the architect of the popular song, as grease monkey or engineer tinkering about in the basement, or as the architect himself? Are we gorillas, builders, hooligans, comedians, or oiled and tattooed athletes with the silken robes and hoodies beloved of the stadium-level prize-fighter?

In the two-drummer King Crimson of the mid-1990s, I "played the part" of Elvin Jones to Pat Mastelotto's Ringo Starr—the former disruptive, blurring, dense, and obscuring the beat; the latter clean, simple, compliant, and revealing the beat.[25] We have all been obliged to adopt multiple personae as may be necessary to make it (the music, the performance) work, from bricklayer to heating engineer to interior designer to the architect responsible for the entire building, and we find creativity in all things. We slide across a continuum of functionality as the situation demands. We find creative meaning in making the (musical) building work as well as (or better than) other buildings, and then articulate a personal aesthetic by making it different from other buildings. We want to make it work and then make it matter. We rightly think we are important because we are: the building is unlikely to fall down if the bass player stops or the saxophonist plays an unfortunate phrase, but it can collapse very swiftly if the drummer gets it wrong.

From the chimera of the one-handed roll to the narrative of the cultural elders' past experiences, all these artifacts and others in aggregate constitute the drum culture. As has long been accepted, creativity builds on what has gone before; it does not come from nowhere. No drummer is working in a vacuum. According to Silvano Arieti, "No living organism is closed; it needs exchanges with the environment to maintain a steady state, and no culture or society is immutable."[26] These cultural resources become tools used by the individual drummer to connect with others in goal-oriented, intentional action. Taken broadly, the most recent revolution in creativity studies is associated with the idea that any satisfactory account of creativity should include the cultural context, not least because culture acts as both a regulator of action and a framework for meaning-making. Culture may be seen as the outcome of interaction with environment, with cultural psychology as the process by which meaning is extracted from that interaction. Feedback from the environment to the organism, or the field to the creator, is both an embedded and useful component in creativity. Collaborative and individual creative action is continually interpreted and assessed by the wider culture and the community of practice; at the highest level, such action may change domain practice. This is how drummers shape the drum culture and the drum culture shapes drummers.

Problematically, however, the link between creativity and the drum culture is mediated by the corrosive influence of the culture's organizing ideology—the articulated system of meanings, values, and beliefs that can be abstracted as the "worldview" of the drum community.[27] Several aspects of the shared ideology act as cultural identifiers, reinforcing distinctions between the culture of drummers and other instrumentalists, and may, in part, be the source of Western music culture's perceived predisposition against the "rhythmatist."[28] Following Juniper Hill, the ideology of the drum culture may be taken as both a fundamental sociocultural determinant of creative activity and the locus of the elements that differentiate the drum culture from other musical cultures.[29] The next part of the discussion is structured around three sets of issues.

A first trope derives from an historical insistence that notions of aesthetics, mind, harmony, and the intellect are superior to hedonism, body, rhythm, and the "natural." It has become embedded in a drum ideology based on a racist misconception, in turn buried deep in 19th-century primitivist myth.[30] We can track this view back to René Descartes and the 17th-century dualist notion of the "mind/body split." Simon Frith traces how the equation of "serious" with the mind and high culture, and "fun" with the body and thus low culture, became established in the United States and Europe in the mid-19th century. He observes how a good classical performance has become measured by the stillness it commands, in contrast to a good rock concert, as measured by the audience's physical response and bodily movement, by how quickly they get out of their seats or onto the dance floor.[31]

This musical dichotomy of aesthetic/mind versus hedonistic/body is depicted by Frith as one effect of the mental/manual division of labor built into the Industrial Revolution, and into the consequent organization of education. Feelings, he suggests, were then taken to be best expressed spiritually and mentally, perhaps in church, or in the contemplation of Art, with a stiff upper lip, but never to be displayed in public. This split is spectacularly evident in the traditional Irish dancer, whose rigid upper body is counterpointed with feverish leg and footwork in popular shows such as *Riverdance*.[32] Bodily responses were, by definition, mindless, now a term of disparagement. The brain came to be associated with art music, brainlessness with popular music. By 1962, it was, on Peter Stadlen's account, "a reliable symptom of Light Music that a minimum of brain activity is required for it to be savoured and understood."[33]

Jazz, also, was not a music that had to be thought about. When popular music engaged with black American music in the early part of the century, a long history of Romanticism stood ready to define black African culture as the "body," the other part of the European bourgeois "mind." American critic Henry Krehbiel, music editor of the *New York Tribune* in the late 19th-century and an important figure in the music appreciation movement of that period, saw rhythm favorably as the "starting-point of music." Unfortunately, he then concluded that it "stirs the blood of the savage."[34] Ted Gioia argues that the French intellectual view of the "primitive," the myth of the "noble savage," meant that jazz was heard as emotionally charged but largely devoid of intellectual content, while the jazz musician was taken to be an inarticulate and unsophisticated practitioner of an art that she or he scarcely understood.[35] A favorable view of the "primitive" precivilized world from the sophisticated overcivilized world thus found primitive people to be innocent, uncorrupted by culture and still close to some undefined human "essence." Such a tortuous logic asserted that African music, held to be more "primitive" or "natural" than European music, had to be more in touch with the body—the difference between the two being the emphasis on rhythm. By such a racist and convoluted ideological route has the Western kit drummer thus become imbued with the primitive, the sexual, and the mindless.[36]

A second ideological trope has its roots in the first, and manifests itself in the downplay of intellect. For years Western kit drummers have been considered, and come to consider themselves, as a breed apart and a breed below. In response to continual questioning of their musical abilities and years of ridicule and trivialization of their skill and the music that embodies it, some drummers have come to perform to type. Downplaying any connection with intellect, they adopt the "us-against-them" approach referenced briefly in chapter 1.[37] Anecdotally, many practitioners and music producers will insist that successful performance in either functional or compositional mode is all about "the feel," but I would argue that musical rhythm is as much a mental as a physical matter. Deciding *when* to play a note is as much a matter of thought as deciding which note to play.

Some drummers choose to foreground their ineptness, espousing a determined incompetence in an apparent effort to distance themselves from technical expertise or knowledge. For Stewart Copeland of the Police, drumming is "something you feel and play *without thought*." However, many who have attempted to coordinate four limbs playing four instruments simultaneously in one coherent rhythm will testify to at least a minimal amount of mental involvement. While asserting that his contribution to Fleetwood Mac's "Go Your Own Way" is a "major part of that song," Mick Fleetwood quickly and tellingly adds that his part came, "I'm ashamed to say, from capitalising on my ineptness."[38] Preempting the British punk-rock movement of the late 1970s, American proto-punks like the New York band the Godz were among the first to articulate the (then) radical premise that anyone could, and indeed should, be a musician. Patrick Burke found the group to be "flagrantly, outrageously, unabashedly incompetent" and admittedly an "extreme case" whose ideas "represented a third stream of revolutionary thought in rock."[39] The conception of drumming as "mindless" will be revisited shortly in the context of the low status of drummers; the take-home point here is the way in which the cultural ideology has given us the drumming, rather than the drumming giving us the cultural ideology. "Of what am I capable?" asks the drummer. "Not much," comes the ideological response.

A third strand to the drum culture ideology, the worldview that does so much to determine the way in which drummers are perceived and perceive themselves, encircles the most obvious difference between drummers and other instrumentalists: the Western drum kit is unpitched, or, more precisely, of indefinite pitch. A prejudice against unpitched instruments, coagulating around the association between drums and noise on the one hand and musical sounds on the other, can be traced back almost as far as their introduction to Western classical music.[40] Disappointingly, the association continues to be heavily promoted to children globally through Roger Hargreaves's "Mr. Men" series of books, in which "Mr. Noisy: The Musician" is, somehow inevitably, a drummer.[41] The origins of our interviewees' strong motivation to achieve, experience, and communicate creativity in performance were not made explicit and can only be surmised, but it is not unreasonable to suggest that drummers may need to assuage feelings of insufficiency or inferiority,[42] to persuade others that they are necessary, and that pitched and unpitched are mutually constituted. The extent to which these motivations may be compensation mechanisms born of reaction to the prevailing pitched-instrument prejudice is an interesting question beyond the scope of this book, which may be answered only with further research.

A powerfully corrosive Western art music ideology has thus nurtured a sense of inferiority of those who perform on unpitched instruments to those who perform on pitched instruments. Embedded in a racist misconception and spawning the falsity of the mind/body split, this ideology exacerbates the separation of thought from feeling and the concomitant downplay of intellect among unpitched or indefinite-pitch practitioners. The supremacy of pitch and the marginalization of those who perform "only with rhythm" has created a circling of the wagons that, one might suggest, finds the less secure practitioner unwilling to engage with the broader musical picture lest she or he be found lacking in inventiveness. The contention here is that 20th-century developments on the drum kit have, on the contrary, evidenced sufficient musical creativity that belated study of the work of this community of practice in the round should assist in a better understanding—and a correction of multiple historical misunderstandings—of the power and place of creativity in our rhythmic culture.

Aligned Feelings and Shared Purpose: Drummers in Community

Drummers' actions, thus governed and regulated by culture, take place within the "intermediate space"[43] of a community of practice, itself enfolded within the broader culture. Drummers tend to be people of like mind, exhibiting remarkably uniform and sometimes intensely held worldviews that sustain them and position them relative to other musicians and outsiders. Writers like Margaret Barrett, who inhabit the terrain between music education and ethnomusicology, have found that children learn music in communities of musical practice.[44] A community of practice is characterized as having mutual engagement, a joint enterprise, and a shared repertoire—dimensions that define a group of people as a community. Drummers substantially satisfy all three criteria.

First, mutual engagement is seen as manifest in specific forms of participation that contextualize meaning, rather than construing it as intrinsic or universal.[45] The action-theoretical approach posits that drummers participate through situated action, and that they participate creatively through the communication of significant situated action. This is supported by the construct of the community of practice, in which people are engaged with one another *in action*.[46] A practice does not exist in the abstract; it exists because people are engaged in actions *whose meanings they negotiate with each other*.

From the moment the beginner emerges from the practice room to engage with others, the engagement is mediated through one or several social structures. Drummers exist as part of a profession, an industry, a market, and a business. They mutually engage at Percussive Arts Society conventions, "Drummer Days," "Drum Festivals," at a single artist "Drum Clinic," or just at a workshop at the local store. At these events, information and gossip are freely exchanged and new community members recruited. The traditional location for the acolyte's enculturation used to be, perhaps still is, the local drum store, where more experienced players would "hang" and share information. More recently, the locus of engagement has both expanded to include real and virtual magazines and websites and contracted as physical retail space dedicated to the drummer has diminished. Band-leading drummers such as those in this study might employ musician X on a Monday, be employed by the same person on Tuesday, and both function as employees in Y's band on Wednesday. Mutual exchange of employment opportunities in this way is one factor promoting a sense of kinship also within other music communities.[47]

Second, participants in a community of practice tend to have a detailed and complex understanding of their enterprise as they define it that outsiders may not share. As already noted, drummers have come to underestimate their skills, downplay their contribution, and save their "best" for appreciation by knowledgeable colleagues at drum clinics and workshops. Studies within the community of jazz improvisers have begun to explore how membership both crystallizes individual identity and helps to conceptualize the very nature of the music being performed.[48] Membership of the drum community provides a similar function for drummers. The community draws on what its members do and what they know, as well as on their ability to connect meaningfully to what they do not do and do not know—that is, to the contributions and knowledge of others. At a Percussive Arts Society convention it is possible to observe the intensity of, for example, the military snare-drum specialist's attention to the presentation of a castanet player from Andalucía. After one such convention I adopted an innovative horizontal and symmetrical layout of the standard drum kit following consideration of the ergonomics of the symphony timpanist of the Amsterdam Concertgebouw Orchestra. Participation in the community, indeed the existence of the community itself, depends on mutual engagement of this sort.[49]

Finally, Wenger suggests that community members will have developed a repertoire for which outsiders miss shared references—in effect, their own language. It is now a commonplace in anthropology not only that the shared language of a community is the most essential carrier of its common culture, but that to study the culture of a foreign people without also becoming acquainted with their language is unimaginable. The drum culture's peculiarly onomatopoeic jargon has already been noted in the context of its pedagogy. Comprehension of this ever-changing technological and pedagogical lexicon is essential for membership of the community. In my experience, to be unable to distinguish the sound of birch from maple, "triple-flanged" drum hoops from wood hoops, or "resonator heads" from "black dots" is to imperil that membership.

The language of melody and harmony shares a commonality with the other musicians in most popular music groups, but the language of the drummer is (perhaps deliberately) arcane. Humans use language as a way of signaling identity with one cultural group and difference from others. Even among speakers of one language several different ways of using the language exist, and different dialects are used to signal affiliation with particular subgroups within a larger culture.[50] Like wine tasters, cymbal manufacturers have developed a large vocabulary to describe the subtle distinctions between, for example, "warm ride" and "dry ride" cymbals in a manner similar to the wine taster's distinction between differing Rhine wines or burgundies. For the majority of drinkers or drummers, these distinctions are those between a better or worse, or a more or less agreeable, wine or cymbal. Wenger acknowledges that our sense of ourselves "includes the objects with which we identify because they furnish our practices. Mastering the wine-tasting vocabulary and being able to appreciate and discuss all the nuances of a good wine can become a source of distinction, pride, and identity." What may seem to the outsider like the fetishization of drum equipment is seen from this viewpoint as part of the desire to belong, and, as such, as part of the interplay between the "participation and reification that makes people and things what they are."[51]

A community is understood less in terms of its topography or as a local social system, and more in terms of the close ties and the feeling of belongingness between its members. A community can describe different social realities, from small groups to organizations and larger social structures. Sandra Jovchelovitch puts it simply: communities exist where they are felt and experienced as such.[52] The notion of community is pivotal in any discussion of creativity because, first, it is within community that descriptions and narratives are meaningfully constructed; and second, community has been identified as a major factor in the analysis of any creative act. According to Lori Custodero, for example, creativity "needs a milieu to invoke influence; the convergence of self and source is meaningful when it finds resonance in community."[53] For Glăveanu, community is both the context for and a major factor enabling creativity. Building on Margaret Boden's bilevel depiction of creativity as either (a) historical H-creativity, which makes a contribution to the culture of a society, or (b) psychological P-creativity, which contributes to the individual's own life sphere, Glăveanu seeks to interpose a third level between the two at the level of community (C-creativity). In this way, he emphasizes the fundamental reality that "humans live and create within communities and each community membership brings with it a distinctive set of resources and practices, a specific knowledge and identity. Placed between the P and H levels, C-creativity focuses on the vital role of communities as social contexts."[54]

Drummers derive meaning as much from community as from culture. Sara Cohen observes that her group of Liverpool rockers drew strength from this vague but crucial feeling of belonging to a community.[55] This is the way in which meaning constructs community, which constructs meaning.[56] Indeed, Wilfred Drath and Charles Palus go so far as to assert that the primary process of meaning-making in collective experience is culture-building.[57] Harris Berger's proposition that different musical cultures lead to different ways of structuring experience and hence to different meanings[58] underpins a central tenet of this book—namely, that the meaning-making processes of drummers are qualitatively different from other groups of popular instrumental practitioners.[59] For example, in much Western popular music, the drummer (or the drumming) tends to start at the beginning of the song and finish or fade at the end in an uninterrupted flow of notes from at least one or more elements of the kit. This contrasts with the contributions of wind, brass, reeds, and vocalists who must necessarily pause for breath, and guitarist and keyboard players who frequently "lay out." In several subgenres of rock (metal, punk, drum'n'bass) there is a very real sense that if the drummer stopped the music would be unable to continue. This would seem to reinforce the idea that the drummer is in "a world of his own": in effect, in a community of practice with its own shared learning,[60] situated within a clearly defined drum culture constituted through its own language, praxis, and mores.

Communication through Culture and Community

Following this important detour to contextualize the meaning of culture and community, we now return to the central proposition of this chapter from which we departed—namely, that the qualitatively different music process or product must be *communicated* to someone as an essential prerequisite to assessment. Adopting the view that creativity is both ordinary and exceptional, Keith Negus and Michael Pickering suggest a requirement for "the capacity to reach others and achieve a resonance with their lives"—in other words, to effectively communicate experience.[61] Borrowing from the aesthetic philosophy of John Dewey, they observe not only that our experience of the world is shaped and given significance by the act of creation but also that the element of communication is an essential component of creativity.[62] Be it material or nonmaterial, an artifact needs to be produced, revealed, and communicated; it is the processes of expression and communication that give form, meaning, and value to the characteristics of experience.[63]

Clearly, communication and assessment have the same object: that which is to be communicated is also that which is to be assessed. Research into classical music performance has shown that the object of the exercise tends to be the communication of emotion to the non-performing listener.[64] Classical pianists are sometimes taught how to develop a personal style of communicating emotion, the successful communication of which entitles the activity to be looked on as creative.[65] The real world of drummers presents an alternative view. The Deweyan approach I am adopting suggests that, rather than the communication of emotion, drummers tend to frame their communication in terms of the expression of significantly different *experience* to co-performing listeners. Everything the performer has done, lived, thought, and performed up to and during the moment of performance constitutes the experience that is expressed (literally, pressed out) during the creative moment. As Martin France has it, it is "the moment where everything that's about you comes out." It thus includes the hours of deliberate practice, the years of experience that provoke the innumerable small selections from among possibilities, and the incalculable microdecisions and selections that lead to (and to some extent become) the work. It is this element that the interviewees were asked to identify in their selections of tracks embodying their own creative expression of experience and the element that they mostly pointed to. (See appendix C.) This is the "something else" that adds value to the functional performance, the alchemical component to be communicated prior to creative assessment.

Creativity in the classical domain, then, does not always constitute creative performance as the expert drummer might recognize it. This discrepancy may have less to do with the differing classical/popular understandings of communication than with the straightforward unpitched/pitched dichotomy. Most research in this area primarily involves expert performers on pitched instruments, but findings from among both expert classical and expert popular musicians show the idea of "playing expressively" as largely defined in terms of "communicating emotions" and "playing with feeling."[66] While we now have some understanding of emotional expression within pitched-instrument classical music performance,[67] further investigation into the communication of emotion by performers on unpitched instruments would help shed light here. Until then, I consider that it is the communication of significantly different experience that remains foundational to the attribution of creativity within and among drummers.

Being Part of the Team: Collaborative Communication

If we accept that all effective music creativity is ultimately the outcome of a collaboration between, at minimum, addresser and addressee, it follows that for music performance to be achieved something needs to be communicated by one to the other. Addresser and addressee may both, of course, be performers. Asaf Sirkis describes something of the process of intra-performer communication below:

> You like their playing, you like their sense of musicality, and their musical sensitivity and they like yours, and . . . when you're playing you're communicating rather than just doing your own thing.

Much importance is assigned to the level of communication between musicians and their co-performers: the topic has been the subject of some research, particularly in the area of movement and collaboration.[68] Playing music together tends to engender a mutual physiological response—"two hearts beating as one"—with communication emerging as a "mutual coordination of intention and action within concrete events in real time."[69] A high level of communication with other musicians is generally understood to be the sine qua non of expert music performance. The creative process of jazz musicians in jam sessions has been found to be "routed in" and strongly influenced by, among other things, communication between participants.[70] My participation in stadium-level performances of progressive rock, however, provides some empirical evidence to support the obverse idea that functional performance may occur quite successfully with minimal intra-performer communication.

As performance moves along the FCC toward the compositional pole, individual co-performers appear to need less overt direction or verbal communication of any kind. The ability of musicians to innovate simultaneously with almost no verbal communication indicates an impressive level of musicianship that has drawn research interest from several disciplines.[71] Despite, or because of, its scarcity, intra-performer communication is highly valued as an important indicator of respect, recognition, and awareness. Visual communication is an equally important conveyor of meaning between co-performers and the audience, confirming recent insights into the centrality of visual communication to the creative experience.

Our experts also attach considerable importance to the ethical quality of the communications between all parties: performer, co-performing listener, and non-performing listener. To be effective, both the performance and its communication must not only be trusting and trustworthy but also sincere and honest. Asaf strives to produce the "most genuine-self drum part." Dylan Howe's performances are enacted as often as possible by what he calls "the best version" of himself. These assertions reflect participants' general concern to serve the music at that moment with integrity. Deviation from these precepts, it is implied, might compromise attainment of the goal of creative performance.

In practice, a collaborative context of aligned feelings and shared purpose seems to afford not only the greatest performance pleasure but a secure, favorable environment in which to incubate difference. The most frequently used metaphor for collaboration was that of the team player:

Thomas Strønen: I want to be part of the team that can change the musical direction; I want my playing to influence the other players.

Martin France: I think I respond more if someone inspires me than if I have the inspiration myself. [...] So if I walk into a band and everything is very creative then I could probably be very creative. But if ... I guess it's like a team player, isn't it?

Being a team player in an interactive ensemble is seen as conducive to creativity. Referencing opera, film, and "larger art forms," Peter Erskine considers that "collaboration allows for bigger things to happen," an observation that might serve in the metaphorical sense in which the "bigger things" are greater than the sum of the parts, offering a creative experience greater than one practitioner may achieve or experience on his or her own. This view is shared by Cindy Blackman Santana who confirms that, although creativity can be enacted by individuals, there is greater creative power in collaboration: "When it's collaborative I think it's even more powerful because you have more impetus than just your own." Mark Guiliana also relies on collaborative interaction—"this back and forth"—to provide forward momentum at the performance level, to

> either confirm a thought, or to amend it later as it's coming out [...] or if you do get stuck, you get into a little rut, relying on your collaborator to maybe inject something new and then "oh, right, okay" and you return to that path.

He parallels the conversational style of our interview, the "back and forth," with the conversational "back and forth" within collaborative music performance.

Against this, Dylan appears to be losing confidence in the value of collaboration, which he sees as predicated upon equality of experience among and between co-performers:

> I think when you're younger and maybe everybody's on bit more of an equal experience thing, or everyone is a bit more open, then creativity is a bit more of an exchange. But the older I've got the more I've found ... you're on your own! [Both laugh]. It's quite sad in a way because musicians generally are untogether, selfish, egotistical, out-for-themselves kind of thing, so to find some simpatico individuals that still can ... it's difficult.

Having accumulated greater experience than his co-performers and elevated himself to the position of bandleader who can perform anything he wants, Dylan's colleagues, retaining a respectful distance, are no longer "simpatico." As the leader, he is on his own. In a discussion of his self-selected tracks, I unpack my Deweyan thinking when I suggest to him that creative performance might be

> *an expression of experience and everything you have done, lived, thought, played up until that minute of playing constitutes your experience, every way you've related to those inputs constitutes your experience, and that is what you express during the creative moment, which you've selected in these particular three tracks.*

With that analysis he readily concurs:

That's so true, that's exactly it, really. [...] Anyone is a sum of everything they've experienced at all times, aren't they, and it's just another
avenue of expression of that, isn't it?

Dylan's insistence that "you've got to play with people who like how you play,
and you like how they play, and that only comes from how you feel amongst
each other" reflects the importance he assigns to his opinion of others and
others' opinions of him within collective collaboration. The consensus beginning to emerge here confirms Thomas's view that, for these mature experts, the greatest pleasure lies in collaborative interaction.

That pleasure, however, seems increasingly hard to come by. Against a
backdrop of the rapid expansion of music technology facilitating the creation and global dissemination of the digital output of a single performer,
some participants, for example, Chad Wackerman, lament the perceived decline of the frequency of collaborative interaction in performance.[72] In a scenario that plays into the idea of the stay-home drummer, Chad, Ralph, and
Peter have all acquired home studios and spend time working alone in
them.[73] In Chad's view "there's less collaboration than there used to be, for
sure." Given that the youngest interviewee was 34 years old, his observation
might or might not hold good for a younger cadre of drummers who have
grown up with the computer, having known little of the benefits of a collaborative music process that the participants appear to hold dear. When Peter,
for example, is recording and he knows

> there's going to be no fixing ... I love that. I love the commitment that
> is required by everyone in the room; the attention level is just a little
> bit sharper.

Conversely, collaboration may act as a disincentive to creativity. We have already noted the inverse relationship between the number of co-performers
in the performing space and the perceived freedom of expression in the context of big band and orchestral work. In her discussion of the co-construction
of musical play among children, Margaret Barrett highlights the notion of
"trialling by performance," which she characterizes as a "process of refine-
ment enacted [...] with friends and the progressive implementation of their
suggested amendments and additions until a satisfactory performative product is reached."[74] This idea strongly echoes the collaborative compositional
approach of the English progressive rock groups of the 1970s, a costly procedure that involved intense rehearsal-room collaboration sustained over many
days or weeks, less prevalent now in an era of easily transportable digital re-

cording technology and much reduced record-company funding.[75] Results could be impressive, though, and you could count me among those who suspect that (a) trialing within popular music groups aids and abets the incubation period classically associated with individual creativity, and that (b) collective creativity may be reduced in the absence of the fierce compositional negotiations involved. With those negotiations came a level of emotional investment that finds approval with Cindy Blackman Santana: "What I like about that process is that it gets everybody involved." Seen as an arena of action, collaboration overarches and suffuses most drummer performance contexts. All drumming that is disseminated is collaborative and given meaning through its co-constructive relationship with community. In this way, meaning constructs community, which constructs meaning in the reflexive process that underpins this (or any) analysis of cultural experience.

Our expert drummers reveal themselves to be social creatures that prioritize the collaborative, supportive role and seek creativity in those pastures rather than on the rockier terrain of solo performance. Their reports generally confirm Keith Sawyer's confident assertion that "collaboration makes each individual more creative" and that "the emergent results of group genius are greater than those any one individual could think of alone."[76] Eva Vass characterizes collaboration as the joint construction of new knowledge, and creative collaboration as the transformation of that knowledge.[77] In that context, a jointly constructed piece of new music might be collaboratively transformed by others in the rehearsal room or in performance.[78]

More specifically, our drummers repeatedly evoke creativity in the context of a close dyadic relationship with a band or group leader—usually an internationally recognized "star" performer. This individual is seen as bestowing not only employment, status, and reflected glory, but also a framework for individual performance creativity. These findings are consistent with the literature; Vera John-Steiner, for example, emphasizes the stretching of one's identity through comparison and contrast with one's collaborator.[79] Referencing the melding, exchange, and appropriation of insights with those of the partner, and the trust and confidence to "live in the other's mind," John-Steiner's collaborator Michele Minnis draws attention to the level of "emotional fitness" needed for the rigors of creative collaboration. Both writers emphasize the generous give and take, the listening skills, the willingness to see the other point of view, all manifest in the sophisticated level of personal interactivity necessary for the sort of trusting creative relationship crucial to effective music performance.[80]

Literature searches in the mid-1990s revealed few if any citations of group creativity. Since then, however, there has been a substantial increase in research and theory developed in the area of innovation through collaboration, but mostly in the organizational and corporate spheres. Large groups, it appears, rarely achieve the sum of the individuals; the desire for consensus leads to premature closure of creative thinking; the voice of dissent is muffled lest it be seen as disloyal to the organization. When allowed to appear, however, conflict among competing positions may raise the quality of decision making and creative solutions.[81]

In the music sphere, some find the production, reception, and consumption of music *inherently* integrative and collaborative.[82] Sawyer sees the key characteristics of group creativity as improvisational, collaborative, and as an "emergent group-level phenomenon, impossible to explain in terms of the individual actor's creative impulses or inspirations."[83] Building on Csikszentmihalyi's Flow theory, Sawyer seeks to recast it as "group flow," a property of an entire group as a collective unit.[84] Further enquiry into individual creativity within collaborative performance should aim to investigate the possible fit with Raymond MacDonald and his colleagues' findings that group levels of Flow are more closely related to higher creativity than individual levels.[85]

To be added, then, to a growing list of social, cultural, organizational, and contextual "external" factors to music creativity is the collaborative ecosystem within which individual drummer creativity seeks to flourish and bloom. While Sawyer points out that small music groups work well as fora for the constant exchange of small ideas from which creativity may emanate,[86] we should bear in mind Salmins's and Erskine's experience of creative performance with large ensembles, which speaks to some of the negative aspects of collaboration. In drummer shorthand, the greater the number of bodies on stage, the less you can play. The extent to which findings from the organizational and corporate domains may be transferable to (or from) music ensembles has yet to be fully investigated.

Getting It: Attitudes to the Receiver and Reception

I am not sure I derived unalloyed personal pleasure from the process of making music, but I found huge satisfaction in its outcomes. They came embodied in both the recorded artifacts and the smiling faces and applause at the end of gigs and concerts. We know that enjoyment of music has multiple origins, only some of which are musical. I had no concern as to why or how the audience appeared to have enjoyed the proceedings, but that they be enjoyed. Our interviewees universally exhibit something of a conflicted approach to non-performing listeners. On the one hand the audience is a welcome supplier of energy and feedback (Cindy), reassurance (Dylan), and, in Ralph's view, transformative power: "If you've got a great audience and they're on board with you," he says, "we all know it can transform a good performance into a great performance." On the other hand, suggests Ralph, listeners are fickle in matters of judgment and taste.[87] They never "get it" or, at best, are unreliable at "getting it": "If you've got an audience who are not getting it [. . .] you still have to put out a performance that is . . . great, to the best of your ability." In Martin France's thinking, "getting it" has a different quality from "liking it":

> Whether they liked it or not or how high they liked it against other da da da in a way is irrelevant, the fact that they got it [. . .] that's enough. Whether they liked it or not, that's up to them.

Certainly the listener can "get it" but retain the right to not like it. That is generally fine with musicians. Liking it for the wrong reasons, as defined by the performer, is the irritant. It is "very important" to Cindy that non-performing listeners identify her as creative "because that is a large part of my makeup." During a long period of stadium-level work with the international rock-star Lenny Kravitz, she was bemused ("I thought it was actually kind of funny") to receive a different reaction from that to which she had hitherto been accustomed, because

> people didn't realize that I am a jazz drummer. And I thought okay . . . and you know what that means is that I'm playing this gig really well, because I'm satisfying what this gig wants and what this gig needs, you know. I just thought it was funny and I thought, yeah, I'm doing my job well.

From her perspective it was a matter of professional pride to ensure that her functional performance ("satisfying what this gig wants and what this gig needs") was hermetically sealed from any trace of compositional contamination. Personifying the gig allows her to satisfy its demands; here, "the gig wants" her to execute the part, not create it. A good musician is always in the service of the music. To serve it well, she may need varying amounts of creativity.

On the topic of whether the listener is seen as a help or a hindrance in public performance and whether it matters either way, opinions are widely divergent. Generally, those such as Strønen and Erskine who habitually occupy the compositional end of the FCC profess a greater indifference to audience reception than those such as Salmins who reside closer to the functional end. Opinions are contingent upon individual perceptions as to the audience's function. Asaf, it has been noted, wants and needs "to be seen," that is, for his performance to be validated. His identity as a musician and as a person is embodied in his performance, which must be verified as proof of existence. As a younger musician, Dylan used to look to the audience and others for reassurance, but "now as I'm a bit older I feel less inclined to look for anyone to reassure me on what I'm doing, because it doesn't really matter now . . . because it's what I'm doing, and so I don't need so many people to say it's good."

Some cultivate a dispassion in the face of audience indifference: "I've gotten better about trying not to freak myself out if there isn't any reciprocation from the crowd in the moment" (Mark Guiliana). Mark takes more positive feedback, however, as a signal for further interaction:

> But, on the flipside, if there is stuff coming back then I just use it to my advantage and to either push to get more, you know, the back and forth . . . or just as a little "okay, this is cool" and not get too high with the highs, you know, the classic thing and not say "oh, they love it, now I'm going to play it faster!" [Laughs].

The level of reaction is carefully calibrated here, lest the listener tail wag the performing dog:

> *Mark Guiliana:* I don't want the good to really take me off course the same way as I don't want the bad to take me off course, just kind of "okay, wow, they're very reserved. I'm going to keep emoting . . ." or "oh, they love it. Okay, I'm going to keep emoting."

Peter Erskine initially expresses a high level of hostility to the listener, but rather grudgingly acknowledges, on reflection, that

> if you're playing music that has a fair amount of kinetic or actual energy . . . if the audience responds in kind, sure, then there's something bigger than the sum of the parts going on; there is an excitement level, and with a good band, the band will focus a bit more.

In another context, audience response of a different kind has an equal but different impact upon him: "But for a lot of the music I play—the stuff that's at the softer dynamic level—if the audience is very quiet and you sense that they're listening (*that's another pleasure*) . . . that's helpful." Finally, Peter softens completely: "It's fun when they like it, I enjoy playing for people, it's a part of the equation of playing music in public and it's gratifying when someone likes it."

Is an audience capable of changing the way a performance unfolds? Interviewees again express a wide range of strongly held opinions. In Asaf's view: "Everything changes how I play. The room, the audience, the musicians, the musicians' mood that same day, you know." On the other hand, Chad refuses to allow the listener to dictate any aspect of the performance. For the performer to deviate from his or her perception of the meaning of the event would be ethically unsound: "You and I both know what would get them on their feet quickly, you know, and I often don't want to do that because that's being cheap." Mark believes that a certain level of audience participation may affirm and assist the performer:

> [The audience is] a help, especially in an improvising context if . . . it's almost like they are as involved as you, depending on how participatory they choose to be.

The degree of participation, however, is highly contingent upon the cultural expectations attendant upon the type of venue:

> How dare you participate as an audience member at [London concert hall] the Barbican? But at [London club] Village Underground they're resting their beers on the stage, yelling and moving and . . . "oh, we must be onto something, they're moving!" you know.

On long tours, differing audience reactions to repetition of the same material has the potential to lift and color the nightly event. According to Ralph, the audience is

> a definite help, and especially we've just done a six-week tour, we've played similar songs every night and we get a different reaction from the audience each night. It's fascinating to see the effect that has on the musicians. It's enormous. It's absolutely enormous.

This sentiment is echoed in Thomas's perception that the sense of security afforded by an appreciative crowd relaxes the performers and can "open up doors": "it can make you feel very secure, which can open up doors; you relax, lower your shoulders and just do things (*Everything sounds good*) yeah."

These observations illustrate both the transformative power of the audience and its complicity in the co-construction of meaning. One of the reasons that you have to "be there" to experience the event in its fullness is that others are there. Be they musicians or listeners, the experience is in part brought into reality through sharing it with others. Asaf suggests that

> when you're playing a piece of music, even if you play a classical piece of music live, where all the notes are written like in classical music, you will always play it differently every night, and that is down to a lot of factors. One of the main ones I think is the audience who's come to listen to you.

On balance, the prevailing sentiment concurs with Chad's assessment of the audience: "I think they're a help, yeah, sure." Live listeners supply energy and feedback, the twin engines that motivate and encourage Cindy, for instance, "to take things farther than I or we imagined we could do." In short, "we need people to play for." For her, creativity is perfectly possible without external verification because the locus of creativity is within her. However, the *experience* of creative performance is "bettered" by having people around because:

> I like touching people, and I like taking people on a journey. I can do that in my own bedroom by myself from now until the sky turns pink and purple and checkerboard. . . . I'm not taking it as far as I can take it because it's only me who's getting the benefit of it. I love touching people, as I said, and the more people who I can touch with love and beauty, with creativity, the better.
>
> I love knowing that somebody came to our concert and left feeling better . . . left feeling that they went on a beautiful journey, left feeling inspired to go home and play or write or create or sing a song or just be nice to their wives or their husbands or their babies. For me that's really the ultimate; I *love* that.

On Cindy's account, playing in front of people is really playing with and for them. "I don't want to play <u>at</u> them, I want to play with them and for them; I want to touch their hearts, and when I feel that that's done . . . man, there's no better feeling."

Assessing the complexities of notoriety and its potential to block or slow the achievement of creativity in performance, Mark acknowledges and agrees that his rising stature brings with it audience demands that may be difficult to fulfil: "*Next thing you know you are performing to expectations and then you're getting pissed with yourself. [. . .] It's difficult that, isn't it?"* "It is; it is." As the IMCM depicts, domain-level expectations of what a successful performance should be intersect with individual-level expectations to mediate action. Ralph, for instance, intuitively seeks to maintain a respectful distance from listener expectations in the preservation of autonomy:

> I think you do have to have a point where you say, "You know what; I'm putting this out to the world, if you don't like it that's okay." I might not get many gigs, but I genuinely believe this is my best offering (*I absolutely think that's the only way*) . . . the only way. Exactly. I think that. [. . .] You've got to do it for artistic reasons. If the audience get on board with it, it's fantastic as well.

On this theme Peter agrees with a third party analysis to the effect that were he (the third party) "playing in a closet by himself or playing on a stage, for him the performance would be the same." This and similar extracts tend to emphasize the cautious "arm's-length" nature of the performer-listener relationship mentioned earlier, which is viewed as on the one hand supportive and helpful, on the other fickle and unreliable.

In so far as they were identified at all, conceptions of supplying some sort of service, product, or function to live listeners were framed in terms of taking them on "a journey" (France, Blackman Santana) or inspiring them by "touching their hearts" (Blackman Santana). The success of the journey is predicated on the absence of humbug and fakery. As France explains:

> You're trying to make them come, without sounding cheesy, on a journey with you, an emotional sort of journey. I think if you just do what you do honestly, and how you feel honestly, to put that through music that somehow the audience will . . . (*smell it?*) yeah, smell it and they'll get on board and become part of it.

Opinions again divide on whether the audience could or should be persuaded that the performance embodies creativity. Chad believes he cannot control the way the audience receives the performance or any meaning they may attach to it ("it's not up to me") and avoids dwelling on it for the preservation of mental health:

> When Terry [Bozzio] and I, we did I think four tours together, double-drum show (*right, I remember*) he used to say "Look, we're were just doing this improvising for, you know, 45 minutes, taking a

break, and doing another 45 minute improvisation, duet, and we're throwing it out there; after that it's up to them. We've done our bit. You know, you can't dwell on it. I think if you did, it'd drive you crazy.

While enjoying public acknowledgment of his creativity, Mark reveals that he has to guard against manipulating the listener:

If I'm thinking about the reception of something and I premeditate the reception, for example, I want to be seen as creative . . . sometimes that could damage the art, and I could make decisions based on like "oh, okay, I want to be perceived as creative. I'm going to write this fucked up odd-meter song and I'm going to orchestrate it for saxophone quartet and tabla" . . . and now here I am, I've just, you know, premeditated this creativity, like broad stroke of "hey I'm creative," and it's not really from my gut and all of a sudden I'm not really being myself.

The production of something deliberately provocative in the hope that listeners will confuse oddness with genuine creativity is a perennial temptation for the artistically bereft. The perceived possibility of premeditating the reception speaks to both Mark's sense of power as a performer and his awareness of ethical concerns. The idea of genuineness and "being myself" as a more direct pathway to creativity than that of posturing and fakery is prevalent throughout the interviews of, in particular, Sirkis, Howe, and Erskine.

In practice, many musicians see a distinction between creating for (or "pleasing") the many as against the few—the two being antipathetical. In the former case, the belief is that sharing or disseminating something as widely as possible is more important in terms of creative achievement than sharing it with just a few people who are highly likely to do something immediately creative with it (such as taking the music and developing it in the moment), as against being inspired by it in some less directly connected way. In the latter case, the belief is that the creative performance becomes in some way compromised or devalued by virtue alone of its wide dissemination. Career goals may be fashioned accordingly. It seemingly falls only to the likes of John Lennon, John Coltrane, Jimi Hendrix, Paul McCartney, Miles Davis, or Michael Jackson to hit the domain-changing sweet spot where both addresser and addressee unite in creative assessment, a possibility whose existence is acknowledged by our drummers but considered so unlikely as to be almost irrelevant. Presumably the short list of performers just mentioned, even if they saw such a distinction, took no notice.

Audiences, then, are generally seen as unreliable and possessing a lower level of listener expertise than co-performers, echoing the anecdotal evidence from some classical musicians.[88] Most of our participants share Thomas Strønen's assessment of audiences as emotionally (and financially) invested in the performance event and thus favorably predisposed to like it: "You know what it's like—people are generous, I feel, at concerts." Listeners to music use strategies to create meaning in relation to their personal agenda and identity,[89] and, as the inexperienced performer may soon come to realize, the meaning they make may be far from the meaning intended. These observations may in part explain why most participants privilege the co-performing listener over the non-performing listener as the appropriate judge of significant difference and the individual whose approbation they sought. Simon Frith's proposition that creativity is not just an action but the way the action is recognized and acknowledged[90] receives strong support from all the participants here, recognition and acknowledgment being valued as indicators of successfully communicated action.

Audiences are nevertheless deemed, on balance, to be of greater help than hindrance in the construction of the action-goal of creative performance. Irrespective of the stance individual participants adopt to non-performing listeners, all acknowledge their collective centrality as powerful co-constructors of meaning in the reciprocal experience of performance. Perhaps counterintuitively, interviewees profess a greater indifference to audience reception of their intrinsically motivated compositional performances than of their extrinsically motivated functional performances. One reason for this might be that, by its nature, the former is invested with a greater sense of personal authorship and ownership—as such it is less available for external approval or critical reappraisal. It also makes the performer more vulnerable, hence the need for ego-defence mechanisms like professing indifference to audience reception. Functional performance, on the contrary, is a matter of what Frank Zappa might call "industrial correctness."[91] It is viewed, by Martin France at least, as "very important that we get it right, put it that way."

Sharing

Many suggest that any experience is heightened through sharing it with others, a notion that doubtless underpins the proliferation of social media. I, for one, was never much good at tourism on my own. John Dewey has sharing as the very "fruit of communication."[92] Common to both constructs of collectiveness—culture and community—is the notion of communicating through sharing, a critical factor underlying creative work. Cultural psychology accords high importance to sharing; its processes emerge from and manifest in shared experiences in lived contexts. Within the drum culture there are multiple sharings: of musical knowledge shared and transformed in rehearsal, of pedagogy, of practical advice, of emotional support, of the groove, of Flow, of the construction of meaning and identity, of the sharing of meanings of experience, and, not least, the sharing of problems. These sharings, either temporary or sustained, are located offstage in collaborative content-generation in rehearsal, recording, or postconcert analysis, and onstage at the point of delivery of the collaborative product for evaluation by a live audience. In this section, I focus on sharing in terms of meaning, groove, Flow, and the sharing of problems.

Sharing Meaning

Much of the above has highlighted how drummers derive meaning from a strong sense of shared community. The way they make meaning of lived experience, and particularly lived creative experience, affects the way they carry out that experience in their actions as musicians, as depicted in the IMCM. In this sense it is the connection or relationships among events that is their meaning. Meaning, however, is not only produced by individuals who register certain experiences as connected to others. Cultures also produce meaning through collections of narratives—myths, fairy tales, histories, and stories.[93] The narrative stereotype of the drummer as a hard-drinking hooligan who defenestrates TVs and drives cars into swimming pools, endorsed by those who seek confirmation that drummers are gorillas, is in turn emphasized by a 2007 television advertising campaign for Cadbury Schweppes in which a gorilla is featured as a drummer.[94] To participate as a member of a culture requires a general knowledge of its full range of meanings. Anthony Giddens notes that cultural stocks of meaning are not understood as static but rather as added to by new contributions from members, and deleted by lack of use.[95] In this regard, the "drum battle," mercifully, appears to be falling by the wayside.

As Harris Berger points out, phenomenology can make a substantial contribution to the interpretation of meaning in any study of expressive culture.[96] My phenomenological focus throughout this book continues to emphasize the meaning-making process of the individual, from his or her point of view. For some musicians, any meaning they might assign to the experience of creativity lies entirely within their own mind and may occur irrespective of background distraction, performance parameters, listener or co-performer approval or disapproval, or indeed the presence or absence of any listener or co-performer at all. At the opposite polarity, creativity is experienced necessarily in conjunction with others and is defined and ratified by their external approval.

In Berger's parlance, the interviewees each adopt an individual *stance* toward meaning and the creative experience. Some consider the experience of drumming to be amplified, "bettered," or made more meaningful if shared in collaboration with attentive co-performers and engaged listeners. It needs to be communicated not only for assessment of its significance (and hence creativity) but also, more pragmatically, because recognition tends to raise career profile. Recognition of Ralph Salmins's cumulative experience by others leads directly to his opinions being sought at the functional level of performance because

> I've got more experience. Just like you would go into a gig and someone would say "Well, what do you think?" and I would say "Well, I think I'd like to play this," and that's welcomed.

There may be multiple interpretations of the creative moment from several perspectives: physical, mental, emotional, spiritual, social, or virtual. To illustrate, the physical experience may be characterized in terms of the rate of heartbeat, raised blood pressure, sore hands, or advanced motor function. The mental experience among improvisers may be interpreted as being under varying degrees of control. The relationship to the passive musical instrument may be intensely emotional, seen as falling in and out of love with drums, drumming, or music, as if these were lovers, or as quasi-religious, "monastic, timeless, and unchanging. It may be a relationship as close as and as exclusive as man and wife, or even more so, as many a spouse will attest."[97] When the Christian drummer in an evangelical rock group dedicates his work to God, he invokes a spiritual dimension to his creativity. For others, the creative moment is experienced socially and irrespective of genre; for them, meaning is located in the social and collaborative. Creative meaning may be experienced entirely online in a virtual garage band or in a collaborative cyber-community of Internet musicians.[98] These and other interpretations assign meaning to performance practice. While the discussion retains a tight focus on action-within-culture, two dimensions of perception from embodiment theory may help to illuminate experience and meaning-making in music performance and should be noted in passing.

First, taking embodied experience as his starting point for analysis of human participation in a culture, Thomas Csordas borrows from the philosopher Maurice Merleau-Ponty to explain our existence in terms of reciprocal interaction, a notion that converges with the present line of thinking that runs from Dewey through Boesch to Eric Clarke.[99] A Deweyan view of this reciprocity would suggest that in the creative moment the performer both expresses experience and experiences that expression. He or she engages with the world of sound as "the one both hearing and being heard."[100] This reciprocal quality demonstrates the state of being both subject (the one drumming) and object (the one drummed to), the one both hearing and being heard. Reciprocity, too, is at the heart of Clarke's observation that "perceiving organisms seek out and respond to perceptual information that specifies objects and events in the environment, and this perceiving is a continuous process that is both initiated by, and results in, action."[101]

A second observation, also drawing upon an embodiment perspective, derives in part from Roland Barthes's musical semiology, which aims to explore "the body in a state of music." According to Michael Szekely it is, for Barthes, "not just important that we hear and feel the voice, but that we hear and feel the materiality of the voice."[102] Szekely goes on to reference Barthes's erotics of music: "the body in the voice as it sings, the hand as it writes, the limb as it performs."[103] Barthes's approach is echoed by Allan Moore when he acknowledges that "the way listeners listen is greatly determined by whatever bodily knowledge they have of producing music." Moore points to current exploration in neurology to advance this claim, from which we may infer that, first, a drummer in performance (always a listener) possesses an involuntary neurological response to drum music determined in part by the intimate physiological experience of producing the drum sounds; and second, that this response will always engage him or her more completely than the response of non-drummers.[104] Drummers, then, respond to, experience, and make sense of drumming differently from others *by virtue of being drummers*.

Sharing Groove

Good drummers care about the "groove," the way it is reliably constructed, produced, sustained, intensified, and relaxed. The groove is characterized here as a sociomusical construct embodied in the practice of one or more in shared performance. The topic of the groove was examined in chapter 4 in its relationship to the metrical lever of control; the emphasis here is on its shared co-construction. Drummers enjoy and share with others the pleasure of what Mark Doffman calls "the mutual tuning-in" accomplished through entrainment.[105] This phenomenon has been characterized as task movements coincident with the rhythm of the music, giving the activity elements of a dance.[106] The human tendency toward rhythmic coordination and entrainment is particularly obvious in activities that require rhythmic coordination to improve work efficiency,[107] but it may also engender a smoothing effect with implications for homogeneity within practice. We have already noted a central paradox within the community of drummers, which, reduced to its barest essence, states that more and more drummers are playing less and less (i.e., are generating diminishing quantities of rhythmic information). One explanation of this reduction in available temporal, metrical, dynamical, and timbral options may have its origins in the co-regulatory smoothing process that writers such as Eviatar Zerubavel and Shinobu Kitayama have identified through a cultural psychology approach to socialization in the "thought community," and which may now be seen to have a close cousin in entrainment.[108] Homogenization is a key constraint on expressivity and I return to the topic shortly in a discussion of the wider implications of homogenization for drummer practice.

Sharing Flow

The Csikszentmihalyian concept of Flow, described as a "merging of action and awareness" and thus a "convergence of knowing and doing,"[109] has received considerable attention in connection with peak performance, group creativity, and jazz performance.[110] Its cultivation and co-construction is a central dimension of the experience of group performance and finds meaning at its intersection with action theory and Deweyan philosophy. We have seen how the former holds situated action as goal-oriented and intentional. In having purpose, it fulfils a central criterion for Flow: "to experience Flow one must set goals for one's actions."[111] For example, deliberate practice on the drum kit prepares the ground for the Flow moment when there is minimal or no delay between thought and action, when the two are completely fused.

When Csikszentmihalyi goes on to state that "the purpose must result in strivings; intent has to be translated into action,"[112] he echoes both the action-theorists and the philosophy of John Dewey. Dewey, we should remember, considered that obstacles or constraints are always necessary for action to become experience. "Undergoing" always precedes "doing" and, at the same time, is continued by it. These interconnected processes take the action forward to become full experience.[113] The concept of Flow gathers these strands of thinking and frames them such as to illuminate the experience of individual creative music performance. Dylan Howe, for instance, characterizes being "in the moment" as both an absence of self-consciousness and the achievement of a "slightly altered state," for him an elusive goal. His approach is to avoid

> any self-consciousness, so you're not kind of thinking how it sounds or what other people might be thinking it sounds like; you're just in the moment. [. . .] I like it when I feel slightly detached and I feel like I'm kind of . . . if it can get in any way into a slightly altered state of being not really there but completely there, then I know I'm enjoying it [laughs].

If one can sustain the being-in-the-moment for even as little as a quarter of an hour on occasion, then

> that's a result, I would think, because most of the time you're nowhere near that.

Dylan's description evokes Csikszentmihalyi's Flow construct while the drummer is quite unaware of it; at the individual level the pursuit of Flow is a good way to find what he seeks. Going further, Elina Hytönen-Ng links shamans and musicians when she suggests that Flow is also the way society accommodates altered states of consciousness without jeopardizing the individual's rationality or mental health.[114]

Sharing Problems

Drummers, then, experience sharing in respect to meaning, groove, and Flow. A final dimension addresses the common obstacles and problems that not only heighten the sense of sharedness, of confidence under threat, but which also mediate creativity. One strand of thought posits culture as arising essentially in response to a problem or set of problems faced in common by a group of people.[115] From this viewpoint, the drum culture is *strengthened* by the very problems with which practitioners must contend. Matt Brennan's astute characterization of the drummer as oscillating uncertainly "between centrality and marginality, between virtuosity and incompetence, between useful supplier of good quality human groove and unnecessary adjunct to the terrain that music technology has now secured as its own"[116] neatly summarizes the prevailing ecology within which drummers are obliged to perform. Crucially, it also highlights the "useful/useless" dichotomy that tends to presage the common understanding of what drummers are for. A good way to usefully unpick the dualities in Brennan's characterization might be to focus on the several interlinked problems loosely grouped within three aspects of practice: marginalization, the relationship between technology and identity, and homogeneity.

As a corpus of popular music instrumentalists, outsiders to the playfulness of pitch by nature of their chosen instrument but insiders to the art of the groove, drummers in particular have been characterized as standing apart from others, with their contribution generally unrecognized.[117] The negative ideological tropes of the mind/body split, the downplaying of intellect, and the pitched instrument prejudice highlighted above have been implicated as possible causes as to why this might be so and need not be restated. The consequences of such denigration, however, may have implications for the action-choices drummers make and their perceptions of creativity.

Elite attempts to construct a socially exclusive, highbrow tradition of legitimated art music in the late 19th-century necessitated a deprecation of lowbrow, "light" (later, popular) music as "an important element in the process of sacralization."[118] On this account, efforts to foreground tonal harmony enlisted and promoted the pitched-instrument prejudice in the concomitant deprecation of the rhythmic element in music. Popular music, itself framed as an object of "disdain, derogation, and disgust,"[119] has only recently been habilitated as a subject for analysis. It comes as no surprise, then, that drummers tend to remain reticent about their skills and wary of allying them with any notion of creativity. A causal connection might exist between the constant misunderstanding and denigration of the art of the drummer from outside the community, perpetuating the "substandard musician" stereotype, and a corresponding lack of creative confidence within, but, if so, its extent has yet to be fully examined.

In seeking to distance himself from such negative introversion, Max Roach found powerful creative motivation: "Drummers who just played straight time never did much for me. I've always felt the drummer shouldn't be a subservient figure."[120] From this I infer that he thought drummers probably *were* subservient figures:

> I always hated the idea that the drums were the musical coons of the band, just the support systems. [...] I played in a way that meant the drums weren't in the background anymore; they were the front line with everybody else.[121]

Joe Chambers offered a similarly Afrocentric point of view when detailing the role drums have played in American history, their overall acceptance in

Western music, and, ultimately, why he no longer wished to be considered a jazz drummer.[122] A causal connection seems to exist between the status of kit drummers as substandard musicians and a heightened sense of the embattled culture of deviancy, an identity that drummers share and from which they take strength.

Recording techniques afforded by the late 20th-century arrival of computer-generated and quantized clock-time, progressively adopted as common practice in Western recording studios, further conspired to marginalize the drummer. In the predigital tape-based era of the 1960s to the 1990s, the drummer's performance was among the first to be committed to tape. The requirement was for, as far as possible, a flawless performance with only guide accompaniment from band members (who generally replaced their parts later) and based on a supposition of what instruments she or he may eventually be accompanying. Other instrumental parts might be considered post hoc in their relationship to a steady, unvarying drum track, to which they could be added or from which they could be removed. Milton Mermikides refers to the provision of this necessary but functional "backing" track as a "playground" for others, revealing "an asymmetry of instrumental function."[123]

Early intercourse with digital technology did not augur well. Under the glare of the ubiquitous computer screen, drummers unsurprisingly tended to avoid the exotic, the excitable, or that which might exist at the limit of their technical ability. All those turn of the century albums that were sent round as audio files on the Internet for colleagues to add their contribution seemed to sound like paint-by-numbers looked. All those early automated drum tracks with the life quantized out of them sounded stiff and unyielding. Through the later decades of the 20th century, marginalization of the drummer proceeded apace through injudicious edits producing "unplayable" performances, inappropriate overdubbing, quantized and automated clock-time, and a flattening of dynamics. The eventual arrival of digital recording systems afforded the wholesale ceding of whatever control remained of the individual's performance to the producer in postproduction.[124] By the turn of the millennium, a long list of real and perceived infringements by the technologists upon the drummer's traditional terrain was questioning appropriateness, lowering expectations and confidence, and promoting the sense that the services of a popular group's dedicated rhythmic specialist were now no longer required, at least in the studio. Over time, however, accommodations were made, benefits emerged. Drummers began to emulate machine precision and perform more accurately. Blair Sinta learned how to "become" a Roland 808 for people such as Melissa Etheridge. On the other side, programmers and software developers became adept at emulating human inflection, touch, and feel. Technology has vastly extended the drummer's sonic palette, further extending opportunities for the construction of difference. Distance and audible distinction between the two camps began to narrow. Now drummers can "play like machines" and vice-versa, although the advantages of this new scenario are not immediately clear.

Some interviewees perceive technology as hastening to sever the beginner from the "old" ways, the cultural modes of learning that not only transfer skills but deliver a cultural context for their appropriate use. The great drumming "originals" have clear connections to the work of their rhythmic forefathers that ensure their cultural value, relevance, and potency, if not their creativity. As we have seen, creative drummers see little inherent virtue in the ruthless pursuit of novelty for its own sake, preferring instead an approach that recombines existing elements usually, but not exclusively, from within the drum culture. Connection to the drum culture becomes a vital component of drummer creativity; a lack of cultural connectedness is one aspect that makes it harder for younger drummers to be creative.

A further obstacle to be circumvented is the perceived homogenization of some dimensions of performance. Cultural homogenization is readily apparent in numerous areas of modern life, from clothing, hotels, and advertising to architecture, car design, and popular music. With respect to the latter, it would seem likely that its component performances are also becoming homogenized, although the results of exploration in this area are not yet entirely convincing.[125] Contemporary work asserting that hit songs are getting louder and more rhythmically repetitive and predictable tends to confirm anecdotal evidence.[126] A number of trends in contemporary Western popular music point toward potentially poorer volume dynamics.[127] A drummer's sound, or timbral presence, is at the heart of his or her character as a musician. To restrict or delimit a drummer's expressive palette is to separate the individual from his or her character, render him or her faceless, and reduce him or her to anonymity. On David Blake's account, it is timbre, more than any other musical parameter, that musically expresses differentiation.[128]

With respect to predictability, a reading of the FCC would suggest that at one end of the spectrum the functional drummer operates with an *intention toward* predictability; at the other, the composing drummer does so with an *intention toward* surprise. In part because of the easily replicable and, arguably, the increasingly predictable patterns of the functional drummer, the computer has impinged most upon his or her traditional domain. Several popular music genres (for example, electronic dance music, house, rap, grime, or hip-hop) are generally layered upon a bed of automated percussion generated from the computer or sampler. This predictability, coupled with a preference toward louder, dynamically more stable music and improving music technology, enhances the possibility of automation, which some see as a threat to their practice.

Evidence here from older practitioners transitioning from the analog to the digital world suggests that they tend to find the latter ethically and aesthetically unwelcoming, underscoring their own sense of inferiority and questioning their competence. My own experiential evidence supports the idea of both an intentional, narrowing homogenization of tempi, dynamic range, and stylistic appropriateness in the mainstream, and an intentional, broadening heterogeneity of timbral and metrical possibilities at the very margins of practice. An oppositional position asserting that Western kit drumming is, on balance, becoming more heterogeneous is difficult to find in the literature.[129]

This increased homogenization of some dimensions of the performed part has had consequences in several areas. First, as has been noted, it has fostered a susceptibility to its reproduction by computer, the human performance being correspondingly surplus to requirements. Second, it has heightened the attention afforded by both producer and practitioner to surface detail, especially in the recorded artifact. Third, it may have shifted the area of innovative work to postproduction. The skilful application of outboard analog and digital treatments (often referred to as "ear candy") locate the postproduction work on the recorded drums in the world of "sound enhancement," of the kind much used in commercial advertising or movies. A drum performance without cosmetic enhancement, for example, now comes to be seen as "authentic" and intimate, the preferred option for many introspective singer-songwriters or jazz performers. Moore's construct of the "sound box"[130] goes a long way toward explaining how any given drum part played quietly and foregrounded in the audio mix with little or no electronic processing possesses a different quality and conveys a different meaning to the same part played hard, heavily processed, and set well back in the mix. This type of postproduction decision making is frequently undertaken by contemporary drummers themselves, whose occupation, especially in the context of the stay-home drummer, is in the process of much redefinition. Such heightened attention to these processes may herald a permanent shift in the meaning of drumming and what it means to be a drummer.

We have no space here for a full examination of the connection between the strength of a culture and its requirement for conformity, but within the domain of music this conformity may be interpreted as playing out in homogeneity. As noted earlier, research within anthropology has observed the smoothing effect of a strong cultural identity, in which idiosyncrasies are smoothed out and perceived within classes of behavior.[131] On this account, personal psychological processes and structures are actively organized to co-ordinate with the pertinent cultural systems of practices and public meanings. In short, it would seem on a balance of probabilities that the drum community nurtures and shares problematic aspects of marginalization, technology, identity, and homogenization about as fast as its members can devise creative solutions.

Summary

This chapter has outlined the purpose or value of communicating difference in the context of drummer performance, and the ways in which such communication is achieved. My remarks were prefaced by a necessary detour in order to fully understand the way communication—the third dimension of the SDCA framework—subsists as a vital component of creative drummer action. We have situated drummers in both culture and community, as a breed apart and a breed below. Their activities are governed by a cultural tradition that regulates and shapes the experience of creative practice, and take place within a community that mediates and promotes the psychological behavior, meaning-making, and choice selection of the individual. This is the case in all community-based activities. Embracing a particularly corrosive ideology, however, the broader drum culture (that enfolds the community) is something of an extreme case.

Three sets of issues were highlighted. First was the extent of the impact of the Cartesian mind/body split upon performance perceptions; second, the degree to which intellect is downplayed in practice; and third was a set of questions about performance on instruments of indefinite pitch. Having brought these negative ideological components into the light, I developed a view as to how aligned feeling and shared purpose allow drummers to nevertheless communicate meaning and collaborate successfully in performance. The notion of communicating through sharing is common to both culture and community; the topic was examined here in respect to groove, meaning, Flow, and the several problems surrounding marginality, identity, and homogeneity in practice. Some of these observations buttress the developing argument that, rather than emotion, it is the communication of significantly different experience that remains foundational to the attribution of creativity within and among drummers.

- Experts' perceptions include the following insights:

  - Creative music performance is a form of communication involving connecting and sharing with others in and through culture and community.
  - Although it may be fulfilled alone, the experience of creativity is amplified, heightened, or made more powerful if shared in collaboration with attentive co-performers and engaged listeners.
  - A collaborative context of aligned feelings and shared purpose affords not only the greatest performance pleasure but a secure, favorable environment in which to incubate and communicate difference.
  - Drummers tend to frame communication in terms of the expression of significantly different experience rather than the communication of emotion.
  - A high level of communication with other musicians is foundational to successful music performance.
  - Recognition and acknowledgment are valued indicators of successfully communicated action.
  - Participants show greater indifference to audience reception of their compositional performance than to reception of their functional performance.
  - The presence of listeners is deemed to be of greater help than hindrance in the construction of creative performance.

7 • I Never Heard It Before

Assessing Significance

The final dimension of creative music performance reflected in the SDCA framework addresses assessment. The performances of the drummers we have been discussing have long since and repeatedly been appraised by colleagues and others in the community of practice and found to possess significant difference, to be creative. I borrow again from John Hope Mason in privileging significance over novelty as the key quality of creative action, and restate the pivotal question, "Does it matter?" The important argument here is that it is the *attributed significance* that is foundational to the assessment of the creative outcome or artifact, material or immaterial. Significance is produced by the articulation of certain ideas, beliefs, and aspirations within a common network of assumptions and meanings: new ideas can only become significant by engaging with that network in order to change it. Thus, while the drawings and paintings of a child may commonly be called "creative," they are, rather, individual; they are insignificant to others except, perhaps, his or her immediate family. Significance itself is fluid, contested, and may be disruptive, but ultimately I join anthropologist Clifford Geertz and sociologist Max Weber in believing it to be foundational to culture. Geertz invokes Weber's powerful image of mankind as an animal "suspended in a web of significances he himself has spun" when he, Geertz, declares: "I take culture to be those webs."[1]

Who Counts? The Arbiters of Significance

Who assesses and retains the selected variants in the putative creative action? Who is to assess significance? The identity of the gatekeepers remains rather unclear and may differ between domains. A Csikszentmihalyian list of gatekeepers in the field of Western kit drumming would include other eminent practitioners, manufacturers and retail store owners, magazine editors, record company executives, teachers, and music critics—in short, all those who wield power and influence. Glăveanu seeks to broaden the social organization of the domain by adding the perspective of "significant others" introduced to or affected by the creation (different groups or communities) to that of the creator (informed by her or his "creative identity").[2] Adopting a more consensual approach to the problem, Teresa Amabile asserts that "a product or response is creative to the extent that *appropriate observers* independently agree it is creative."[3]

In practice, expert drummers tend to find such characterizations of the gatekeepers in their particular domain somewhat nebulous. As noted in the previous chapter, the opinions of non-performing listeners tend to be regarded with suspicion or dismissed. Within a somewhat inward-looking community, encircled and surrounded by "pitched" practitioners with arguably a different quality of creative music experience, the wisest heads, the most appropriate observers, the most significant others, it is suggested, are co-performing colleagues and other drummers. It is to them that the question "Does it matter?" is addressed, and their answers are reflected in changed practice. I return to this idea shortly.

The fact that creative assessment is usually made in retrospect, sometimes after many years, should not necessarily invest it with any greater virtue than "in the moment" assessments made by musicians on the bandstand that minute, that day, that week, although it may act as a "double lock" on quality. Neither is long-term assessment necessarily any more stable than short-term, as shown in the critique of Csikszentmihalyi's system model in chapter 2. As yet, we have no single metric for knowing where or when variation becomes newness. In the sphere of music performance, all variation is in some way new, *but not all is significant,* and it is precisely the significant variation that begets creativity in the context of drummer performance. This observation gives us the key to unlock an operational definition of creative performance. In the context of Western kit drumming, *creative music performance resides in the ability to effect and communicate significant difference.* If there is to be an "everyday life" creativity to be had at the drum kit, it may well be novel, useful, and appropriate, but its difference should qualify as significant to appropriate observers.

In the previous chapter, I considered our experts' attitudes toward, and expectations of, the non-performing listener in respect to reliable assessment. What of the co-performing listener? Dylan Howe asks himself the pertinent question that might well have been asked of all interviewees: "Who are you playing for: the audience, the group, or yourself?" Unsurprisingly, in view of the fickleness they attribute to the non-performing listener, a clear majority of participants reference the co-performer as the primary agent to whom difference must be communicated. According to Dylan:

> Things always go well, or better, if you feel there is a good feeling in the house and there are enough people, and they are enjoying it, and they are with you, but generally that only happens if you completely ignore that they're there [laughs] and you play to the other guys on the stand.

His creative process hinges on communicating the appropriate feeling within and among his co-performers first: "That's the only way round to do it. I think the moment that you try and second-guess what you think the audience would like you're on a hiding to nothing [not going to gain anything]."[4] The co-performer tends to seen as the most appropriate judge of difference, whose acknowledgment is crucial to the creative attribution. A clear majority of interviewees consider a positive assessment of their creativity by others in the domain to be important, with the primary assessors being co-performers and other drummers. Such an assessment is valued not only for pragmatic reasons to do with employment opportunities, commercial concerns, and status, all of which impact upon dissemination of the product (i.e., the creative performance), but valued also for confirmation that one is heard and, perhaps, a state of Flow recognized. For Asaf, what co-performers think of him is

> very important because all these thoughts, all these things are really . . . just another thing that will invite, encourage, allow more creativity to come.

Assessment by the few within the domain, then, is sharply prioritized over that of the many without.

The importance to Peter of other people considering him creative is only "to the extent that they're listening, if 'other people' would mean the other musicians I'm working with. If they are listening, then they are tacitly acknowledging the creativity and we get a better result." He instinctively prioritizes the considerations of his co-performers who acknowledge his creativity by paying attention. If they are not listening, one might infer that they have nothing much to listen to, and at that time Peter is exhibiting insufficient creativity. He situates music creativity in close relationship with listening, "which," he insists, "I'm not good at." He again references the act of listening—"truly listening"—in the context of "being open to receiving the other," commonly cited as a prerequisite of creative sharing.

Others approach from a different angle. Ralph characterizes creativity as being "about trust and . . . about permission," permission being withheld if "others" (such as prospective employers) do not consider him creative. "It is important because otherwise they're not going to let me be creative." Martin takes creative attribution as certification that a drummer can perform to a certain standard, that he or she is "creative enough" to be able to assess the musical situation and, frequently under a time constraint, provide an entirely appropriate performance. The perspective of both musicians is thus partially framed in terms of potential employment. Matthew Peacock notes how the mechanics of the discipline thus create gatekeepers of creative attribution in the form of employers (and potential employers), similar to the way in which other professional disciplines involving creativity have formally or informally appointed gatekeepers.[5]

Most, then, prefer to frame the communication of significant difference in terms of intra-performer communication rather than anything to do with non-performing listeners. The creative work, they report, takes place *entre-nous*, and if the audience "gets it" that is all well and good. In reference to some recent (2014) recording sessions of his improvising quartet, Mark Guiliana finds the music "fulfilling" even with no audience other than that of his co-performers:

> I feel those situations are satisfying, more than enough fulfilling on their own. . . . I wouldn't choose that option if it was one or the other, but it would still be a fulfilling experience without an audience.

The "private" audience in front of whom he is playing may be small and not paying, but it is nevertheless of crucial importance to his "fulfilment." Only one participant states unequivocally that he makes music for himself. Self-motivated and critically self-contained, Thomas Strønen creates from a position of confidence and thus strength: "If I'm happy with the gig then it's a good gig, and if I get one out of five stars the day after it doesn't really bother me at all. So I think I make music for myself."

Earlier we have noted an interesting subtheme developing around the degree of intra-performer communication necessary prior to and during effective music co-operation: much of the negotiation surrounding performance in jazz groups is unspoken. Martin France maintains that "you fathom out the people that seem to have the same . . . concept as yourself, you know, but not necessarily ever talking about it." Minimal verbal communication is also implied by Chad Wackerman, to whom the speed of the catalytic reaction ("it all happened and then it was over") comes as a surprise:

> Jimmy [Johnson] just came up with this little riff and I said, great, let's do that, let's count it off—roll tape, count it off—and it turned into something I've never heard anybody do before because we're all . . . It's on the latest record. [. . .] It all happened and then it was over and it was like . . . oh . . . no one else would . . .

Creativity here is seen as residing in both the spontaneous combustibility of the music and its uniqueness, music that Chad has never heard anyone else produce.

If verbal and visual modes of communication between performers are generally kept to a minimum, their scarcity only confirms them as vital indicators of respect and awareness. The smile is interpreted as a powerful communicative device in performance because it confers recognition. Peter Erskine is "always watching," but "I'll instinctively look up and I'll see him [arranger Vince Mendoza] smile and I enjoy that because he's done all the writing and he's conducting and I'm pleased that he enjoys that thing." From this, he concludes that "the important part of the creative process, I think, is acknowledgment or recognition by one of the collaborators." The question as to why a collaborator's acknowledgment appears intrinsically more valuable to Peter than that of the lay listener was not directly addressed, although the foregoing suggests several possible reasons. Peter's testimony seems to support existing research suggesting that informative or constructive evaluation or feedback recognizing creative accomplishment can be conducive to further creativity.[6]

Ingrid Monson observes that, within the jazz community, to say that a player doesn't listen is a grave insult. This may be applied, according to Nicholas Cook, "with equal force to classical musicians"[7] and arguably to all musicians. In the context of the intimacy afforded the musicians in small-room jazz performance, Asaf Sirkis describes the extensive implications of his gestural communication with "one of the guys" in the band:

> I find that sometimes when we all play and it's like heads down and [the music is] complicated and everybody's trying to do his best, and trying to play well and all this kind of thing, and then you know I just lift my head, and look at one of the guys and smile at him, just because he did something I like; that's just enough . . . that little moment to,

er . . . <u>millions</u> of different ideas to come out and the wonderful, joyous creative thing you know so, you know, it's really important . . . I
think that a connection is really important whether you're playing
your music or another music, it can be a change from one to ten, it can
turn over a whole gig from being just an intense "muso" [musician
overly concerned with technique] kind of a thing, where everybody
tries to impress other people and hope that, you know, it doesn't lose
a beat, and then . . . just a really joyous process with, you know, people
just communicating and playing together.

This contrasts rather sharply with my experience within stadium rock, which
was one of an unsettling disconnectedness within and between performers
and audience, exacerbated not least by the many meters of open stage and the
vast size of auditoria. The predominant if surreal feeling was that, in the absence of meaningful sharing, everything might just keep going even if I, or
perhaps all the musicians, departed.

Within the context of the current debate as to whether creativity should
be assessed by the critical acclaim of experts or by popularity with the masses,
the evidence here strongly supports the former approach, with the added nuance that it is current practitioners who are the appropriate assessors by virtue of their swift adoption of anything deemed new or useful to performance.
If "difference" is detected in their own or another's performance, then that
performance matters and is deemed thus to be creative, irrespective of any
domain-changing potential. This is the sense in which "making it matter"
matters, and it is important because it demonstrates the strength of the opinions and actions of "other guys," namely the gatekeepers of significance, the
people for whom this matters most.

Am I Creative? Reflecting on Personal Creativity

Before the interviews, I had asked all our experts to identify recorded examples of their work that they considered to be creative. Assessment of significant action tends to be confused by a reluctance to separate the person
from the process/product (i.e., the performance). "Am I creative?" is frequently conflated with "Is my performance creative?" Given that the focus
remains on what meanings the notion of creativity may be made to carry, a
clear distinction between the two appears to be both impractical and unnecessary to establish. There was little convergence in the degrees of importance interviewees attached to considerations of their own creativity. A

wide range of responses branched out into a general assessment of creative strategies, actions, and processes.

A surprisingly large minority of our drummers downplayed the whole idea of assessing their performances as creative. In Chad Wackerman's case, there is no necessity to think about it consciously because "the gigs I'm doing, it feels like they have room to be creative. (*So it comes with the water?*) Yeah." Martin France is "offered a lot more creativity" than others (by which is meant that the musical situation affords him the space to enable creative action), which is problematic because he doesn't consider himself creative: "I've never really been that sort of player." He finds himself lacking in comparison to others: "He was playing after me, and just seeing that guy play, I was just gobsmacked how creative he actually was. It made me look like I was sort of just . . . you know." Even though Martin is well respected internationally as a jazz drummer, he firmly rejects the idea that he is possessed of a creative direction. For him, creativity is simply a matter of providing the right thing at any point on the FCC. The provision of this in the context of a tightly constrained musical theater gig may involve searching for those "little corners of creativity":

> Even though I've played it 100 times, I might try and look for a little . . . I'm not feeling completely straitjacketed. There might be little corners where I can have a bit of freedom, even if it's just playing rolls on a cymbal and then, changing it slightly, the dynamic or something or . . . just being able to find it . . . little corners of creativity in everything. Whether it's playing with [pianist] Gwilym [Simcock] or something like that, or doing something like this or playing and interpreting a piece of music where someone's only written half a drum pattern and you come up with the rest.

The hunt for the "little corners" is associated here with "a bit of freedom," and echoes the "putting something of yourself into the music," which for most musicians is synonymous with creative performance.[8] Of course, like all the interviewees, Martin's self-assessment is built upon his own definition of creativity, which may be encumbered by the familiar misconception that creativity has to be about big, noisy, original ideas that hit you in the face rather than about being ingenious enough to find creative possibilities within tightly confined problem spaces.

Thomas Strønen finds it hard to feel creative in part because he finds it difficult to surprise himself:

I don't feel creative as a person because I . . . know all my skills, good and bad, and I know what I'm capable of and so it's very hard for me to surprise myself.[. . .] I don't think about it being "outside the box" or "different" or not within the "normal parameters."

While collaboration with an audience alone in solo performance may be fruitful ("Sometimes it's enough with yourself—you can do a solo concert and it really works"), collaboration with other musicians affords the possibility of being led into new areas:

Thomas Strønen: So what happens is that when I play with others they might in a way <u>lead</u> me into something that I wouldn't have done. . . . Some musicians you play with, you know, they make you a better musician. Some musicians do something to you that takes you to a different level, and it can make you focus. If I play with [pianist, composer] Bugge Wesseltoft I'll be very aware of the beat and time because he's got such a good beat and he's so distinguished and it does something to me. While if I play with John Taylor, for example, on the piano, I feel like I can be very loose and open and wide; I feel I can stretch time; I can really work around his playing.

Some, such as Thomas and Peter, frame their creativity within a stylistic confection from which they derive their respective voices, "really an emulation of what I like most about the drummers I've enjoyed listening to" (Peter). Peter's modest evaluation of his most creative moments amounts to no more than being "pretty cool," which is "as far as I'm willing to go with it." He tends to see his most creative work as within a constraining framework, preferably one that he characterizes as "antidrumming," by which he means "not meeting the expectations of the drum dolts or geeks but also finding another path by means of the drum." This represents a good example of creativity arising in resistance to something, be it the expectations of others or other forms of restrictions in what is considered acceptable performance. His chosen audio environment as the leader of a trio exhibits a stripped-down drum style in which, he says, "every single cymbal pulse starts to carry a lot of meaning."

In contrast to the hesitations and circumscriptions of many participants, Cindy has a singular perception of the locus of creativity. Her affirmative response to the question "Do you consider yourself creative?" resonates through several passages of her interview. Creativity is within her as "part of the way that God made me," and always running in her head. She is "blessed to be designed" with creative ability and the desire to be creative. She cannot turn it on and off like a tap, but she can choose when to use it, a choice she sees as mediated by her taste and professional judgment. She does not need anybody else to be creative with, although the experience is certainly heightened in the company of others.

Mark is similarly straightforward: asked if he feels creative, he responds with a simple "Yes." For him, creativity is made manifest principally within his own band where the quality of the decision making can be in no doubt: "I can make any decision I want at any moment and it's right because it's mine, which sounds very ignorant..." Asaf and Chad agree it is important to think of themselves as creative, but offer no specific explanation as to why this might be. It is important also for Ralph to allow his "creative side to come out," and

> it has to be given credence even if you come up with an idea and it's wrong and it doesn't work. [...] You think "I fancy playing that" and if it doesn't work, that's okay. But I do support my own creative urges and I try to be as creative as I can.

These extracts demonstrate a desire to be close to or express the phenomenon of creativity and to seek it out. While a small majority places creativity squarely at the center of their music consciousness, a substantial minority downplays the centrality of the phenomenon in performance and assign it less meaning than might have been expected. To answer why that might be so, it might be instructive to survey the ways in which participants ascribe significance to their own, and others', strategies, processes, and performance outcomes.

I Never Heard It Before: Attributing Significance to Self and Others

What's creative about it? Participants' judgments reflect multiple ways in which their perceptions of creativity are brought into reality and given meaning. One much-trodden pathway to difference lies within the avoidance of what others are doing. Peter assesses some of his own work as creative because "that's not something I've heard other guys do." This speaks to the FCC's distinction between the quantitative improvement of functional performance—the doing of things because other drummers do them (or the doing of the same things better)—and the qualitative difference of compositional performance—the doing of things because other drummers do not do them (or do them differently).

In this extract, Dylan describes why his self-selected performances are creative:

> They just kind of illustrate when you're not feeling self-conscious, when you're not feeling you have to subscribe to anything particularly, externally. You are yourself, in the best version of yourself, so that's what you want. . . . They say that when I was doing that recording I was just as completely free as I can be, and in the moment, so that's something rare, really.

He attributes creativity on four grounds: that his cited performances are unselfconscious, that they are intrinsically motivated, that they exhibit the "best version" of himself, and that they communicate an expressive freedom. His construct of the "best version" of himself accords with Asaf's "genuine self," but differs in that he can conjure it only infrequently ("it's something rare, really"). Nevertheless his creativity is framed within a rising self-esteem, a diminishing need for reassurance, and a feeling that he's "not just bluffing it out."

Chad assesses one of his recordings, in current use for instructional purposes at the college level, as uniquely creative because "it does sound really different and it doesn't sound like anybody else." Interestingly, he did not attribute those qualities to it at the time of performance, evidencing his fluid appraisal of the outcomes of action over time. Other attributions of creativity within the interviews emerge from memories of process, of "allowing the creative process to happen" (Ralph), of entering a (mental) space "where everything was possible" (Thomas), of "really concentrating" to get a result that was "probably as good as it can get" (Thomas). Martin found creativity in extending his work from the audio to the video domain: "If you introduce that other element of the video then the music takes on a different form. It takes on a different purpose." Asked to describe, in his self-selected samples of creativity, why he assesses some as more creative than others he might have selected, Ralph supposes simply that "it's the creative process involved in putting the right [drum] parts to the music."

Allan Moore draws the distinction between popular song and popular music.[9] Our participants made no mention of any such distinction; the interesting possibility of performance being approached differently within each context did not surface. Anecdotally, most popular music is vocal music. Drummers generally play to support the song, and may seldom if ever engage with entirely instrumental music. "Playing for the song" is a notion designed to highlight the selflessness of the drummer and downplay her or his ego.

However, interviewees' selections of their "solo" music (i.e., their self-directed performed output) almost entirely avoided the song-based vocal form. This may be coincidental, or it may support the idea that many drummers consider it easier to be creative in instrumental forms of music as distinct from the song-based or vocal variety. In the latter, instrumental parts are traditionally sublimated toward the effective communication of any lyric meaning, in support of the song. The removal of such a constraint may allow creativity to appear in a different way. One approach to the sung vocal is to regard the voice as another instrument that may or may not carry meaning for the instrumental performer. In my own performing experience, I tended to listen from the bottom (drums and rhythm section) up (to vocals and lyrics). I took the rhythm and texture of any vocal as being the key components; the much discussed "meaning" of Jon Anderson's lyrics in Yes was a battle in which I declined to engage. His words had plenty of pitch and rhythmic information and their sound had sufficient grain and texture to communicate experience: that was all I needed.

Interviewees were more effusive in the detailed discussion of the work of a small number of former and current members of their community of practice who had successfully communicated significant difference. Ralph references the drummers of the big band era of the 1930s who "sort of changed the landscape in a way, and sort of rewrote the book." In another era, drummer Jack DeJohnette

> created another language . . . took the need to even keep time out of it, necessarily; that's a concept, that's a big, big concept, that not many other people have ever succeeded in achieving but, he's done it, people can do it . . . he was massive.

Peter Erskine reports that Bernard Purdie took "whatever was happening with R&B [and] he codified it and did a thing in the delivery of it that I never heard before or since." This yardstick for creative assessment of the performances of others being whether the interviewee had "ever heard it before" is of course the same yardstick that Chad uses to assess his own performance.[10] Beyond that heuristic, participant reports of the creative strategies and processes of influential performers and co-performers are thick with references to many of the emblematic dimensions of creative performance already mentioned, such as exploring, allowing, omitting, limiting, avoiding the obvious, game playing, problem finding, problem solving, and the rapid shift of expressive emphasis:

Martin France: He [drummer Joey Baron] seemed to be able to explore the music—all corners of the music—at the drop of a hat . . . [to] be able to move quickly [. . .], to get inside the sound that's being created with what they're involved in right at that specific moment . . . being able to change and create with sympathetic sounds.

Martin France: He [pianist John Taylor] will never play the same thing twice. He always wants something different. He'll always play something different. He'll move it around; he won't want to play the obvious.

The ideological compulsion to be "different," sometimes even at the expense of the music, is also noted. Strønen expresses exasperation with the jazz musician's aesthetic of perpetual renewal:

If they play something and it really worked out and it's because of the circumstances and all that, you know . . . but still, if you find a way to solve something, and it works, and then so many people feel that the next time they have to do something completely different, because it's "improvised."

Erskine finds a "very highly developed" creativity in the crafted functional performances of drummer John Robinson, a man who "knew how to come up with a part." He interprets this skill as a mastery, often linked by creativity theorists to creative expression.[11] In Peter's view, mastery is both "craft" and a "form of creativity." "The master knows that the most important part of a pencil is the eraser . . . so a lot of the creativity comes from, let's say, a seasoning, of knowing maybe the best option, a note-to-self, don't try that one again." In respect to domain-level innovation, Peter appreciates but doesn't like the most recent developments, finding much contemporary performance simultaneously "mind-blowing" and unlistenable, and possibly inappropriate:

All the pioneering work that drummers have done in terms of metric modulation, superimposition, and then you know like the mind-blowing stuff which [Dave] Weckl and Vinnie [Colaiuta] did, which then led to . . . when I hear what Chris Dave is doing now I'm fascinated by it, I appreciate it intellectually. Do I want to hear it again? No, I can barely make it through a whole performance.

Appropriate performance glues the music together, and is thus a central tenet of what a drummer does creatively. To violate that appropriateness tends to be generally seen as a major transgression of the rules of drum performance.

Like Chad, the attributes that Peter points to as emblematic of creativity in other people's performances are the same that he points to in his own. He finds the pursuit of creativity less noble than the pertinence of action, the making it work. Drummer Mel Lewis's choices were "almost never outrageous but they were always perfect." Together with Carlos Vega, "it just seemed like everything they played was just kind of perfect and there's a wonderful creativity in that." When he watches Levon Helm of the Band, it strikes him as "a perfectly played drum part. There is nothing outstanding drumming-wise except for the mere fact that it feels so damn good. It's just the right thing." In this view, creativity is embedded and experienced in an appropriate performance that evokes qualities of subtlety, understatement, "perfection," and concealed virtuosity. It may not need 10,000 hours of deliberate practice, but it demands a high level of musicality that may in turn be "so creative that . . . the listener's not even aware it's going on. Which is, I think, a very creative way to do things."

The most frequently cited individual in these discussions of creativity in other drummers' processes and outcomes was Elvin Jones. According to Cindy, Elvin "was a very creative musician" because he was able to resolve the central paradox of drum kit performance that Sinta grappled with (see chapter 2) and that drummers everywhere try daily to surmount—how to keep the music moving forward while making it feel laid back:

> His triplet style—there was a propulsion in that that just kept the music moving forward, even though he played so laid back that it sounded like he was in last week sometimes [*laughs*] . . . moving forward forward forward because of the triplet propulsion.

In Thomas Strønen's opinion, "[Elvin] was adding another energy to the drum playing . . . it was loud, and it was a <u>lot</u>. [. . .] It was just floating, but still he also did something with the way he was going round the set. He was changing sort of the perception of the drummer being (*stretching the bar line*) stretching the bars and also making the sound so big, you know." Thomas describes the powerful emotional effect of experiencing Jones's creativity under the most adverse of conditions. The performance

> was <u>incredible</u>. The band was really shit, it was really bad (*oh, bad?*) yeah, the <u>band</u>, and his playing was very limited, he was not in good

shape, but when he touched his old "K" cymbal, it made my tears come.

To Erskine, Jones was both a "whirlwind[12] of creativity, a whirlwind of poly-rhythmic expression," but also an enigma, because "you can't find a lineage that you might find with most other drummers."[13] Peter considers current thinking on the topic, citing the man himself:

> Elvin talks about Shadow Wilson . . . probably Jo Jones and then even Philly Joe, undoubtedly some Max. [His creativity lay] not only [in] the triplets but the dynamic shape of the way he played on the kit (*in between the cracks, as they sometimes say*) well, not even that, but some-thing a little more . . . just the soft to loud and the loud to soft, and I sometimes wonder if it was just the way the drums were recorded, that some drums seemed to leap out a little more than others.

By contrast, Dylan Howe characterizes Jones's original contribution to the domain as no more than "a slight alteration"; "you can hear how Elvin took everything that Roy [Haynes] was doing and then slightly altered it," but Roy "informed and inspired all of the drummers, I think." In short, most participants see the creative process in music as inherent in real-time inter-action with others and as essentially strategic, finding ways to make things better or different.

In asking our experts to reflect upon and assess the actions, processes, and creative worth of self-selected others, I was hoping that such an approach might not only reveal fresh perspectives on participants' own creativity but also provide a yardstick by which to assess and measure significant difference. Drummers maintain that it can take years to forget the mistakes and errors made in the sometimes traumatic process of a recording session, the fruits of which having nevertheless been long since assessed as creative by others. This factor references again the time dimension etched into creative work and its assessment, noted earlier in the case of the Pre-Raphaelites or progressive rockers, and rightly highlighted by Glăveanu in his 5A's framework.

In recognition of the unverifiable, subjective nature of creative self-assessment and its dependency on the individual's personal definition of cre-ativity, which may be more or less stringent, I deliberately addressed the topic only obliquely in the interviews, preferring rather to solicit perceptions of performance practice. These reflections on many years of high-level perfor-mance have proved useful in examining the way people conceptualize their own creativity.[14] All our participants were familiar with a wide variety of examples of the work of other drummers across a plethora of genres, eras, and styles. (Knowledge of the output of current and past practitioners not only certifies one as a member of the community, but potentially provides directions to unexplored territory.) The primary metric for creative assessment within the community of practice is both subjective and pragmatic. It asks "have I heard it before?" and then, quite rapidly, "how can I use it?"

It is community that privileges functionality and utility over novelty, and community that attributes significance. Nicholas Cook points to research within both developmental studies and classical performance indicating that musical difference is significant "within a musical community whose participants—listeners as much as performers—are highly sensitive to nuance, to the meaningful, negotiated shaping of the notes."[15] One way drummers appear to distinguish the significant from the insignificant is by interpreting the former as meaning-creating. In this view, performing upside down may constitute difference, but the action is likely to create meaningfulness only for the individual or onlooker rather than appropriate observers, and thus remains insignificant.

Expert drummers may be creative at the highest level, but that tends to be exceptional and unrepresentative of participant views of the phenomenon. Taking something and slightly altering it may have profound domain-change capability; taking something and substantially altering it may serve only as a minimal contribution to the domain. Max Roach's choosing to play a few notes less per measure on the bass drum was a minor alteration that caused uproar; it was the shot that was heard around the world. Bernard Purdie's hi-hat "barks" behind singer Aretha Franklin in the 1970s crystalized a nascent hi-hat technique and reconceived the role and function of the hi-hat as a key instrument in the kit in a way that *mattered* to drummers. On the other hand, while Gavin Harrison's sophisticated rhythmic illusions have radically altered notions of pulse and meter, they have as yet had slower adoption in the domain. In Hope Mason's terms, and within the context of the current discussion, they matter less.[16] The speed of the adoption of the variation into the domain may be interpreted as an indicator of its attributed significance.

It is generally recognized that attributions of creative worth within the arts are notoriously unstable, subject to multiple changes of assessment criteria within shifting sociocultural landscapes. Within music, producers, performers, and receptors may shift their view over time, leading to a perception that, while important, assessment is beyond performer control. Just as music is constrained by its ability to be understood as music, so drumming is constrained by its ability to be understood as drumming. Many failed to understand "free jazz" when it was "invented." Was free jazz drumming an invention or an adaptation in the domain? Did its move to freedom and its wholesale removal of constraints of rhythm and form constitute a creative leap? How far do you have to leap to make a creative leap? As Sheila Henderson has noted, some inventions leapfrog technology, such as the lightbulb versus the candle lantern, and some improve on existing technology, such as amoxicillin versus penicillin.[17] Can we say the first is a creative invention, the second a non-creative improvement? Which drummers have executed the Big Leap Forward? Max Roach, certainly; Rashied Ali and Andre Cyrille, probably; Ringo Starr (under some collaborative guidance from George Martin), possibly; Gavin Harrison, eventually. Terry Bozzio surely exemplifies incremental creativity in his extension of Roach's work in establishing the drum kit as compositionally self-sufficient. With one foot beyond the scope of this study, Pete Lockett's recombinational creativity has brought the Carnatic and Hindustani rhythms of India to the Western drum kit.[18] But attributions like these remain subjective and contested within the community. As we have seen, while most participants rate Elvin Jones as a master who changed the domain, Dylan Howe sees his work as a series of small improvements on Roy Haynes. Creativity modeling, such as we have it, has further to go before it can cast a more focused light on in-the-moment performance creativity.

Summary

Chapter 7 has addressed several issues surrounding the fourth and final dimension of the SDCA model—the assessment of significant difference. Experts have been asked to reflect upon and assess their own actions and processes and those of self-selected others, in the expectation that such an approach might not only reveal fresh perspectives on their own endeavors but also provide a yardstick by which to assess and measure significant difference.

Am I creative? Who says I am or am not creative? Who counts? While a clear majority of interviewees consider a positive assessment of their creativity by others to be important, they are uncomfortable with notions of the "field" as originally constituted within the organizational or business spheres, finding them too nebulous. Its members are deemed insufficiently qualified "to navigate a myriad of domains driven by technological and powerful modalities of temporal action that draw upon the digitization of music and art, and unprecedented shifts in the concept of musical work."[19] Expert drummers take the primary assessors to be co-performers and other drum community members, and the important yardstick is *does it matter*?

Emerging here is a domain-specific creativity that prefers to frame "everyday" drummer creativity in terms of a symbiotic collaboration with another or others, the principal goal of which is to make the music work. Then, something further is needed to make it matter. As suggested, the explanation appears to be, in part, cultural psychological. We have seen how drummers think not only as individuals and human beings, but as members of a particular community with distinctive cultural traditions that allow them to ascribe meaning to creative experience, and to circulate and exchange that meaning (see IMCM). In the context of a broader culture that avoids associating drummers with creativity, drummers prefer to see it not as an end in itself but as something to be pursued *as may be necessary to make the music work*. This is one way in which they do things *because they are drummers*.

• This chapter has collated the ways in which drummers distinguish between significant and insignificant action in two thematic strands. The first addressed perceptions of personal creativity and the second sought meaning in the creative actions of self and others. Our experts offered the following insights:

- The co-performing listener is privileged over the non-performing listener as the appropriate observer who might assess significant difference.
- A small majority of this cohort prioritizes the pursuit of creativity. A substantial minority downplays the importance of the phenomenon in performance and assigns it less meaning than might be expected.
- A positive assessment of experts' creativity by others in the domain is considered to be important.
- One common strategy for the realization of creative performance is to address its reception, to control elements of the social, musical, and audio environment (the "situation") in which it might be heard.
- The primary metric for creative assessment asks "have I heard it before?" and then "how can I use it?"

The preceding chapters have looked at each of the four dimensions of the SDCA framework—selection, differentiation, communication, and assessment—sequentially but in isolation. I now want to suggest some of the ways drummers conceptualize creative music performance in its totality by seeking our experts' perceptions, first, of what it is and how it is experienced, and, second, what meanings they assign to that experience.

8 • The Experience That Disappears

Perceptions and Meaning

Creative Performance Is . . .

It was J. P. Guilford's 1950 address to the American Psychological Association that first alerted psychologists to the neglect of the subject of creativity. Yet after some 70 years of steady endeavor, creativity theorists remain unsettled on a precise definition of the phenomenon. Phillip McIntyre's formulation, however, has proved robust and useful over the course of this discussion.[1] It may seem odd to some that I have had little interest in asking our expert drummers to define creativity as they see it. I approached the topic only obliquely, preferring to seek perceptions of its meaning to them in the context of their music performance. My aim was to get the interviewees to talk *about* creativity, to consider their perceptions of the phenomenon and any meanings it may hold for them. As Allan Moore observes, sometimes we don't know what we mean until we express it, however partial or incomplete that expression might be.[2] For the creator, much of the striving associated with creative action lies in the struggle to communicate an idea, or a song, or some drumming so that she or he might come to know its meaning, to make sense of it. Much of the value associated with it lies in the almost getting there.

Asaf Sirkis kicks off with an inclusive, holistic view of the phenomenon. Creativity is "something that everyone has." Creativity "has no address . . . it is not dependent on time or place. You can invite it, you can allow it, but I don't think you can actually cultivate it, and accumulate it. It's not a commodity." Ultimately, it is "the expression of human worthiness," and, "like oxygen," vital to human survival. In the following extract he grapples with the nature of creative music performance:

When you play you don't play what you practiced anymore, when you are creative. You are taking your skill to the next level, basically. Where it's not the actual thing what you do is important, but the music; you know, what you want to express is more important than the actual means of doing that, OK? It's simply that for me. It's when everything connects together. All what you have, all what you learn is coming together and you're using in that particular moment when you're creative only the things that you really need for your creative process.

On this account, creativity is evidenced by the degree of departure from the prepared text. His assertion that "you don't play what you practiced anymore" neatly describes the typical approach of the expert jazz musician and contrasts with the detailed practice and close rendition of the prepared piece in classical performance. In Asaf's depiction, the *creative* performance requires the music to be reduced, focused, and taken to "the next level." Anything superfluous to the expression is jettisoned; technical concerns evaporate as individual performance is seamlessly connected to the whole in the "interpretive moment," a construct that resurfaces shortly.

Drummer creativity is further conceptualized as contingent upon intra-human interaction predominantly, and human/machine interaction secondarily. Most interviewees see it as something done with somebody else, an interaction with other human beings, the process and products of which will probably surprise you or others. It depends on interpretation and "taking it [the music] further" in the moment (Cindy). Peter, however, assigns no great importance to the phenomenon, likening it to a playground, a "marvelous three-dimensional spatial universe . . . filled with those possibilities." Asked to play recordings of some examples of his work that he considers to be creative, he avoids any clear explanation as to why he thinks of them as such.

Differences in opinion arose as to whether creativity is optional or nonoptional—that is, the extent to which one might choose to be creative or not as the environment might require. Asaf suggests that the phenomenon is unavoidable because there are always challenges that make one think in another way "so you have to be creative." On Cindy's account, the *use* of her creative thinking is optional and subject to professional constraints, while nevertheless being permanently available to her. She hears possibilities but cannot always act upon them. Her creativity

is within me; it's within my control as a professional to choose when to use it or not. It is always running through my head, you know; so I don't know that I can turn it off, I can just choose to use it or not . . . because even when I'm playing in a situation that is not creative, I still hear things going on in my head; I still hear things that could happen in the music . . . whether they are allowed to happen or not.

Where Cindy might choose to withhold the creative impulse as a matter of professional judgment, Asaf surrenders to it entirely. Far from being optional, creativity is for him "just one of these things we always have. We always drink water, we always breathe, and we always have to be creative, otherwise we cannot survive." He insists that he has "no other choice" but to play differently, because *everyone* is different. Stay true to yourself, he advises, and your singularity will eventually shine through in your music. The only way of "being unique or being special or developing your own sound" is by being "genuine and honest about where I come from and . . . being at <u>peace</u> with that, with where I come from and my influences." Others adopt a more pragmatic approach. When Chad Wackerman reflects that "any kind of gig you're doing, you have the option to be creative," he joins Cindy in implying that there are certain gigs on which one may choose, or be compelled, to *avoid* creativity. The idea that creativity is not always welcome in some traditional genres of popular music was briefly discussed in the introduction of this book and has considerable support both here and in the literature.[3]

Despite much modern thinking to the contrary, creativity continues to have a spiritual dimension in the perception of some interviewees. Asaf's expression of our human worthiness, "or divinity, or whatever you call it" [. . .] "expresses our 'beyondness' as human beings. [. . .] I really think, and I'm not religious or anything, but I really think that creativity . . . does not come from this life." Cindy has an equally powerful understanding of the origins of her creativity:

It's like my hair . . . my hair is the color that God made it, my eyes are the color that God made them, my skin is the color and texture that God made it, my creativity is part of the way that God made me . . . [and thus it is] not something that I can turn off.

While from her perspective creativity is something she possesses in perpetuity rather than co-constructs in moments of significant action, it remains for others largely a psychological construct:

Thomas Strønen: Just the word creativity . . . maybe I feel it's more a state of mind than what you actually do. And the case can even be that you are being creative even though the outcome isn't very creative. (*Oh, that's an interesting idea . . . creative thinking?*) It can be creative thinking, and it's not always [that] you're capable of bringing your ideas out in the right way.

Here Thomas draws a distinction between creative thinking processes and creative outcomes, which, on his account, do not always coexist. This has echoes of the view propagated by Brian Eno and others that the intention is more important than the execution, that one has permission to fail or make mistakes on account of insufficient technical capacity, and that the creative performer should honor his or her hidden intention—a view that has played into much European avant-rock in the last three decades.[4]

. . . The Experience That Disappears

How do drummers engage with the world of sound to create and communicate meaningful experience? Experience is indeed a useful and valuable tool; the value of a deep well of knowledge is limited without experience of the outcome of its application in a variety of contexts. It is experience that provides the appropriate musical gesture. For Peter Erskine it is experience that says "I've been here before" and provides "a seasoning, of knowing maybe the best option, a note-to-self 'don't try that one again.'" Asaf points out that everyone has a different experience of creative expression. His experiences (the small instances that go to make up the single notion of "experience") are predicated on being calm under tightly constrained circumstances that may be extramusical. A lifting of those constraints enables "a sudden release, and a sudden explosion of things that really wanted to come out for a long time." Experience is, in his perception, something that can be passed on through teaching. He hopes to give to those "who might have problems with rhythm" so that they "might experience something that I've experienced before." His experience tells him that a highly motivated creator in the band can promote creativity in others in the band: "When you feel better about your playing you affect the people in the band that's playing with you, so everybody's, you know, feeling better, playing better, being more creative."[5]

Thomas experiences music in a profound way, as "quite materialized. I feel there are still concerts and feelings, receptions of sound, that I can still feel the flavor or taste of that experience, of how the cymbal sounded." Articulating the creative power of another drummer in a performance from years earlier, he highlights the longevity of the experience: "It's still alive inside me." Here he describes the steps leading up to a surprisingly powerful experience of creativity and its consequent assessment:

> I think what happened was . . . I had an idea where I wanted to go . . . and immediately entering the studio we came—not physically but mentally—we came into this room where everything was possible. And I remember being very unsecure [*sic*]. [. . .] So I was really concentrating to be able to . . . you know, be in the music and deliver as good . . . (*you survived?*) I survived (*you delivered and you were surprised at yourself?*) yeah, and I listened to it and I thought this is probably as good as it can get.

While Mark locates his "richest experiences" in heavily improvised music, close to the compositional pole of the FCC, he nevertheless acknowledges the creative potential in premeditated, part-based music. His creative goal is to find those "uber-creative and uber-open-minded moments" as frequently as possible, the pursuit of which he has earlier likened to an addiction. He characterizes his collective experience as crucial to decision making:

> And you know for example playing with [bassist, leader] Avishai [Cohen] I felt like . . . of course, over time there was a strong rapport and we developed this relationship where a lot of decisions were based on intuition and experience.

Echoing Peggy Phelan's ontology of performance,[6] he offers the following passionate articulation of the uniqueness of live performance; I make no apologies for extracting from it both the title of this chapter and the subtitle to this section:

> The beauty of live performance is that it is this unique experience that, even if it gets captured on YouTube or even if it gets recorded, it still is this experience that disappears . . . that true personal experience . . . you have to be there to experience it. I can't expect everyone to come to me, so I can stay home, so you do go out and there is a certain thing about, you know, just being expressive in front of a wide variety of people and that's . . . the music grows from that, yeah.

What remains? What haunts? What lasts? One of the reasons that one has to be there to experience it is that others are there, be they musicians or listeners; the experience is in part brought into reality through sharing it with others. For Mark, that is the subsoil from which his music grows. My summative assessment of the locus of his creative experiences as being on stage (rather than in the studio) meets with a crisp, repeated affirmative: "Totally, totally."

. . . Fun

Most interviewees strongly associate the experience of drumming with fun and pleasure for themselves and others: "I looked at the drummer and thought this looks fun." The strong emphasis on the last three words of Ralph Salmins's youthful observation indicates a bottom-line appraisal of how drumming should be for both practitioner and listener—an aspect of performance that should be present as much of the time as possible. Fun is identified as an attraction to the art of drumming in the first place, as inherent in the action of drumming, both alone and in the company of others, and as attached to various dimensions of drumming, such as its unpredictability and capacity for surprise. Fun is frequently associated with the primary processes of acquiring the tools for creative performance—namely, drum lessons and practice sessions. Ralph's early teacher "used to sit down and play 'Lady Be Good' . . . get me to jam along with him, which was fun." For Cindy it was "never a chore to play my drums. [. . .] I love to practice." Describing how he spends his time with a few precious hours in a quiet house, Thomas will "compose music just whenever I want to, as long as I want to, and I will play the drums. That's what I love to do. I might not talk to any people . . . I would just do that." While he gets pleasure from working solo in concert, nevertheless "the biggest pleasure is playing with others, I think." In this view, the pleasure resides in performing *with* others (a group of peers) rather than *for* others (an audience).

Creative strategies often have an emergent quality manifest in unpredictable outcomes of the sort described by Mark. His radical change of both instrument and approach to his practice sessions only made practice more fun. "It was the most fun I'd had in a long time, actually, at the drums [. . .] and it was bringing out new ideas, and I was able to play more fluently and more quietly." The clear linkage developing here between having fun and being creative is underscored by Peter Erskine. If Peter is not having fun, there is little likelihood of a creative outcome. Referring to the preparation of some new music, he is

> having as much fun or more playing it in the solitude of my studio
> than I anticipate I'll have [. . .] I mean it is just part of the gig, I have

to do it. I'm having more fun just kind of working on it. So creativity is definitely possible in the solo environment.

Ambivalence arises, however, in his account of making it fun for others:

It's fun when they like it. I enjoy playing for people, it's a part of the equation of playing music in public and it's gratifying when someone likes it, but actually a weird thing happens to me, Bill, when I play. A lot of times by the end of the concert the last thing I want to do is say hello to anybody. I want to hide away, and so if the audience liked it, or didn't even, doesn't affect my perception of what happened on the stage. I'm not that... I don't really give a fuck about the audience. You can quote me on that.

Here the warmth of Peter's opening words is undermined by the derogatory outburst in closing, indicating a conflicted sense of obligation to the audience in his desire to protect his perception of events. Any pleasure the listener may derive from his performance is irrelevant to his perception of any creativity it may or may not exhibit. Much less discussed was the absence of fun, the disappointments and difficulties experienced by most drummers at some time in pursuit of the creative moment. That may have been, of course, because the effects of the few negatives encountered had long since been neutralized or recycled into fuel for further creativity.

It is commonly accepted that to become expert in any field, one is going to have to learn from mistakes, failures, and errors. Some come to interpret their mistakes as hidden intentions, as mentioned above. The few early disappointments that arose in part from poor or nonexistent teaching appear to have had little permanent effect upon participants' creativity, as evidenced by the measure of success in evoking the phenomenon in later life. The North American cohort had few complaints in this area; all spoke of the consistently high quality of the instruction they received, frequently from nationally known teachers or older musicians.

... A Slightly Altered State: Temporality and Being in the Moment

Notwithstanding its lack of attention in the creativity research literature, the temporal immediacy of performance—the being "in the moment"—was frequently alluded to by our interviewees and is casually discussed within the community. With its connotation of a psychological state of complete immersion, "being in the moment" in music performance shares some aspects of Flow but has a greater equivalency to what Keith Sawyer calls "group genius" on account of its social dimension.[7] Creative drummers gravitate toward the "interpretive moment" because it is there that they see fertile ground, a "sunlit place where at last the music is there, pouring out, easy, conversational, technical concerns now sublimated to the greater good of music-making, the hours of practice producing the phrases that you want, when you want them, now."[8] This place, according to Asaf, is one where "everything connects together" and in which "no moment is like any other moment and you're a different person in every moment."

Across all interpretations, being "in the moment" is valorized as something to be desired and achieved, but there may be obstructions to its acquisition:

> *Chad Wackerman:* Jake Hanna didn't give many clinics but gave this one and somebody asked him what perfect coordination was, and he said "it's when you think it and you play it at the exact same moment" and ever since then I've been trying to be exactly in the moment and not having these kind of demons that say I'm not playing creative, or I missed that one, or . . .

In the extract above, Chad's "demons" block creative Flow by separating and delaying thought and action, permitting untimely creative self-assessment.

Some identify the ability to be in the moment as a source of additional creative power, as extra wind in the sails that might be depended upon to blow one through the creative doldrums. Acknowledging his unfamiliarity with a particular genre of music, Mark Guiliana says he

> might not be able to deliver the exact sticking that would be the most appropriate for a certain pattern, but I'd like to believe that my being in the moment and my intuition and the way I'm listening to the guys, I could deliver an appropriate sound and feel.

Mark associates being in the moment with the demands of constant decision making. Exactly what demands the music will make of him he cannot know in advance, so he must be prepared: "So I show up empty and therefore I have all this room for new ideas, to take them in, and then it's what I do to them in that moment that becomes its own vocabulary." "Being prepared" generally means having constant access to multiple options which, for Dylan, is "the point of practice."

These perceptions of altered time in peak performance support those documented elsewhere.[9] While the composer generally has time to revisit or reconsider in private before unveiling the artwork to the public, the performer creates and unveils simultaneously, usually in the company of others. Given the immediacy of performance decision making, characterized by both the rapidity of instinctive reaction to incoming information and the interpretive moment that embodies both listening and "speaking" (the simultaneous reception of incoming data and production of the outgoing response), some have called for a reappraisal in respect to creative performance.[10] I connected my personal experience of the Flow state to wellness and meaningfulness when I described it elsewhere as like "making circles in the air with a feather duster, a somewhat childlike activity that required no effort and produced an enormous sense of well-being. Imbued with a kind of undeniable rightness, such occasions are what people like me struggle to create for much of our professional lives."[11]

Expert drummers position creativity somewhere between the individual domain-changing variety evidenced by Roach and espoused by Csikszentmihalyi and Arieti and the inclusive variety attendant upon practically all musical performance as proposed by, for instance, Barrett and Burnard. In the latter view, creative performance is characterized less as an expression of individual will and more as an activity constrained by and mediated between multiple actors in different contexts. It has collaborative or interactive elements, enhanced by an ability to control or affect outcomes. Jason Toynbee's proposition[12] that the musical creator is restricted in how much difference he or she can make at any given moment is cautiously supported by participants, who nevertheless see creative action as available to some degree at any moment and in any context or mode of performance.

In brief, creative performance is conceptualized as not only recombinational, exploratory, or transformational, or a combination of these, but also as a set of social-psychological actions (making others "comfortable," achieving group Flow) and music actions (the provision of good groove) whose goal is to enable or assist others to be creative. Creativity is situated within and mediated by the performance context in the moment; such contexts are characterized in terms of receiving, sharing, or giving direction. While all music situations are construed as more or less supportive of creativity, playing *with* others rather than performing *for* others tends to be seen as affording both the greatest pleasure and the greatest exposure to creative possibility. Successful performance acknowledges that creativity is not always welcome or necessary in popular music performance, with the unsurprising consequence that its pursuit is not always prioritized.[13]

Creative Performance Means . . .

How do drummers assign meaning to the lived experience of performance, and what meanings are assigned? Our drummers confirm that even though the performance may be captured in repeatable form, the experience of its creation is unrepeatable, an ephemerality neatly captured in Guiliana's phrase "the experience that disappears." Creative performance is not merely the collaborative or interactive experience (although it may embody both), it is the outcome of music action that is communicated and judged to be significant. Recognition of that experience within the broader music community is considered to be crucial before a drummer's opinion is sought and he or she is granted permission to determine outcomes.

If drumming is creative action, then drummers are not only agents of change but they also make meaning from their participation in change.[14] Viewed through the Deweyan lens, it is the cumulative experience of action over time, in a continuous cycle of doing and undergoing, that constitutes experience that, in turn, informs meaning for the creative music performer. We have seen how there may be multiple interpretations of the experience of action from several perspectives, including but not limited to the physical, mental, emotional, spiritual, social, or virtual. The mental experience has previously been discussed in terms of the possession, surrender, loss, or absence of control, but it may also be invoked in relation to learning. When musicians describe something as a "learning *experience*," they typically also identify a substantial creative element in either the learning itself or its outcomes. Expert drummers tend to learn through creating, and to continually learn through continually creating.[15] One important purpose of creation, we should not forget, is to make meaningful sense of the creator's world.

Mature peak-career practitioners were selected for interview not least to gain access to the depth of their accumulated experience over many years of practice. This experience is the outcome of countless functional and compositional performances under multiple variations of environment, constraint, and complexity. Accumulated experience informs current practice and gives rise to further action, as previously depicted in the IMCM (chapter 1). Some of these component (everyday) experiences are significant and judged to be creative by self or others; some are insignificant and adjudged uncreative; and some go unjudged. The quality of these assessments is seen as beyond practitioner control, although drummers certainly prefer assessment (and thus acknowledgment) to indifference.

One important aspect of music experience is its appreciation or enjoyment by self or others, or both. Interviewee reports already cited support the observation that entraining our bodies to musical rhythms brings pleasure.[16] The performance experience is amplified, heightened, or made more powerful if shared in collaboration with attentive co-performers and engaged listeners, although it may be fulfilled alone. This converges with thinking in the areas of both individual Flow and Flow within collaborative performance, which asserts that people experiencing high levels of Flow are generally more motivated and creative in both work and leisure.[17] Subjective descriptions of successful performances often revolve around the fundamental traits of a state of Flow, where a balance of skills and challenges is prioritized.[18] Within positive psychology the two traditions of hedonism and eudemonia are held to be necessary in the pursuit of happiness, and a balance is required between the three components of pleasure, engagement, and meaning in order to achieve a state of subjective well-being and authentic happiness.[19] Participant reports strongly support current thinking in this sphere, which suggests that greatest performer happiness lies in those domains that can both accommodate and welcome the personal expressive input of the performer and afford him or her a sense of control over his or her own performance.[20]

I make no apologies for introducing an element of caution at this point. Professions of positive affect may be more forthcoming in interviews than professions of negative affect, even within the context of anonymity and a supportive and understanding researcher-participant. The pain, disappointments, and difficulties occasionally experienced in pursuit of creative performance have been rather less discussed, as already noted. Musicians rarely focus on negative experiences when discussing musical issues, preferring to comment instead on ideal communal experiences, in pursuit of what Melissa Dobson calls "professional sociability."[21] While my own experience of performance with little or no positive affect might serve as an example of an unsuccessful creative process, it is unlikely that my case is an isolated one. Other musicians may also have communicated significant difference effectively without the accompanying positive affect identified by Emery Schubert.[22] In general, however, the collaborative context of aligned feelings and shared purpose identified above seems to afford the greatest performance pleasure, adding further weight to the evidence connecting creativity to wellness within performance.

The meanings drummers assign to creative action initially seemed to be so diffuse that collating them coherently might prove impossible. Three extracts (framed in terms of action, interaction, and discovering or finding something, respectively) will suffice to give a flavor of the variety of participant approaches to the topic. First, Asaf Sirkis adopts an action-theoretical perspective, a central plank of which asserts, very broadly, that we are what we do. When we are creative it is about "joyously being, you know, joyously being here and joyously creating, *and joyously being what you're supposed to do*." Second, Ralph Salmins speaks for many when takes creativity in music to mean interaction; "the interaction of musicians together, creating something, for me is probably what the definition of what creativity as a drummer is to me, yeah. That is the crux of it really." Third, Martin France suggests that creative performance means being skilled enough to find or discover exactly the right thing for the music. It means finding "little corners" of creativity in everything. Many rereadings of the interviews eventually suggested four further subthemes that encapsulate participant perceptions of the meaning of creative performance: allowing, trusting, connecting, and surprising. Each is now addressed in turn.

. . . Allowing

First, interviewees made multiple references to the circumstances of allowing, or being allowed, that afford creative action. The idea is characterized in terms of (a) allowing mistakes to be made and things to go wrong; (b) allowing a creative process to come to fulfilment; (c) allowing "me to be me" (a theme already touched on in the second performance context of working with a leader); and (d) allowing as an act of will. In Asaf's opinion

> you have to allow [laughs], you can allow, you're able to allow; when you're relaxed in your mind you can allow creativity, musical creativity. [. . .] You can invite it, you can allow it, but I don't think you can actually cultivate it, and accumulate it.

He considers it "very important" that others consider him creative, because "all these things are really just another thing that will invite, encourage, allow more creativity (*yeah*) to come." In keeping with his assumption that creativity is unavoidable, he is thus "forced to be creative, so you can either accept it or allow it, or you can be very bitter about it or you can be very angry about it or very frustrated about it."

For both Chad and Ralph, the concept of allowing is strongly connected to the idea of "allowing me to be me," turning the corner from identity sublimation to identity projection. This reveals an interesting distinction between, on the one hand, the implications of the "complete sideman" role, seen as one in which no input is required other than as specifically directed;

and on the other, the preferred "allowing me to be me" situation, in which personal input and identity projection are encouraged. Ralph explains how producers are beginning to hire him for what he can bring to the session:

> It's <u>very</u> encouraging because . . . it's much more creative. I think the product that you get at the end, the musical product, is much better, and I even do that. . . . I have been doing that for years but I only just realized it probably about 10 years ago, that people give me pieces of music [i.e., written scores or charts] . . . I just completely disregard them. I just don't . . . (*and they don't even know you've disregarded them!* [Both laugh]. *You play what's appropriate*). You play what's appropriate and that, I think, is one of the central tenets of what a drummer does creatively.

Reflecting on his decision-making process, Mark assesses the extent to which "a given situation allows me to essentially truly make my own decisions," concluding that "the more open the environment, the more creative I feel."

The actions of "letting" and "allowing" are essentially a matter of choice. For Peter, "everyone is creative every day of their lives if they choose to be open to receiving the other." The interesting question as to whether creative performance may be achieved and experienced if there is no "other" to receive it has already been addressed more comprehensively in chapter 3. Tangentially to this, interviewees were asked to imagine a scenario in which they were no longer allowed (or able) to perform in public. Many thought this prospect catastrophic, a position somewhat at odds with their low estimates of the importance of an audience to the effective communication of creative performance revealed earlier.

. . . Trusting

In a second subtheme about the meaning of creative performance, our experts variously saw a need to trust themselves, others, the leader, and the music in different times and places. From a broad perspective, both Ralph and Peter ultimately situate Chad's "allowing me to be me" in terms of trust and permission. As mature experts, there is every reason they should be trusted to provide elements to make the music work, or work better, that may have been overlooked:

> *Ralph Salmins:* I think it's about trust and it's about permission, and you know, like, a lot of the great musicians, probably . . . being <u>the</u>

number one in my opinion, is a guy who booked musicians and he didn't tell them what to do, in general. [...] He booked guys for the way they played and then he let them do that, and it was a bit like ... get all these guys in a room, now what comes out? Mmm, that's interesting.

Peter Erskine: I enjoy the leader who trusts my choices and lets me do my thing; they concentrate on the bigger picture, but don't provide too much direction. [...] I think when you get to a certain age it's just like ... a lot of times they'll go "oh, I've never thought of that, that's a good idea."

Creative performance means trusting and being trusted by co-performers. Developing an instinct for whom or what is trustworthy is an important skill, one that is central to effective creative action and underpins, for example, Asaf's entire approach to performance. He is "able to <u>trust</u> my hands to do the right thing" so long as "I know the music first." His desire to "know the music first," in order that the knowledge will inform his performance, which will be "improvised on the spot," identifies a compositional approach, that is, that the music from which he is deriving this knowledge is stable enough to allow him to improvise in this way. How he chooses what to play in the event that the music is *unstable*, that is, he cannot know the music first, remains unresolved.

A satisfactory outcome in the context of high compositional performance "with no nets" with Frank Zappa depended, for Chad, on the trustworthiness of colleagues: "You had to trust that this is going to be really good. And we all have enough ability here where we can all make this really good, whatever he [Zappa] throws at us." Interjection, interaction, or "interference" in the performance are all permissible so long as the level of trust among collaborators is and remains sufficiently high. Cindy emphasizes the responsibility that comes with interference and the attributes necessary to interject effectively without causing disruption:

I love to create, and I love to be able to interject my opinion and I think that when you have people you can trust to be able to interject, and interjection is a responsibility because it takes taste, it takes intellect, it takes heart to do that and keep the music swingin'. I don't mean the swing rhythm; I just mean the feel to keep it swingin', to keep it happening.

She speaks from experience. In the following vignette, her understanding of the different interpretive requirements as between the recording of a song in a studio in front of a handful of people and the live performance of the same song in front of tens of thousands does not accord with that of the group's rock-star leader, Lenny Kravitz:

> We were playing parts. You were playing the part that was on the record, and for me, as we went along I would add little things here and there and improvise some stuff there because what's on a record, to me, doesn't always translate, firstly to what's appropriate for a live situation. You might need to really fire something up at a certain point, much more than it is on the record, or you might need a different feel here or there, so for me I would temper that to what I thought was necessary at the moment.

In this stadium-rock example, Kravitz has decided that the live rendition has drifted too far from the recorded artifact, irrespective of the drummer's perception that what is on the record "doesn't always translate" and is inappropriate in the live situation. Cindy is being "too creative." The tension between the demand of "live" and "studio" is resolved in the interest of "making it work": "He [Kravitz] might say to me or to all of us 'hey, let's get back to what worked on the record.'" From the leader's perspective, Cindy's inappropriate interference causes sufficient disruption as to jeopardize the trust that was between them. From Cindy's perspective, her accommodation of the leader's instructions underlines her professionalism, reestablishes trust, and avoids further confrontation. The incident further demonstrates the subtle and unspoken shifts of trust, power, and emphasis to be negotiated in different performance contexts.

In a surprising response to the seemingly unrelated question *"How important is it to you that other people think you're creative?"* Ralph frames his answer in terms of being trusted and trusting. On the passive side, he wants to be trusted to interfere correctly in the professional context of the recording studio. The "number one guy" in his opinion is the producer or client who books people for the way they play and then allows them to do just that. The producers and clients who employ him are more likely to grant him permission to act creatively if they associate him with that phenomenon and the skills surrounding it. On the active side, he sees trust as a two-way street, and he needs to be able to trust that the leader is competent to lead:

> It does remove a level of responsibility from me, and I don't mind it so long as the person telling me what to do knows what they're doing,

you know. Now there have been many producers I've done sessions for; they put something on a demo, then they get me in and they just get me . . . You know what it's like, you just . . . chase the demo, and it never works (*and in the end they end up throwing the demo away anyway*) They do! [. . .] Whereas if you're working with people who are in full possession of what they need to know to make the music work, then it's a different thing.

Recognizing the need for trust with non-performing others, such as employers, employees, collaborators, and clients, Peter echoes Ralph in emphasizing the reciprocal nature of the trust. He points out that "part of the creative equation often has to do with the other side—if people are willing to trust the practitioner." In support of this he attributes to the movie director Seth MacFarlane (for whom he has worked) the admirable quality that he "was able to trust those whom he had brought into the larger creative whole, and he was able to let go." When Peter works with graphic artists in the role of client or producer, his "general instinct" "is to choose an artist based on the trust that I'm going to like what they come up with, and I very rarely send them back to the drawing board." Trust sits on the borderline between the "for a leader" and "with a leader" performance contexts and becomes an increasingly essential requirement as the individual moves to the compositional polarity of the FCC.

. . . Connecting

> Only connect! That was the whole of her sermon. Only connect the prose and the passion, and both will be exalted, and human love will be seen at its height. Live in fragments no longer. Only connect, and the beast and the monk, robbed of the isolation that is life to either, will die.
> —E. M. Forster, *Howard's End*

A third quality of action that gives meaning derives from participant reports of the intra-human connections between and among performers and listeners, seen as not only crucial to successful performance but that also make it meaningful. Distinctions between the notions of sharing and connecting are not germane to the analysis and need no further expansion here. I highlight only that the two activities are both sequential and consequential; one must connect to share, and yet one connects through sharing. Most of the interviewees see creative music performance as contingent upon connecting with others and then sharing something with them through effective communication, although it has been noted that some—for example Thomas, Cindy, and Mark—feel they can perform creatively entirely on their own.

Following Etienne Wenger, drummers might be described as connecting and sharing ideas with co-performers in a negotiated joint enterprise.[23] These ideas are built on, elaborated, and reworked such as they emerge as shared understandings for and across the group, rather than belonging to any one individual. Pamela Burnard neatly parallels the distribution of melodies, harmonies, and rhythms with the distribution of ideas.[24] Such an enterprise requires a high quality of sharing across the collective, the "willingness to allow" that Cindy speaks of above. Dylan describes the best connections between co-creators in terms of a rare "special chemistry." Asaf, too, emphasizes the centrality of the quality of the connection with his co-performers and links it to creativity. Referencing the practice of drummer Jack De-Johnette, Asaf sees the connection between Jack's actions and the listener as afforded by Jack's genuineness: "because Jack is so natural and so genuine about everything he does, it just connects everything he's doing, you know."

At domain level, drummers are connected to the dominant drum culture. The attraction of the community elder is that his or her playing is connected to and resonates with the history of the culture, manifest in the countless small decisions that give life to musical personality, in the same way as the walls of an ancient building ooze history. Distinguishing such drummers from the hypertechnical young modernists, Chad problematizes the lack of cultural connectedness of the younger group:

> Some people don't go very far back. Like a friend of mine said if you want be a funk drummer and you entered music at Tower of Power, you haven't heard James Brown and you haven't gone back to R&B or even Robert Johnson blues; or today if you start at Dream Theatre or you start at Rush you have . . . (*you've got a way to go*). Well, you're kind of starting at a funny point, I think. . . . Steve Smith says if you start at that point there is no swing in anything, there's no jazz, there's no lope. It's all very strict and mechanical and accurate.

Creative music performance, then, implies an effective connection to the listener, in respect to which Martin sees "honesty" and Asaf "genuineness" as key components. In Martin's view "the honesty with which you do something is really important. People are quite open-minded like that; it doesn't matter what it is, if it's good and they get it, and it's coming from the right place, it doesn't matter what it is, they'll connect with it." This chimes with my experience. It appears to me that audiences are remarkably adept at distinguishing the bogus, fraudulent, and faked, the purporting to be someone you're not, from the genuine, honest, and sincere.

. . . Surprising

The fourth and final subtheme addressing the meaning of creative performance encompasses references to the notion of surprise. In communicated performance the process of selection from possible courses of action frequently results in surprise at the effect of that selection upon either addressee or addresser. The idea that the unforeseen or the surprising are foundational constructs of creativity is becoming commonplace.[25] The "unforeseen" is linked though its Latin etymology to the notion of improvisation, a key skill of the jazz performer as she or he deals literally with the unforeseen in real time. These understandings invoke Whitney Balliett's astute title for his collection of articles on jazz as *The Sound of Surprise*, a genre in which good jazz musicians tend to surprise themselves and others.[26]

The idea of surprise as an indicator of creativity is further evident in the work of Margaret Boden. Her background in artificial intelligence leads her to assert that for a computer program to show exploratory (as opposed to combinational) creativity, it must "inhabit, and explore, a conceptual space rich enough to yield indefinitely many surprises."[27] Greatest creativity may lay with those whose imaginations inhabit such rich conceptual spaces, those who exhibit what Gregory Feist has termed "ideational fluency."[28] While surprise for practitioner or listener (or both) may or may not be an essential component of creative music performance, it arises so frequently in the discourse that it may usefully be considered an indicator of significant creative action.

A majority of participants drew attention to the emergent quality of performance when they expressed being surprised by, or surprising another with, the results of their own or others' musical actions. Thomas Strønen goes so far as to consider it an obligation or responsibility to surprise his co-creators:

I feel that my responsibility in a band is . . . if we've been playing together . . . I have to surprise you. You can't take everything I do for granted. I can't just do what you've heard before and what you expect; I have to lift you out somewhere so that you do something you wouldn't have done.

Thomas sees the connection between surprise and creativity as an important determinant of his action-choices, invoking an ability to surprise himself as a personal creativity litmus test. He finds this hard to do because "I know what I'm capable of," leading him to conclude that he does not feel particularly creative as a person. On Asaf's account, surprise is an inevitable consequence of improvisation in the moment: "You can only surprise yourself, nothing but surprise yourself." The surprise lies in the sudden brief glimpse of how it could be or sound, a pivot point around which "you've found another way of doing something in a moment where all the old ways of doing it do not work for you."

Hidden capabilities within an unfamiliar musical terrain can be surprising in their outcomes. Does Ralph Salmins sometimes surprise himself?

> Yeah, because I think I don't know if I can do that. I don't really do that much drum'n'bass so that was something I'm not familiar with, so sometimes if I'm out of my comfort zone.

Describing a "classic moment for me personally where I thought I could actually be a little bit nervous here," Martin France "went the other way and I think I managed to pull it off to my own surprise." In a discussion of his compositional approach, Martin explains: "I did surprise myself and I was glad I did it and it was something that I achieved and got together." The lesson that Dylan took away from his encounters with composition was that "you only know everything you need to know about building a house after you've already built it [laughs]. (*Were you surprised at the type of house you'd built after you'd built it?*) Yeah." With the discussion focused primarily on surprising and being surprised by co-performers' products and processes, only Thomas raises the prospect of surprising the listener. He reports that the audience is less easy to surprise these days (2015), with the happy outcome that the drummer has a "freer role." "People don't get surprised if the drummer is a leader . . . if he's playing out of time while the band's playing time or vice-versa."

Cultural psychology, we recall, suggests that drummers think not only as individuals, but as members of a particular community with distinctive cultural traditions. Everything is relational. Donald Polkinghorne's "narrative discourse" approach, outlined earlier, offers a powerful lens through which to view the "apparently independent and disconnected elements of existence as related parts of a whole."[29] Within the drum culture, for instance, the multiple participant references to the influences of a small group of community elders accord with his idea that preexisting cultural traditions offer a store of plotlines that are used to configure events into stories.

The drummer acts in the drum culture and in doing so progressively constructs a personal history. My drumming relates me to my drumming history: "[e]very action or experience relates to other actions or experiences, near or far in time or space, more conscious or less."[30] I take my drums to go and play a gig. Following Boesch, the drums, the gig, and the act of drumming are all cultural features and action possibilities, or possibilities within an action field.[31] It is axiomatic of this approach that the performance of the action may itself be more important than the outcome.[32] For example, within jazz performance the listener is invited to observe a series of engagements with music as an ongoing process rather than the delivery of an end product. Any creative endeavor may have secondary meanings attached to it that are as important (or more important) than the overt concrete goal (in this case, creative performance); some examples emerging from our experts' reports might include Howe's desire for reassurance or Blackman Santana's spirituality.[33]

Meaningfulness in Action

The notion that experience is meaningful and human behavior is generated from and informed by this meaningfulness encapsulates the basic phenomenological premise of this project, which concerns the structure of lived experience. The interviews show how the drummer engages with his or her performance. Should she wish to seek meaning in that engagement, to make sense of it, she must actively bring it into lived experience.[34] Her interpretation of that experience gives it meaning, which in turn informs further action, as depicted in the IMCM.

An action-theoretical account suggests that through his or her experiences with the object, in this case the interactive experience of performance with others, the subject not only gives it meaning but also personally experiences his or her *potentialities* of action. This brings the subject to the construction of the individual's meaning as person, that is, his or her identity.[35] For example, a heterogeneous collection of objects are likely to have many different meanings. The first drum kit I perform upon might carry the meanings that not only were my parents generous in assisting in its acquisition, but that it was the same color, size, or resonance as that of my drum hero. We have seen how our experts make their drum performances carry multiple varied meanings at the individual level: of reassurance, of belonging, of learning, of negotiating constraints, of problem solving, of trusting, of connecting, and of sharing lived experiences. To experience meaningfulness is profoundly satisfying and reassuring.

To experience meaninglessness, on the other hand, is for things to make no sense, or to be nonsense. Imagine you are a professional drummer hired for a straightforward recording session, the sort you have done many times before. You set up your small drum kit, dwarfed by the cavernous studio. It is to be an overdub session with others to be recorded after you, a common enough practice and not a problem. The control booth is high up on a mezzanine floor. The lighting reflects off the glass, making it difficult to see the occupants. Donning headphones, you are played a simple, expressionless, electric "piano-plus-click" track that you assume is to become a song. You listen once. The piano timing and rhythm seem to have little to do with the click, and oh, by the way, this is a guide part, the producer says, which will probably be replaced anyway.

What should you play, and how should you play it? Where is the music? Is there any music? What are you playing to here? Do you play with the click or the piano, or aim somewhere between the two? The default strategy is to aim for the click with the simplest two and four backbeat that you can manage and await feedback. Unhelpfully, the disembodied control booth voice says you can play anything you like. In the absence of an interaction, any audible humanity, you have no desire to play, but you have to play anyway. The sound you make is pathetic; perfectly matched, in fact, to the dismal guide piano. You stop the take and try to get a grip. Take two is worse and breaks down earlier; take three, worse, and breaks down earlier still.

The huge studio floor is dark except for spotlights illuminating you in your small loneliness. You can be seen alright, and can just make out the shadowy bus queue of musicians assembling in the control booth waiting to overdub on your perfectly grooving drum part. With each take the voice in the headphones gets nicer and nicer—"just take your time, no rush, it's going to be great"—but the music and your contribution get progressively flaccid. *You can detect nothing recognizable as music*, for, in truth, there *is* no music. You can detect no meaning. Your inner self is screaming "What are you doing? Go home." In the absence of meaningfulness, you watch your four limbs struggle to play something any child could play, let alone a cool up-and-coming young London player like you with a million seller or two to your name who should be able to nail this in one take. You want to shout: THERE IS NO MUSIC HERE. The professional in you wrestles with your internal psychological mechanisms, which are closing down fast, and loses. You just about complete something with lots of drop-ins and edits (which will take time and money to fix in postproduction, thus ensuring you will be offered no further work by this producer) and leave without a word.

Such was one of my several personal experiences of meaninglessness. This anecdote has much to say about the production of late 1970s pop and rock records, and what was expected of a drummer. Given a sow's ear, the drummer, then as now, was expected to turn it into a silk purse, largely on guesswork as to the producer/client's intent. It also says much about the powerful psychological effect of meaninglessness in performance. Any drummer action generates a tangle of meanings to the actor, some of which might signify as creative. The meaning of an object (such as a drum performance) never derives from the object alone, but also from its embeddedness in larger contexts; in this case, in the drum culture and my self-assigned place within it.

This is important in the understanding of drummer agency because the way a drummer acts toward creativity is based on the meaning creativity has for him or her, with creativity and meaning being connected through significant situated action in context. Within functional performance, for instance, creativity might mean making the other person comfortable. Within compositional performance, it might mean oneself being comfortable with the uncomfortable, or making the other person uncomfortable.[36] Drummers derive meaning also from both their participatory discrepancies and the "unpredictable thousands of mis-intonations, uncontrollable hundreds of combinations of sound-colours, and uncountable variations in rhythmic phrasing [. . .] collectively known as expression."[37] As I have argued, these domain- or individual-level meanings are informed by and inform the drum culture and are mediated by its psychology at the domain level of action (figure 3). Mediated action is taken forward to become full experience, the communicative performance of which may be assigned creative significance by contributing to or changing the domain. This is how action links creativity to meaning.

We have seen how creative music performance means connecting with and trusting others in a negotiated interaction that allows something to happen in a musical way, that cannot be fully premeditated and that tends to cause surprise.[38] While the phenomenological project recognizes that nothing can be understood perfectly, and at best the researcher attempts to make sense of others making sense, the thinking in this chapter may be as close as one can get for now to understanding how expert drummers conceptualize and make sense of creative performance. All our drummers report engagement in "the unending search for and the construction of meaning,"[39] even if the meaning is only sometimes creative. When Asaf Sirkis earlier explained that "when you are creative [you are] joyously being what you're supposed to do," he cast creativity in action-theoretical terms. In this sense, drummers are what drummers do, and what they do takes place within an intricate socio-musical web of people and artifacts.[40] Meaning makes sense of our performance, our life, our existence. Like other musicians, expert drummers strive at meanings, the better to relate themselves to their world. To ask what this or that *means* is a basic question for all human beings.[41]

Summary

In the chapter I have tried to untangle some of the ways in which drummers conceptualize creative music performance by asking our corpus of expert drummers (a), what it is and how it is experienced, and (b), what meanings they assign to that experience. My aim was to get the interviewees to talk *about* creativity, to consider their perceptions of the phenomenon and any meanings it may hold for them. The ephemerality of the performative experience is neatly captured in Mark Guiliana's phrase "the experience that disappears." Creative performance is not merely the collaborative or interactive experience, it is the outcome of music action that is communicated and judged to be significant. It is also a set of social and music actions whose goal is to enable or assist others to be creative. Creativity is situated within and mediated by the performance context in the moment; such contexts are characterized in terms of receiving, sharing, or giving direction. While all music situations are construed as more or less supportive of creativity, playing *with* others rather than performing *for* others tends to afford both the greatest pleasure and the greatest exposure to creative possibility. I have identified and briefly addressed four subthemes that encapsulate participant perceptions of the meaning of creative performance: allowing, trusting, connecting, and surprising.

• The interviewees offered the following insights into their experience of creative performance and their perceptions of meaning-making:

- Most acknowledge the collective centrality of listeners as powerful co-constructors of meaning in the reciprocal experience of creative music performance.
- Even though a performance may be captured in repeatable form, the experience of its creation is unrepeatable.
- The experience of being "in the moment" is something to be desired and achieved.

- Drummers in performance are at once making and listening to the music, and experiencing it in the moment; they may then interpret it (which is to assign it meaning) post hoc.
- Perceiving, experiencing, acting, and evaluating are all enacted through a nexus of meaning-making, meaning-transmission, and meaning-circulation encapsulated in a personal "plotline" or narrative.
- The performer is simultaneously perceived, experienced, and evaluated by two groups of hearers—co-performers and non-performing listeners—who are to a greater or lesser degree sharing the same nexus of meaning-making with him or her.
- The notion of reciprocal interaction suggests that in the creative moment the performer both expresses experience and experiences that expression.
- Some genres of popular music discourage musical interplay or interaction. These genres lack "letting" and "allowing" and inhibit decision making, a central component of creative action.
- Creative performance is contingent upon trusting and being trusted by co-performers.
- The element of surprise may be considered an indicator of significant action.

9 • Breaking Down

Conclusions

As set out in the introduction, the key objective of this book was to provide a more nuanced description of creativity in drummer performance than hitherto by understanding the lived experience of expert practitioners. While what governs the choices and actions of the Western kit drummer has occasionally been interrogated within the literature, the voices of drummers themselves have been less heard. Those whom one might imagine to have most to say on creative music performance, the eminent or the expert, have been heard even less. The aim here has thus been to deepen and broaden the discourse by presenting evidence from within the domain of unpitched practitioners. Extrapolating from the line of thinking that suggests that the capacity for creative thought is the rule rather than the exception in human cognitive functioning,[1] the evidence suggests that the capacity for creative action is similarly the rule rather than the exception among drummers.

So what can we now say about how drummers go about their business? Analyzed according to the precepts of flexible thematic analysis, 100,000 words of testimony generated rich insight indeed. I have been able to demonstrate that drummer creativity tends to be instrumental in *making it* (the music, the performance) *work* and *making it matter*, rather than an end in itself. Making it work is, in the first instance, making it work for others, and drummers' action-choices are mediated by both the sociocultural and sonic environments. Every drum student's first lesson might usefully encompass the idea that the music is not there to serve the musician; the musician is there to serve the music.

I have argued that drummer creativity is a process that brings experience into meaning; that it does so through situated, mediated action in context; that such action is regulated and given meaning by the drum culture; and that creative drum performance is the ability to effect and communicate significant difference. As drummers, as much as human beings, we are what we do, and what we do is largely governed and defined by culture, embedded in a social matrix of people and artifacts. The sharing of lived experience is one way that we shape this culture and one way that we make sense of our world. This meaning-making process, while not qualitatively different from that of other groups of popular instrumental practitioners, may be considered atypical by virtue of the nature of our instrument of indeterminate pitch.

This much seems relatively uncontroversial now, many pages after I first asked the question: How do expert drummers construct, communicate, and assess significant difference? To get at an answer I synthesized a range of views from action theory, cultural psychology, and expert practitioners to interpret perceptions of creativity and meaning in Western kit drummer performance. Drawing together and developing the work of Csikszentmihalyi, Dewey, Boesch, and Glăveanu, I argued that the construct of "significant action in context" provides the conceptual and methodological framework within which to begin analysis of this relationship of mind to cultural setting. It might also serve as the central determinant by which meaning is established in creative drummer performance. I tested and critiqued several creativity and cultural psychology models, but they require extension or adaptation to cast a more focused light on the meaning of creative performance for drummers.

Three new tools were fashioned to sharpen focus, reduce the substantial area of interest, and frame conceptual thinking. First, I drew a subjective subset of four key dimensions of creativity from the literature to form sure footings for a selection/difference/communication/assessment (SDCA) framework of performance creativity. The purpose of this construct was to frame and contextualize the process of creative performance within the specific domain of the Western kit drummer. Second, I offered a trio of artificial constructs to connect the drummer to the decision-making process: "functional performance," "compositional performance," and the "functional/compositional continuum" (FCC). These constructs were useful in modeling the action contexts perceived as meaningful for the interviewees themselves. Third, I constructed an integrated model of the circulation of meaning (IMCM) to explain how drummer action generates lived experience, which informs meaning. Meaning forms a basis for possible change in practice. Within this theoretical and analytic framework, we have crystallized the essence of creative music performance as a post hoc judgment by others of the outcome or outcomes of significant action that is different and effective, probably producing a reaction that may surprise receptors without necessarily changing the domain.

There appears to be a disjunction between expert drummers' experiences of creative music performance and the conceptions of a broader music culture that seems unable to decide what drummers are for. Since the invention of the instrument, the Western kit drummer has been cast sequentially as the vaudevillian stick twirler (someone to watch); as swing-band drummer (someone to dance to); as co-constructor of African American high art (someone to listen to); as rock god (someone to reach oblivion with); and, perhaps coming full circle, as a re-creator (someone to watch on stage as she or he "nails" the groove already nailed by the ubiquitous and ever-prurient computer). This book has hopefully clarified something of the "what" and "why" contemporary drummers do what they do and how they give meaning to the experience of doing it. Some of its contents may reduce the distance between what drummers think they are for and what they do, and what others think of these things. Drummers can be creative in ways that are important to our understanding of music creativity and creativity in general.

I have attempted to capture a rounded picture of the expert Western kit drummer in his or her natural environment to show how the individual engages with the world of sound to create meaningful experience. As mature, successful, peak-career performers, our participants enjoy an international status derived from the repeated attribution of creativity to their "products" (i.e., performances), even though the acquisition of such an attribution may not have been the primary intent. Their purpose, rather, is to make the music work by making it swing or making it groove, often by making others comfortable. They want to make their performance better, or different. They want to make it matter, and make it mean something to themselves, to other drummers, and, collaterally, to the listener. Indeed, an early desire, common among young musicians, is expressed anecdotally as wanting to "make it," that is, to be successful. This returns us to one of creativity's simplest characterizations as the act or process of *making something* new.[2]

Chapters 3–8 have all concluded with a summary of the key perceptions that emerged from analysis of the relevant interview material. As individual interviewees, each drummer was of course privy to her or his own perceptions and to those of no other. As researcher, on the other hand, I was privileged to be able to collate, analyze, and interpret their observations as a whole in the context of both my own experience and the literature. With that in mind, I highlight the following propositions, overarching or additional to those presented in-chapter, that represent reasonably secure, virgin territory regarding what we can now assert about the relationship between creativity and the Western kit drummer.

(A) Creativity in drummer performance:

- Creative drummer performance is sociocultural, intersubjective, and interactive, an action in between actors and their environment rather than a psychological phenomenon entirely located within the individual mind.
- Greatest creative satisfaction inheres in those performance contexts that can best accommodate and welcome expressive input and afford a sense of control of outcomes.
- Creativity is viewed as a means to an end rather than something pursued for its own intrinsic value.
- A capacity for creative action is the rule rather than the exception.
- The importance of technical control in music invention lies in its affordance of possible options from which to select.
- There exists no direct linear connection between technical dexterity (or the amount of deliberate practice needed to achieve it) and creativity.

(B) Meaning-making in drummer performance:

- Creative performance is embedded within a meaningful shared experience around collaboration and community.
- Creative meaning lies in making it (i.e., the music embodying the performance) work, and then making it matter.
- Creative meaning is conceptualized less in terms of changing the structure of the domain than in contributing to it.
- "Making it work" is interpreted as the meaningful action-goal of appropriate performance that occupies most drummers most of the time.
- Creative meaning is derived less from the expression of emotion to a non-performer, and more from the expression of experience to a co-performer.
- Unique aspects of a pronounced cultural ideology are important determinants of drum community practice.

- If this book has a particular strength it lies, I believe, in the unusual level of access afforded me by a group of people who have not hitherto been researched. Prior studies of music performance seldom gained access to the lived experience of internationally known peak-career performers. As researcher-participant (to academics) and tour guide (to lay readers) I knew what questions to ask and was able to contextualize and interpret responses within the broader music culture into which I have long since been enculturated. Participants' willingness and enthusiasm for a topic that most considered valuable and underresearched spoke to an underlying preoccupation with it. This process came with the caveats highlighted in the introduction, and they need not be rehearsed again here.

Such an exploration of the way drummers make things work, make things matter, and make sense of both has utility in several ways. First, in light of the proposition that perceptions of creativity and meaning within pitched-instrument classical music performance have only limited transference to a group of unpitched popular music performers, the study has begun to fill a gap in the knowledge by constructing a more comprehensive picture of creative music performance as viewed by expert drummers. The findings I present have several implications for neighboring disciplines, including but not limited to music education, developmental studies, and the psychology of performance.

Within music education, I believe this study contributes to a fuller understanding of the creative process, illumination of which is of use to teachers and researchers in determining the ways in which teachers define and set targets for students in creative music invention in the classroom.[3] The book may be used to help develop or improve a performance curriculum in which students may aspire to, and attain, even greater musical inspiration and creative individuality. For example, key skills necessary to "make it work" include an entrepreneurial willingness to embrace change, the ability to think on one's feet, to learn, to adapt and to relearn on the job, to tolerate risk, and to confront the gap between what is past and what is now. Explicitly or implicitly, knowingly or unknowingly, all our experts exhibit these traits and infuse their creativity strategies with them to varying degrees. Students, teachers, and those seeking to invoke any form of creative drummer performance may consider inculcating these traits with the same fervor, at least, as that with which they inculcate the technical dexterity and stick control embedded in deliberate practice.

To be sure, all drummers are not the same, but I contend that there is sufficient commonality adhering to our practice within a strong drum culture to permit cautious generalizability. With "thick description" as a database, a judgment can be made as to possible application to other settings. If, as Nicholas Cook states, "better practices of teaching [...] depend on better models of creativity,"[4] this book may have implications for the teaching of drummers through the application of certain of its findings. Within developmental studies, too, the ways in which people learn through creating is a central area of interest.[5] While I make no claim to originality in interpreting and drawing upon the works of others, the nuanced action-theoretical understanding of significant, mediated action-in-context presented here should promote a clearer understanding—and a correction of multiple historical misunderstandings—of the power and place of creativity in our rhythmic culture. Most studies of the psychology of artistic creation have hitherto taken place within the visual, literary, and plastic arts rather than the performing arts. This volume joins others in seeking to redress the imbalance.

Critical Review

In retrospect, the limitations, challenges, strengths, and weaknesses of the work are in need of some critical reappraisal. I took much care in a participant selection process that prioritized the widest possible range of backgrounds, styles, and contexts to capture as broad a picture as possible of contemporary expert Western drummer performance. Constant attention to the responsibilities and obligations of a complete-member researcher proved sufficient, in my view, to balance the emic and etic positions. The harder challenge in this type of research was to know whether interviewees had knowingly or unknowingly misinterpreted or misrepresented their experiences. While prior research has found that performers possess an adequate vocabulary for the expression of music and emotions, and can accurately describe performance situations, I can only explore the kinds of experiences participants choose to report and any commonalities in those experiences.[6]

It is worth noting that while the sample group covered as broad an age range as possible, the youngest was already aged 34. These mature professionals' perceptions of creative performance and the meanings they assigned to their actions in context were thus, broadly, shaped in a predigital environment. Postdigital, mainstream popular music appears to be increasingly unsupportive of the type and level of skills these digital-immigrants evidenced. Further investigation with a younger cadre of digital-natives might reveal different insights born of a different set of attitudes, skills, and assessment mechanisms.

Throughout the book I have compared and contrasted participant reports against my own lived experience in a subjective attribution—a fact that points to the high degree of subjectivity in this type of research. The subjective relativism at the core of this study assumes that what is said to be "the way things are" is really just "the sense we make of them,"[7] which is why I have been assiduous in teasing out this aspect of the participants' experiences. Individual drummers have different accounts of their lived experience of creativity, in which truth and reality are individually defined and subjectively assessed. I have avoided the positivist approach, which attempts to measure the output of humans objectively with the goal of directly assessing the performer. That approach unfortunately tends to exclude those aspects of creativity that many find to be the most important and interesting, the "mainly subjective ones."[8]

Several questions remain unanswered or partially answered, not because they are unimportant but because they are tangential to the scope of this book. For example, while we have been able to go some way toward an improved understanding of some dimensions of the performer/listener relationship at one level of expertise, I take on board Alexandra Lamont's suggestion that exploration of similar experiences in a wider sample of participants at different levels of musical achievement is necessary to investigate how important the audience is for providing the appropriate level of motivation for high-quality performance experiences.[9]

In the introduction, I delimited the object of analysis to the "playable" performance. This may have been useful in framing the discussion, but of course avoids the larger question of what indeed constitutes performance in this "age of digital reproduction."[10] In the interest of maintaining a sharp focus on the real world of drum performance I have arguably neglected a fuller discussion of creative collaboration in the virtual world. With increased computer storage capacity and improving Internet connections, the holy grail of latency-free real-time collaboration is edging closer,[11] bringing with it implications, for example, for the meanings of competence, mastery, and virtuosity in a reduced rhythmic ecology, be it virtual or real.

On the face of it, the proposition that popular instrumentalists might be expert in some way seems to be counterintuitive. Is not one of the singular attractions of popular music that anyone can do it, that all can partake? The music broadly espouses a simple but effective methodology—variously three chords and the truth, three chords and a backbeat, or even fewer chords and plenty of words. While much else surrounding this simple framework may be highly sophisticated, especially in the areas of recording, postproduction, and interactive and collaborative skills, the essence of the music remains inclusive. It is therefore paradoxical that areas of considerable exclusivity remain. Musical eminence and expertise persist, notably in the world of the highly skilled studio musician, the improvising jazz musician, and the multifaceted Western kit drummer sliding along the FCC as needs dictate. Her or his expertise resides in an encyclopedic knowledge of what is appropriate for the performance context (or situation) and the ability to produce and perform it at short notice, through fine adjustment of the principal parameters of performance—temporal, metrical, dynamical, and timbral.

Technical dexterity in drum performance has advanced far past the modest requirements of the architects of the popular song, leading to the aberrant behavior of such dexterity being on display primarily for the admiration of other drummers at specially convened events, such as drum workshops and drum clinics. At these events, creativity and virtuosity make uneasy bedfellows. As virtuosity holds court, creativity seems to evaporate. Virtuosity appears to need a substantial element of overt technical dexterity and desires to generate much heat in a bright light. The enigmatic fungus of creativity, on the other hand, conceals her covert dexterity and seems better able to flourish in the shadows. While not mutually exclusive, the two phenomena appear disconnected. We admire the virtuoso, but often remain unmoved. To the extent that we *are* moved, this book has tried to show how creativity may be implicated, and where in the performance it might it be found.[12]

Future Direction and Implications for Further Research

With the collapse of the long-established functions of composer, performer, and producer into the singular occupation of the music inventor, one now evidently available to all, we may be watching the evaporation of the function of the drummer as it has been understood these past 80 years or more. Perhaps we are evolving a cultural approach to our popular music instrumentalists akin to those older cultures that inculcate only a very loose idea of the instrumental specialist. In Javanese, Balinese, and some African music-making, for instance, there appears to be a less defined use of the word "musician," less sense that such a musician might be, or might wish to be, individually creative outside the context of the music's communal cultural functions.

Operating within wholly different cultural parameters, we Western kit drummers are probably more creative than we realize, and are certainly more creative than others perceive us to be if our low status is to be taken seriously. This book has tried to address the urgent need for a fuller understanding of creativity in a young discipline that is still finding its shape within a rapidly developing music performance ecology. The idea of a bordered, definable role for the kit drummer in offstage performance (for example, as a studio musician) appears to be dissolving as drummers turn their hands to the multiple associated creativities afforded by music software in home recording, but that do not actually involve playing the instrument. The discrete categories of popular music devised and developed decades ago by record company marketing departments will continue to have diminishing salience and can safely be abandoned within practice, even if that is impossible outside practice. Indeed, the discrete categories of instrumental performer and the associated nomenclature (the drummer, bassist, "rhythm section," "front line," and so on) carried over from the big-band era also seem to be collapsing under the more generalized notions of what it means to make music.

The accelerating use of electronic drums in "playback" practice to prerecorded material, so useful to those living in small apartments, may change the skill set of those hardy souls who wish to become or remain "just a drummer." An ability to extract expressive timbral variation and a full dynamic range from the acoustic instrument, for example, may become surplus to requirements in the homogenized ecology whose emergence was problematized in chapter 6. Those who fear the inexorable decline of the small group rhythmic specialist into an "unnecessary adjunct to the terrain that music technology has now secured as its own" of Matthew Brennan's nightmarish scenario can take succor from the sheer visceral power of the drummer on stage where she or he remains, for the time being at least, the conduit to the rhythmic epicenter of the music, adding visual and audible value to the communal experience.

While I might be accused of producing an overbroad conclusion, it seems to me that the discourse involving the purpose and function of the contemporary drummer exhibits a certain circularity. For much of its existence, the music in which the drum kit has been used has been associated with the degree of metrical consistency required for dancing, typically manifest in the steady pulse of the bass drum playing four notes per measure. The late 20th-century application of technology accorded the drummer an asymmetrical function as a lesser instrumentalist who *kept* time rather than created it and whose performance "discrepancies" were to be eliminated. Ironically, the increasingly sophisticated use of this technology has generated contemporary research and analysis of the drummer's art supporting the idea that such fluctuations and variations are musically meaningful and part of the creative life force of the music.[13] This position, drummers might reasonably argue, is convergent with what they have "felt" rather than "known" all along.

Several of the insights I have revealed have not hitherto been considered in the music performance literature. While findings broadly concur with the ethnographical and phenomenological work upon which I have built, there is significant divergence from some understandings of music performance within the Western classical tradition. Meanings of creativity in performance, of how it is enacted, and the extent to which it may be invoked; perceptions of perfection and of what it is that is to be communicated— this much at least appears to drift substantially from understandings within classical music. Expert drummers, we now know, tend to derive creative meaning less from classical performance understandings of the expression of emotion to a non-performer, more from the expression of experience to a co-performer. Drummer creativity typically resides in the moment of performance in the presence of others rather than in the pre-preparatory creative work behind the highly practiced performance typical of the classical tradition.

Expert popular instrumentalists do, however, share some of the concerns of their classical counterparts: for example, the amount and quality of deliberate practice, the appropriate degree of expressive input, and the relationship between control over outcomes and performance "wellness." In regard to the last of these, I can do no more than suggest that greater performer control may lie within popular music performance rather than within its classical counterpart, and that anecdotally that idea constitutes one attractive dimension of the former to those contemplating a career in either domain. The linearity of the relationship between control of the dimensions of performance and wellness, a key concern within the discipline of the psychology of music, is given added weight here. The extent to which unpitched practitioners in popular music differ in perception from their pitched-instrument classical brethren with regard to the topics of creativity and meaning is substantial but poorly understood; further work is needed because the degree of transference of research from the latter to the former, and within both traditions, is low.

Conclusion

My closing comments emphasize the relational, everywhere implied but seldom foregrounded throughout the preceding pages. The notion of relationship has been invoked in several contexts and on multiple occasions: between the individual drummer and the composer; between the individual and technology; between culture and community; between action, experience, and meaning; and in the shifting of the analytic spotlight away from the individual drummer or the sociocultural environment and onto the *relationship* between the two. I have sought throughout to establish that drummers achieve creativity in playable music performance by the effective communication of significant difference: they find creative meaning in making it work and making it matter.[14] Crucially, both sets of actions entail the making of relationships.

Existing creativity models are being recalibrated to tell us more about the immediacy of the creative performances of dancers, actors, and musicians. Glăveanu's Five A's framework of distributed creativity represents an adapted, expanded systems model that accounts for a lower-level personal creativity that neither seeks nor demands domain change, and that foregrounds the role of the sociocultural milieu in which the creative action takes place. I have made extensive and appreciative use of it in this study of the expert drummer in the popular music tradition. I borrow again from the author when I emphasize that creativity is not a thing, it is a relationship that connects two or more people in a common (and creative) search for meaning, for understanding. The experience of creativity has both neuropsychological and sociocultural components, and the latter appear to trump the former in drummer experience. Put another way, it is not only (or even primarily) about cognitive capacities and personality characteristics. In James Greeno's view, creativity involves reorganizing the connection or relationship an individual has with a *situation*, rather than reorganizing that which occurs within the person's mind.[15] Ultimately, music creativity is a quality of relationship—of that between the drummer and the *situation*, that composite of musical experience, competence, cultural practice, people, instruments, and instructions that together constitute the sociomusical environment in which she or he must live, breathe, and perform.

Appendix A

Participant Biographical Data

Biographical Data	Date of Interview	Most Creative Drummers
Cindy Blackman Santana. Born: 1959. Age at interview: 55. Active in the profession: >30 years. African American. Cindy has been for many years a stadium-level rock drummer as a "day job" and a prolific leader of her own jazz ensembles "on the side." She has numerous credits with others, and eight album recordings as a leader.	April 8, 2014	Art Blakey Elvin Jones Tony Williams
Peter Erskine. Born: 1954. Age at interview: 60. Active in the profession: >42 years. Anglo American. Peter is a jazz drummer and composer who has been a session drummer, recording and touring with many famous jazz and rock artists. He also has a vibrant, multi-album solo career. Unusually, he has rare experience of performing in the modern classical idiom. He also produces teaching materials, such as books, videos, and online content.	August 18, 2014	Elvin Jones Burnard Purdie Paul Motian
Martin France. Born: 1964. Age at interview: 50. Active in the profession: >30 years. British. Primarily a jazz drummer on multiple recordings for other leaders, Martin teaches and records under his own direction: two albums to date. His activity is principally in Europe rather than North America. He has recently completed a run in a London West End show, a somewhat different discipline.	February 17, 2014	Joey Baron Tony Williams Jack DeJohnette Ringo Starr Max Roach Zigaboo Modeliste

Biographical Data	Date of Interview	Most Creative Drummers
Mark Guiliana. Born: 1980. Age at interview: 34. Active in the profession: >14 years. Italian American. Conceptual synthesist and youngest participant in the study. Of all the participants, Mark has most successfully connected the rhythms of the community elders from bebop through hip-hop to the sine-waves and oscillators of the gaming generation. A prolific touring musician and recording artist, he has released four titles under his own direction, and multiple titles in conjunction with others.	June 18, 2014	Jim Black Jeff Ballard
Dylan Howe. Born: 1969. Age at interview: 45. Active in the profession: >25 years. British. Dylan is a drummer, bandleader, session musician, and composer. He has played on over 60 albums by others, and produced five "solo" albums, primarily in the jazz vein. He has also performed and interpreted music by classical composers at one end of the spectrum and rhythm 'n' blues artists at the other.	August 22, 2014	Roy Haynes Tony Williams Bill Bruford
Ralph Salmins. Born: 1964. Age at interview: 49. Active in the profession: >30 years. British. Drummer/producer/composer and a professor at two prestigious London music academies. His ability to traverse musical styles that include jazz, rock, rhythm 'n' blues, funk, pop, and classical music has enabled him to work as a London-based session musician with internationally known names in the music business. His credits include radio and TV commercials, motion picture soundtracks, and performances on countless albums with artists from around the world. Alone among the participants he has no commercial releases under his own name.	January 8, 2014	Philly Joe Jones Jack DeJohnette Tony Williams Steve Gadd
Asaf Sirkis. Born: 1969. Age at interview: 44. Active in the profession: >25 years. Israeli-British. A fiercely committed jazz drummer, bandleader, and composer, Asaf began his career in 1990. Alongside multiple credits as a sideman on jazz dates for others, he has written, directed, and produced seven CDs of original material over some 15 years.	September 23, 2013	Elvin Jones Gary Husband Jack DeJohnette Jim Keltner Terry Bozzio

Biographical Data	Date of Interview	Most Creative Drummers
Thomas Strønen. Born: 1972. Age at interview: 42. Active in the profession: >20 years. Norwegian. Thomas is a jazz musician and composer, known from more than 60 albums and much collaboration with internationally acclaimed musicians worldwide. In the way of jazz musicians, he is simultaneously in several collectives, drawing on a wide group of primarily European players. He has a distinguished record as composer or co-composer of multiple commissioned works, and he teaches at a national conservatory. Of all the participants, Thomas is the most versed in solo improvised performance.	May 2, 2014	Jon Christensen Tony Oxley Elvin Jones
Chad Wackerman. Born: 1960. Age at interview: 53. Active in the profession: >30 years. Anglo American. Since Chad's career began in 1978, he has toured and worked globally and steadily for internationally celebrated leaders in rock and jazz. As a bandleader and composer, Chad has five critically acclaimed CDs and he has written music for other jazz and rock musicians and for television. His primary performance experience is in rock groups, jazz groups, and drum duets.	November 18, 2013	Jim Keltner Terry Bozzio Vinnie Colaiuta Steve Jordan

Appendix B

Interview Questions

Preliminaries included a reminder that it was the participant's personal experience that was being sought, from their point of view; what sense he or she makes of it, and how if at all that meaning informed action. There were no right or wrong answers. The interviewee was free to withdraw from the interview at any time.

1 **How did you come to be a drummer?**

   This "gateway" question addresses multiple issues surrounding the choice of instrument, degrees of parental support and encouragement, formal and informal learning and training, attitudes and actualities of practice. It is intended to shed light on the manner and extent to which appropriate skills and tools are acquired and musical identity constructed.

2 **Is it important to your creativity to have choice and control over what you play?**

   Issues of choice, selection, and control are at the core of the continuum of control between functional and compositional practice.

3 **If and when you have choice and control, how do you decide what you play?**

   From what raw materials does the autonomous practitioner begin to construct significant action?

4 **Turning now to how you think about yourself, do you consider yourself creative?**

   Probe: What, if anything, does creativity mean to you?

5 **How important is it to you to consider yourself creative?**

6 **What motivates you to be creative?**

7 **How important to you is it that others identify you as creative?**

To what extent do the opinions of others count in the enabling or disabling of potentially creative action?

8 **How important to you is it to develop your own distinctive voice, and work with or resist the influence of others?**

This question addresses the perceived requirement of developing (or obscuring) a distinctive approach, "standing out from the crowd."

9 **Turning now to composing or writing, could you tell me something about how and why you came to do this?**

To what extent did the individual begin writing or band-leading as a deliberate strategy (a) to control the musical environment in which his or her distinctive musical voice might develop and grow, or (b) to gain status and control, or (c) because she or he or others saw drumming as inherently or insufficiently creative? When did it become a decision?

10 **Can you say something about collaborating with others, and how, if at all, that might determine your understanding of creativity?**

To what extent does the collaborative give meaning to the individual? To what extent is creativity construed by this participant as embodied in the individual or the collaborative? Is there a sense in which creativity is enacted in "the space between": self/other, orthodoxy/iconoclasm, or, from a practitioner's perspective, the space *between* the notes?

11 **Tell me a little about your selections of creativity in your own work.**

This request is designed to enlighten a set of issues about their performance process. Had the participant come to understand something about this music (or himself or herself) in a way that hadn't been understood before? Had something new emerged in the approach to the music? Had the participant learned something that would help him or her to be more creative or original in future performance?

12 **Is there any thread running through these examples, something they have in common that enabled your creativity?**

The intention here is the reconstruction of experience.

13 **What is it that makes you describe what you experienced in these particular examples as "creativity" rather than as something else?**

14 **Could you name three drummers, living or dead, whom you consider creative, and why you consider them so?**

Here the question looks for participant convergence or divergence on previous practitioners whose work may be considered emblematic of creativity. How does meaning circulate within the domain? It also aims to elicit insight into the participant's own practice by contrast or comparison.

15 **Have any changes in the drum scene since you started made creativity more or less possible?**

Has the arrival of the digital age made creativity more or less possible? Multiple ripples run out from this into the ecology of drummer creativity: the heterogeneity or homogenization of tempo and dynamics, stylistic fragmentation, the use of music technology, electronic v. acoustic drums, and so forth.

16 **How do you see the audience or listener in respect to your creativity?**

What attitude is taken to the listener—co-performers, paying audience or other receivers? Are they seen as a help, a hindrance, or essential partners in a co-creation?

17 **Can you tell me a bit about what you like or dislike about performing in public?**

The latent question here concerns the degree of importance attributed to performance. How important is playing in public to practitioners' sense of themselves as drummers?

18 **Given everything you've said so far about creativity in your work, what does it mean to you?**

This asks participants to reflect on meaning. How do they construct notions of creativity and assess potentially significant action in themselves and others?

19 **That's just about all the questions I've got. Is there anything else on the subject that we haven't covered?**

This question allows the participant to lead into areas that may have been overlooked.

20 **Just about the interview itself and how it felt: What have been the positives and perhaps negatives involved in taking part?**

Appendix C

Participant Examples of Own Creative Performance

Participants were asked to provide samples of recordings that embody their own creative performances. They are indicated in **bold text**. Other examples of an individual's work indicate other contexts in which she or he performs, and have been selected by the author. They are indicated in light text.

The constraints associated with large ensembles tend to necessitate a high level of direction. Such performances thus gravitate to the high functional. In the opposite direction, the lack of constraints associated with solo or duo performances tend to cause such performances to cluster at the high compositional end of the FCC.

Peter Erskine

● FUNCTIONAL PERFORMANCE

	For a Leader	With a Leader	
		Example 1	Example 2
Artist	Steely Dan	**Bob Mintzer Big Band**	Peter Erskine-Alan Pasqua Trio
CD title	*Alive in America*	*Gently*	*My Old New Friend*
Track title	*Reelin' in the Years*	*Timeless*	*Wichita Lineman*
Catalog	Giant Records 9 24634-2	DMP CD-534	Cryptogramophone CG122
Web link	https://www.youtube.com/watch?v=TqKC38A8QjI	https://www.youtube.com/watch?v=Zbyj1E6WjcU	https://www.youtube.com/watch?v=mWqfcwDXrrA

● COMPOSITIONAL PERFORMANCE

	As a Leader	Without a Leader
Artist	**Peter Erskine-Alan Pasqua Trio**	*None selected*
CD title	*The Interlochen Concert*	
Track title	*Wichita Lineman*	
Catalog	Fuzzy Music: 19	

Martin France

● FUNCTIONAL PERFORMANCE

	For a Leader	With a Leader	
		Example 1	Example 2
Artist	**NDR Big Band**	**Kenny Wheeler Big Band**	**John Taylor Trio**
CD title	*The Hamburg Suite.* Composer: Gwilym Simcock	*The Long Waiting*	*Afterthought*
Track title	*All tracks*	*All tracks*	*Angel of the Presence*
Catalog		Cam Jazz: CAMJ 7848-5	Cam Jazz: CAMJ 7778-2
Web link		https://www.youtube.com/watch?v=snMpz2Vvf0k	https://www.youtube.com/watch?v=KKLijPVV0Tk

● COMPOSITIONAL PERFORMANCE

	As a Leader	Without a Leader
Artist	**Martin France: Spin Marvel**	*None selected*
CD title	*Infolding*	
Track title	*Canonical*	
Catalog	RareNoise records	
Web link	https://soundcloud.com/rarenoiserecords/01-spin-marvel-canonical	

Mark Guiliana

● FUNCTIONAL PERFORMANCE

	For a Leader	With a Leader	
		Example 1	Example 2
Artist	*None selected*	**David Bowie**	**Avishai Cohen**
CD title		*Blackstar*	*As Is . . . Live at the Blue Note*
Track title		*Blackstar*	*Feediop*
Catalog		ISO Records 8887 5173871	Half Note Records: HN 4531
Web link		https://www.youtube.com/watch?v=kszLwBaC4Sw	https://www.youtube.com/watch?v=4gkHLunG-ig

● COMPOSITIONAL PERFORMANCE

	As a Leader	Without a Leader
Artist	**Mark Guiliana**	**Mehliana**
CD title	*Beat Music: The Los Angeles Sessions*	*Taming the Dragon*
Track title	*All tracks*	*The Dreamer*
Catalog		Nonesuch 7559-79579-5
Web link	https://soundcloud.com/markguiliana/sets/beat-music-the-los-angeles	https://www.youtube.com/watch?v=b06L3svIbUs&index=6&list=PLemtoUQ96XC9HN6tSfw4Csj0syTv7XKbh

Dylan Howe

● FUNCTIONAL PERFORMANCE

	For a Leader	With a Leader
Artist	*None selected*	The Blockheads
CD title		*Staring Down the Barrel*
Track title		*Greed*
Catalog		EMI: 5099969750724
Web link		https://www.youtube.com/watch?v=4cTT4pD4fNA

● COMPOSITIONAL PERFORMANCE

	As a Leader	Without a Leader
Artist	**Dylan Howe**	**Howe-Butterworth Duo**
CD title	*Subterranean*	*Stravinsky: The Rite of Spring Pt.1*
Track title	*Neukoln - Night*	*Introduction 2*
Catalog	Motorik Recordings MR1004	Motorik Recordings 5032796022923
Web link	https://soundcloud.com/dylanlhowe	https://www.youtube.com/watch?v=0G-CznIjnXE

Ralph Salmins

● FUNCTIONAL PERFORMANCE

	For a Leader	With a Leader	
		Example 1	Example 2
Artist	**Guy Barker Jazz Orchestra**	**Van Morrison**	**Nitin Sawnhey feat: Imogen Heap**
CD title	*The Amadeus Project*	*The Healing Game*	*London Undersound*
Track title	*Overture: The T Dance*	*The Healing Game*	*Bring it Home*
Catalog	Global Mix GM2CD-02	Polydor 537 101-2	Cooking Vinyl MBB20039
Web link		https://www.youtube.com/watch?v=HlVZtzSJi70	https://www.youtube.com/watch?v=FUlFTJZUs0k

● COMPOSITIONAL PERFORMANCE

	As a Leader	Without a Leader
Artist	*None selected*	*None selected*

Cindy Blackman Santana

• FUNCTIONAL PERFORMANCE

	For a Leader	With a Leader
Artist	Lennie Kravitz	Spectrum Road feat. Jack Bruce
CD title	*5*	*Spectrum Road*
Track title	*Fly Away*	*All tracks*
Catalog	Virgin CDVUS 140	Palmetto Records 2152
Web link	https://www.youtube.com/watch?v=EvuL5jyCHOw	https://www.youtube.com/watch?v=miDyI69NfAM

• COMPOSITIONAL PERFORMANCE

	As a Leader	Without a Leader
Artist	**Cindy Blackman**	*None selected*
CD title	*Works on Canvas*	
Track title	*Three van Goghs*	
Catalog	High Note HCD 7038	

Asaf Sirkis

• FUNCTIONAL PERFORMANCE

	For a Leader	With a Leader
Artist	*None selected*	**Tim Garland Group**
CD title		*One*
Track title		*Sama'i for Peace*
Catalog		Edition Records EDN1072
Web link		https://www.youtube.com/watch?v=gyApxYDdtaM

• COMPOSITIONAL PERFORMANCE

	As a Leader	Without a Leader
Artist	**Asaf Sirkis Trio**	*None selected*
CD title	*Shepherd's Stories*	
Track title	*All tracks*	
Catalog	Stonebird Productions SBPT 002	
Web link	https://soundcloud.com/asaf-sirkis/shepherds-stories-taster	

Thomas Strønen

● FUNCTIONAL PERFORMANCE

	For a Leader	With a Leader
Artist	**Trondheim Jazz Orchestra**	*None selected*
CD title	*Unavailable*	
Track title		
Catalog		
Web link	https://www.youtube.com/watch?v=YZHwyc26kyk	

● COMPOSITIONAL PERFORMANCE

	As a Leader	Without a Leader
Artist	**Time is a Blind Guide**	**Food: Live at Nasjonal Jazzscene**
CD title	*Time is a Blind Guide*	*Unavailable*
Track title	*Time is a Blind Guide*	*Unavailable*
Catalog	ECM 2467	
Web link	https://www.youtube.com/watch?v=0_DSnBuD3RA	https://www.youtube.com/watch?v=4yL9bn-quTo

Chad Wackerman

● FUNCTIONAL PERFORMANCE

		With a Leader	
	For a Leader	Example 1	Example 2
Artist	**Frank Zappa**	James Taylor	**Allan Holdsworth**
CD title	*Zappa in New York*	*Gorilla (original CD)*	*All Night Wrong*
Track title	*Black Page #2*	*Mexico(live version)*	*Water on the Brain Pt. 2*
Catalog	WEA, Discreet: K69204, 2D 2290		**Sony Music/Favored Nations FN2330-2**
Web link	https://www.youtube.com/watch?v=CtkZxnkbjtI	https://www.youtube.com/watch?v=qLcTuRAPvps	https://www.youtube.com/watch?v=inHbczTE1-Y

● COMPOSITIONAL PERFORMANCE

	As a Leader	Without a Leader
Artist	**Chad Wackerman**	**Terry Bozzio-Chad Wackerman Duo**
CD title	*Dreams, Nightmares, and Improvisations*	*DW DVD: D2-Duets Two*
Track title	*Bent Bayou*	*All tracks*
Catalog	Audio Cave: ACB-002–2012	GSM Entertainment
Web link		https://www.youtube.com/watch?v=xRiZNOvC5J8

Bill Bruford

• FUNCTIONAL PERFORMANCE

	For a Leader	With a Leader	
		Example 1	Example 2
Artist	**The Buddy Rich Big Band**	**Chris Squire**	**King Crimson**
CD title	*Burning for Buddy – A Tribute to the Music of Buddy Rich. Vol. 2*	*Fish Out of Water*	*DVD: The Noise- Live at Fréjus*
Track title	*Willowcrest*	*Lucky Seven*	*Waiting Man*
Catalog	Atlantic 7567-83010-2	Atlantic K50203	DGM 0401
Web link	https://www.youtube.com/watch?v=Qgc4EFz9Pmk	https://www.youtube.com/watch?v=WS29bnX45H0	https://www.youtube.com/watch?v=PJ2uDTqD_OU

• COMPOSITIONAL PERFORMANCE

	As a Leader	Without a Leader
Artist	**Bruford, Towner, Gomez**	**Bruford, Borstlap**
CD title	*If Summer Had Its Ghosts*	*The Summerfold Collection (double)*
Track title	*Thistledown*	*The 16 Kingdoms of the 5 Barbarians*
Catalog	Summerfold Records BBSF002CD	Summerfold Records BBSF022CD
Web link	https://www.youtube.com/watch?v=ydwHoAcNk-4	

Appendix D

List of Persons Mentioned

Anderson, Jon: singer, songwriter (1944–)
Blakey, Art: drummer, bandleader (1919–90)
Bonham, John: drummer (1948–80)
Bozzio, Terry: drummer, bandleader (1950–)
Colaiuta, Vinnie: drummer (1956–)
Dave, Chris: drummer, bandleader (1968–)
Davis, Miles: trumpet player, bandleader (1926–91)
DeJohnette, Jack: drummer, bandleader (1942–)
Dodds, Warren "Baby": drummer (1898–1959)
Gadd, Steve: drummer (1945–)
Grohl, Dave: drummer and multi-instrumentalist (1969–)
Haynes, Roy: drummer, bandleader (1925–)
Helm, Levon: drummer, vocalist (1940–2012)
Jones, Elvin: drummer, bandleader (1927–2004)
Jones, "Philly" Joe: drummer (1923–85)
Lewis, Mel: drummer, bandleader (1929–90)
MacFarlane, Seth: actor, movie director, singer-songwriter (1973–)
Manne, Shelly: drummer, bandleader, club owner (1920–84)
Mason, Harvey: drummer (1947–)
Mastelotto, Pat: drummer (1955–)
McShann, Jay: pianist, bandleader (1919–2006)
Mendoza, Vince: arranger, composer, conductor (1961–)
Porcaro, Jeff: drummer (1954–92)
Purdie, Burnard: drummer (1939–)
Rich, Buddy: drummer, bandleader (1917–87)
Roach, Max: drummer, composer, bandleader (1924–2007)
Robinson, John (J. R.): drummer (1954–)

Scabies, Rat (a.k.a Christopher Millar): punk drummer (1955–)
Scott, Ronnie: saxophonist, bandleader, jazz club proprietor (1929–96)
Smith, Steve: drummer, teacher, bandleader (1954–)
Thompson, Ahmir "Questlove": drummer, music journalist, producer (1971–)
Vega, Carlos: drummer (1957–98)
Watts, Jeff "Tain": drummer, bandleader (1960–)
Wilson, Steven: musician and record producer (1967–)
Weckl, Dave: drummer, bandleader (1960–)
Williams, Tony: drummer, bandleader (1945–97)

Glossary of Terms

Blasticks: Strikers that are softer than sticks, but harder than brushes. They perform like sticks but produce a soft and full sound.

chair: Position held in a jazz group, as in "the saxophone chair," or "the drum chair."

"Chameleon": Track from Herbie Hancock featuring the funk style of drummer Harvey Mason.

Charleston: Popular American dance of the 1920s.

chart: Written instrumental part.

chops: Technical ability.

click or *click track:* Any type of automated metronome, typically played to the drummer through headphones and designed to keep him or her in time.

clinic: Technical display, demonstration, or workshop.

clock-time: Accurate tempo measurement, usually computer- or machine-generated.

comp, comped: Derived from "accompany" or "accompanied" (another musician).

crush or crushed roll: Drum rudiment of military origin.

D.C.I: U.S. company specializing in the manufacture of instructional drum videos.

demo: Demonstration recording to indicate preliminary intentions.

Feels Good to Me/One of a Kind: The author's first two albums as a drummer-leader.

fill: Either a noun (a fill) or a verb (to fill), a short musical passage to sustain rhythmic propulsion during a pause in the music, frequently linking one section or phrase to another.

flam accent: A rudimental sticking pattern.

GarageBand: A digital audio workstation and music sequencer that can record and play back multiple tracks of audio.

gear: Equipment.

head: Abbreviation of drumhead, a membrane, now typically synthetic, stretched over one or both of the open ends of a drum.

Heritage Rock: A U.S. radio format that features artists who focus on their past achievements or recorded "heritage."

"K" cymbal: A grade or type of cymbal produced by the Zildjian Company and much favored by the late 20th-century drum masters.

"laying out": In music performance, not playing.

lead-sheet: A form of music notation that specifies the essential elements of a popular song: the melody, lyrics, and harmony.

lick: (noun) A short pre-prepared phrase or pattern.

M.D.: Musical director.

Messengers: Abbreviation of the Jazz Messengers, Art Blakey's long-standing group.

pad: A "bed" of sustained chords fleshing out the sound under the melody line, typically on a synthesizer in pop music. In a different context, also refers to an instrumentalist's printed music for a show (e.g., the "drum pad").

pocket: Drummer near-synonym for groove.

pre-set: A preconfigured synthesizer or electronic drum patch available for instant recall.

Pro-Tools: A digital audio workstation widely used in the audio industries for recording and editing.

quantization: A process within digital music technology that results in performed notes being set on beats and on exact fractions of beats. Such notes may have some rhythmic inconsistency due to expressive performance: quantization transforms them to an underlying musical representation that eliminates imprecision.

Rhodes: A type of electric piano.

ride: The ride cymbal, upon which, post 1940, the rhythmic continuum generally is kept.

Ronnie Scott's: A London jazz club.

set: An uninterrupted block of performance for popular musicians, who might play two or three "sets" a night.

Sibelius: Music-writing computer software package named after the celebrated composer.

situation: In this context has the meaning of a performance situation. It connotes the sociomusical environment around somebody's band, ensemble, or recording session.

sock-cymbal: Early name for pedal-operated hi-hat cymbals.

song: In U.S. musician parlance, this typically refers to the music under discussion or being performed, irrespective of whether or not it embodies any singing.

subs: Abbreviation of "sub-woofer loudspeakers" dedicated to the reproduction of low-pitched audio frequencies.

"trading fours": In jazz performance, trading fours usually occurs after each musician has soloed, and typically involves alternating four-bar segments with the drummer.

turnaround: See ii—v—i.

ii—v—i: Jazz musician's shorthand for a common harmonic device.

"wide open": In respect to drum tuning, the drums are left undampened.

Notes

Introduction

1. Pamela Burnard points to John Blacking's discussion of empathic experience in the context of African drumming, in which two drummers might achieve such an experience "unavailable in any other way." Pamela Burnard, *Musical creativities*, 161.

2. Such as scientists like Parag Chordia, cited in Miles O'Brien and Marsha Walton, "Music and creativity"; authors like John Howkins, *The creative economy*, and Richard Florida, *The rise of the creative class*; and government agencies like the British Department for Culture, Media and Sport.

3. My use of the term "experience," a phenomenon unpacked in chapter 1, has a collective quality in that it embodies both the small instances that go to make up the single notion of experience and the cumulative outcome of interaction with the environment, also known as experience. Which meaning is meant is determined by the context in which it used.

4. The terms "unpitched," "indefinite pitch," "indeterminate pitch," and "semidefinite pitch" are used synonymously throughout, both to denote an attribute of the drum kit and to act as a descriptor of the drummer who performs upon it, as, for example, an "unpitched practitioner." A pitched note may be identified as a tone of clearly discernible fundamental pitch. The instruments comprising the Western drum kit generally do not have discernible fundamental pitch; they are of indeterminate or indefinite pitch. It is quite possible, however, to roughly detect "higher" and "lower" between two sounds of indefinite pitch. The high, medium, and low tom-toms of many drum kits afford an approximate sense of a melodic contour. Wilson elaborates the concept of melodic drumming in the work of Terry Bozzio and Max Roach in Ronald Wilson, "Melodic drum set compositions."

5. Caroline Palmer, "Music performance," 119.

6. For more on action theory, see Ernst Boesch, "Cultural psychology in action-theoretical perspective," or James Wertsch, *Mind as action*. The relationship between action and experience is discussed in depth in John Dewey, *Art as experience*, and Vlad Petre Glăveanu et al. "Creativity as action." Creative worth is examined from a historical perspective by John Hope Mason in *The value of creativity*.

7. Promoted by, among others, John Rink in his book *The practice of performance*, and through the AHRC Research Centre for Musical Performance as Creative Practice.

8. Keith Negus and Michael Pickering, *Creativity, communication and cultural value*, vii.

9. This term has a somewhat specific use in the drummer discourse and will be foundational to the argument. Folkestad suggests that it connotes that composite of musical experience, competence, cultural practice, tools, instruments, and instructions that together constitute the sociomusical environment around an individual's band, ensemble, or recording session. Göran Folkestad, "Digital tools and discourse in music," 197.

10. See, for example, Matt Dean, *The drum*.

11. Ralf Krampe and Anders Ericsson are cited in Eric Clarke, "Creativity in performance," 2014.

12. See, for example, John Hayes, "Cognitive processes," or Scott Kaufman and James Kaufman, "Ten years to expertise."

13. Malcolm Gladwell, *Outliers*.

14. See Philip Auslander, "Performance analysis and popular music," 3. Writing as recently as 2004, the author observes that "those who take music seriously, either as art or culture, dismiss performance as irrelevant." The selection of participants who are both composers and performers is designed to render the venom less potent. One exception was permitted in the interest of covering the broadest possible range of practice; interviewee Ralph Salmins has hitherto deliberately avoided the nurturing of a parallel solo career in the interest of his development as a studio drummer, remaining thus "just" a performer.

15. See Gareth Smith, *I drum, therefore I am*.

16. Interviewees are listed in alphabetical order. Names in parentheses are those of a few of the prominent artists with whom the individual has worked.

17. The occupation of the drummer is in the process of much redefinition. Recent technological advances have enabled the emergence of the "stay-home" drummer—broadly, one who is able to work entirely from home by some combination of teaching and music production for colleagues or clients, typically through the exchange of music files from a home studio.

18. Barbara Tedlock, "From participant observation to the observation of participation."

19. Pamela Maykut and Richard Morehouse, *Beginning qualitative research*, 123.

20. Stephen Cottrell, *Professional music-making*, 19.

21. Sonya Dwyer and Jennifer Buckle, "The space between," 54. Dwyer and Buckle lay out the case for insider academic research, promoted by others such as Teresa Brannick and David Coghlan in *In defense of being "native"*.

22. Ference Marton, *Phenomenography*, 147–48.

23. Norman Denzin and Yvonna Lincoln, *The Sage handbook of qualitative research*, 636.

24. The research data that informs this work was derived from anonymous interviews in the first instance. Each interviewee subsequently granted permission for their words to be attributable for the book.

25. Etienne Wenger, *Communities of practice*. Wenger's construct of a "community of practice" is both foundational to and frames much of the ensuing discussion. It is examined in greater depth in chapter 6.

26. Borrowing from Anne Danielsen, further questions might ask: What is expected of drummers? What does the culture expect, the public expect? What do other musi-

cians and drummers themselves expect, and how do we respond to those expectations? See Anne Danielsen, *Musical rhythm in the age of digital reproduction*.

27. See John Hope Mason, *The value of creativity*. The main trends in the creativity literature have been reviewed by, for example, Robert Sternberg and Todd Lubart, "The concept of creativity"; Ian Fillis and Andrew McAuley, "Modeling and measuring creativity"; Alane Starko, *Creativity in the classroom*; Phillip McIntyre, *Creativity and cultural production*; and Vlad Petre Glăveanu, "Paradigms in the study of creativity."

28. Systemic approaches might include those of Mihaly Csikszentmihalyi, "Society, culture and person," and Howard Gruber, "The Evolving Systems approach."

29. Donald Treffinger, "Creative problem solving," 302.

30. See Robert Weisberg, *Creativity*, and Peter Webster, *Creative thinking in music*.

31. The first construct in each pairing is usually attributed to Howard Gardner, "Seven creators of the modern era"; the second to Margaret Boden, *The creative mind*.

32. See Silvano Arieti (1976) and Mihaly Csikszentmihalyi (1988) for more in this regard.

33. Pamela Burnard, *Musical creativities*, 14.

34. See, for example, the work of Charles Limb, "Your brain on improvisation."

35. This point is emphasized, for example, in Mihaly Csikszentmihalyi, "Implications of a system perspective."

36. McIntyre's definition appears in Janet Fulton and Elizabeth Paton, "The systems model," 41. I make appreciative use of McIntyre's definition to underpin the action theory approach developed in chapter 1 and throughout this volume.

37. See Vlad Petre Glăveanu, *Distributed creativity*, 68. Glăveanu draws on Jaan Valsiner for his definitions of "microgenesis" (the emergence of action within here-and-now contexts) and ontogenesis (the development of the individual across the lifespan). On the latter level, the drummers following Max Roach's useful (and creative) performances were simultaneously relieved of onerous performance demands and offered a new framework within which to perform appropriately. See Jaan Valsiner, *Culture and the development of children's action*.

38. Johannella Tafuri, "Processes and teaching strategies," 135.

39. See Eric Clarke, "Creativity in performance," 17–21.

40. John Hope Mason, *The value of creativity*, 233.

41. Philip Auslander collates some of the thinking of those who dismiss performance and the performer as irrelevant: Philip Auslander, "Performance analysis and popular music," 2–7.

42. Farmer is quoted in Paul Berliner, *Thinking in jazz*, 285.

43. Stephen Cottrell, *Professional music-making*, 111–16. Cottrell's assertions accord with my own observation.

44. This observation has been borrowed from Philip Tagg, *Music's meanings*.

45. A close identification of the classical composer with his or her composition renders performance as something that may happen to the composer, who may tell you she or he "has been performed" at various festivals, for example. Such an unusual ontology is generally alien to the popular songwriter.

46. Schoenberg is cited in Nicholas Cook, "Music as performance," 204; Pierre Boulez in Simon Frith, "Creativity as a social fact," 67. See also Bruce Ellis Benson, *The improvisation of musical dialogue*, 12–14.

47. Paul Berliner notes that not all jazz musicians welcome a fancy beat from the drummer. Paul Berliner, *Thinking in jazz*, 410.

48. Theodore Gracyk, *Rhythm and noise*, 137.

49. See Gerhard Lock, "Musical creativity in the mirror of Glăveanu's five principles of cultural psychology," 124. The topic is addressed in Lock's discussion of "non-creational" processes. He takes such processes to mean "purely imitating, reproducing, acting without individual will and genuine ideas, being part of a system without having the possibility of interfering, quoting purely secondary sources, etc., because mechanically produced art and science are considered to be non-organic and without value."

50. See Christopher Small, *Musicking*.

51. Pamela Burnard, *Musical creativities*, 124.

52. Ibid.

53. Ibid., 142. See also Nicolas Cook, "Beyond creativity?," and Christopher Small, *Musicking*, 10–11.

54. Folkestad makes this point in Victoria Armstrong, *Technology and the gendering of music education*, 9.

55. Carl Seashore, *Psychology of music*.

56. This history has been drawn out effectively by Matthew Brennan in "'Instruments of a lower order.'"

57. See Alf Gabrielsson, "Music performance research at the millennium," for a thorough review.

58. In this regard, see the valuable work of Raymond MacDonald and Graeme Wilson, "Constructions of jazz."

59. See, for example, the view of Patrice Pavis, cited in Philip Auslander, "Performance analysis and popular music," 5.

60. This list of qualities approximates Simon Zagorski-Thomas's notion of "linear performance," by which he means "performing a recorded work from start to finish." Writing in 2010, he asserts that this action "remains central to the notion of professional competence amongst both musicians and producers." In the few short years between then and now (2017) the veracity of that assertion has become highly questionable. Simon Zagorski-Thomas, "Real and unreal performances," 207.

61. In positive psychology, "Flow" or "being in the zone" is the mental state of operation in which a person performing an activity is fully immersed in a feeling of energized focus and full involvement in the process of the activity. The concept was named by psychologist Mihaly Csikszentmihalyi, and is widely referenced across a variety of fields including music. The concept embodies qualities of being "in the moment" and of being in a "slightly altered state," all sensations frequently evoked by the drummers here. It gathers and frames these ideas such as to illuminate the experience of individual creative performance. Flow theory is capitalized here and throughout to distinguish it from other uses of the term "flow." See Mihaly Csikszentmihalyi, *Flow: The psychology of optimal experience*.

62. See Ingrid Monson, *Saying something*, 27, for further discussion of this idea.

Chapter 1

1. See, respectively, Henri Poincaré, "Mathematical creation," and Herman von Helmholtz and Russell Kahl, *Selected writings*. Graham Wallas suggested that the cre-

ative process had four distinct stages—preparation, incubation, illumination, and verification. See Wallas, *The art of thought.*

2. See, for example, Claude Shannon and Warren Weaver, *The mathematical theory of communication.*

3. David Hargreaves et al., "How do people communicate using music?" 7–17.

4. Gerhard Fischer et al., cited in Vlad Petre Glăveanu, *Principles for a cultural psychology*, 156.

5. See Mihaly Csikszentmihalyi, "Society, culture and person"; Howard Gruber, "The Evolving Systems approach to creativity"; and Pamela Burnard, *Musical creativities*. Gerhard Fischer et al., for example, attempt to go beyond binary choices: their work is cited in Vlad Petre Glăveanu, "Principles for a cultural psychological of creativity," 155–56.

6. Vlad Petre Glăveanu, *Distributed creativity*, 8.

7. Ibid., 9, emphasis added. The Five A's framework is depicted on page 27.

8. Ibid., 27.

9. The argument that much of contemporary performance practice, rooted in the 19th century cult of the virtuoso, has overemphasized technical display is particularly apposite within a contemporary drum culture that places excessively high value on overt technical dexterity.

10. Vlad Petre Glăveanu, *Distributed creativity*, 76.

11. Ibid., 37.

12. Pamela Burnard, *Musical creativities*, 38.

13. John Hope Mason, *The value of creativity*, 225. I draw further on Hope Mason's insights as the narrative develops.

14. In particular, I borrow from Glăveanu's 2013 Action Theory of Creativity. See Vlad Petre Glăveanu et al., "Creativity as action."

15. Keith Sawyer, "The interdisciplinary study of creativity in performance," 15.

16. John Dewey, *Art as experience.*

17. Keith Negus and Michael Pickering, *Creativity, communication, and cultural value*, vii.

18. John Dewey, *Art as experience*, 1.

19. Ibid., 89.

20. Ibid., 86.

21. Ibid., 112.

22. Ibid., 113. Emphasis added.

23. Ibid., 245–46.

24. These views were and are propagated by, among others, Lev Vygotsky, *Thought and language*; Ernst Boesch, "Cultural psychology in action-cultural perspective"; Bonnie Nardi, "Studying context"; and Michael Cole, *Cultural psychology.*

25. Bonnie Nardi, *Studying context*, 40.

26. For an elaboration of the nuanced debate within cultural psychology as to which is the most effective route to a successful integration of culture into psychology, see Lutz Eckensberger, "Activity or action."

27. Michael Szekely, "Gesture, pulsion, grain," paragraph 4.

28. The Porter and Davies BC2 bass drum monitor system is one example of such a reinforcement system.

29. Silvano Arieti, *Creativity*, 4. See also James Wertsch, *Mind as action*, for further discussion of cultural psychology's interpretation of the uses of cultural artifacts.

30. There may be an involuntary component to this. Miles Davis allegedly said "I have to change; it's like a curse." Aaron Rogers, "Miles Davis," 1.

31. Lutz Eckensberger, "From cross-cultural psychology to cultural psychology," 43.

32. Ralph Rosnow and Marianthi Georgoudi, cited in Lutz Eckensberger, "From cross-cultural psychology to cultural psychology," 43.

33. Ernst Boesch, "Symbolic action theory."

34. Jean Lave cited in Bonnie Nardi, "Studying context," 36.

35. Christopher Small, *Musicking*, 109.

36. Bonnie Nardi, "Studying context," 36.

37. John Hope Mason, *The value of creativity*, 7.

38. See, for example, Christopher Small, *Musicking*; Irène Deliège and Marc Richelle, "Prelude"; or Lori Custodero, "The call to create."

39. Irène Deliège and Marc Richelle, "Prelude," 2. Original emphasis.

40. Vlad Petre Glăveanu et al., "Creativity as action," 2–3.

41. Ibid., 1.

42. In this regard, see Keith Sawyer, *Group creativity*.

43. Vlad Petre Glăveanu, "Principles for a cultural psychology of creativity."

44. Ibid., 156.

45. John Dewey, *Art as experience*, 108.

46. Donald Polkinghorne, *Narrative knowing*, 1.

47. Jonathan Smith et al., *Interpretative phenomenological analysis*, 16.

48. Not all cultural psychology theorists agree on appropriate unit(s) of analysis in the discipline, but the history of this disagreement is not germane to the introduction of the IMCM. Andrés Santamaría et al. offer a detailed discussion of the issues surrounding the unit of analysis in cultural psychology. I adopt the position stated succinctly by them, and situate the notion of "mediated action" as the unit of analysis at the heart of the model. Santamaría et al., "Thinking as action," 86–89.

49. See Howard Becker, *Outsiders*.

50. Silvano Arieti, *Creativity*, 306–9.

51. See Wilfred Drath and Charles Palus, *Making common sense*.

Chapter 2

1. Gerhard Lock, "Musical creativity in the mirror of Glăveanu's five principles of cultural psychology," 124.

2. Use of the notion of situation within the drum community chimes well with its use within the psychology community. Warning us against a reductive approach in the psychological treatment of experience, Dewey states that "What is designated by the word 'situation' is *not* a single object or even a set of objects and events. For we never experience nor form judgments about objects and events in isolation, but only in connection with a contextual whole." Dewey cited in Michael Cole, *Cultural psychology*, 132, original italics.

3. Keith Negus and Michael Pickering, *Creativity, communication, and cultural value*, 19.

4. Philip Tagg, *Music's meanings*.

5. Personal correspondence, October 8, 2013.

6. These general remarks on creativity in the recording studio are based upon no more than my experiential evidence in the field. It is conventionally one of the producer's tasks to weigh the time and cost involved in creative trial and error, or experiment, against possible outcomes.

7. Roach's solution to performance problems at extremely fast tempi has been well documented. Jo Jones situated his own creativity in being constrained by limited equipment when he was traveling with a carnival: "With this limited amount and kind of equipment I had to do something." Jones is quoted in Paul Berliner, *Thinking in jazz*, 818, n2.

8. Monson also situates this kind of subtlety within bass playing. See Ingrid Monson, *Saying something*, 9.

9. Blair Sinta, "Capturing the 4th Street feeling," 72. The album was recorded at the House of Blues studio in Los Angeles. The track may be heard at https://www.youtube.com/watch?v=G8dAYNjb-_Q

10. This comment refers to an electronic drum sound from the Roland Corporation's TR-808 Drum Machine. Introduced in 1980, it had already been heard on several international hits by the time Phil Collins used it in his solo work between the mid-'80s and early '90s. Many of his ballads, including hits like "One More Night," "Do You Remember," and "Can't Turn Back the Years" used the 808 sound. http://www.vintagesynth.com/roland/808.php (accessed November 9, 2013).

11. "Riding" is the drummer's term for the playing of a repeated pattern, usually one-handed, on the hi-hat or cymbal, which carries the forward momentum of the rhythm.

12. See Andy Bennett, "Subcultures or neo-tribes?," for a sociological perspective on musical taste groups.

13. For example, Treffinger has brought forward a creative problem solving framework that understands problems as "opportunities and challenges for successful change and constructive action" in which a problem might be defined as "any important, open-ended, and ambiguous situation for which one wants and need new options and a plan for carrying a solution successfully." Donald Treffinger, "Creative problem solving," 303–4.

14. Pamela Burnard, *Musical creativities*, 135. Burnard's understanding accords with the recent thinking of other music educationalists who find individual creativity situated "within social communities where members practice problem finding, problem solving, and productive evaluation." See Margaret Barrett and Joyce Gromko, "Provoking the muse," 227.

15. See Mark Gridley, "Clarifying labels," for more in this area.

16. Pamela Burnard, *Musical creativities*, 81–84.

17. An entirely subjective list of drummers who gravitate primarily to the compositional might include Stewart Copeland, Joe Morello, Jeff "Tain" Watts, Gavin Harrison, Tyshawn Sorey, David Garibaldi, Sonny Murray, Terry Bozzio, pushers of technical boundaries such as Thomas Lang and Virgil Donati, and most of the interviewees.

18. Evelyn Glennie, "How to truly listen."

19. For Boulez's views, see the discussion in the introduction to this volume.

20. Jonathan Impett, "Making a mark," 403.

21. Margaret Boden, "What is creativity?"

22. See Simon Frith, "Creativity as a social fact," for a fuller discussion on monetizing and rights ownership in popular music.

23. For further discussion of the fiscal climate that favored the birth of bebop, see Scott DeVeaux, *The birth of bebop*, 285–87.

24. As outlined in Orrin Keepnews, "Max Roach, a founder of modern jazz."

25. See, for example, Ingrid Monson, *Saying something*, or Paul Berliner, *Thinking in jazz*, for further discussion of this aspect of intra-performer communication.

26. Roach, cited in Rick Mattingly, "Max Roach." The architecture is visually evident in transcriptions of Roach's work. For an example, see Chris Munson, "Max Roach." Some of the drummer's favored techniques within the AABA 32-bar song form, such as the stretching, compressing, and fragmentation of rhythmic motifs and their redeployment around multiple combinations of drums and cymbals may be heard on Max Roach's solo piece, "Big Sid."

27. The drummer was a 1988 MacArthur Foundation "genius grant" award winner in the United States, and named Commander of the Order of Arts and Letters in France.

28. Csikszentmihalyi found it useful to invoke the work of Richard Dawkins: "to think about creativity as involving a change in memes—the units of imitation that Dawkins (1976) suggested were the building blocks of culture." Mihaly Csikszentmihalyi, "Implications of a systems perspective for the study of creativity," 316. In his book *The selfish gene*, Dawkins famously interpreted the "domain" as a system of related memes that changes over time. On this account, Roach's domain-changing creativity might be interpreted as memetic—that is, as structured information embodied in a meme, the valuable and memorable "unit of imitation" transmitted from one generation to the next.

29. Shelly Manne cited in Ira Gitler, *Swing to bop*, 51.

30. See Vlad Petre Glăveanu "Distributed creativity."

Chapter 3

1. See Wilfred Drath and Charles Palus, *Making common sense*.

2. The italicized comments in parentheses throughout the interview extracts are those given by the author during the conversation.

3. The subtlety of the distinction between performing "for" or "with" a leader is brought to the fore in Wackerman's case. His gigs with James Taylor and Frank Zappa represent two extremes of functional performance. The former carries an implicit, unstated requirement for simplicity and a low density of rhythmic information, and comes with minimal direction. The latter carries explicit instructions embodied in written music requiring both complexity and a very high density of rhythmic information. Chad's anecdote about the necessity to lead the conductor would further indicate that he performs "for" rather than "with" Frank Zappa, and "with" rather than "for" James Taylor.

4. Etienne Wenger, *Communities of practice*, 105.

5. Ibid., 109.

6. Throughout the interview extracts, bracketed ellipses (i.e., "[...]"), indicate that a portion of the conversation has been removed.

7. This thread emerges in, for example, Pamela Burnard's *Musical creativities* and Margaret Barrett's *A cultural psychology of music education*.

8. Drummer Phil Jones offers the following description of the enabling quality in some functional practice: "They were looking for a sort of 'groove doctor' to assist in

keeping everyone happy. It wasn't my job to make it happen, but more to help smooth things out between different people." Phil Jones, cited in Kelly King, "Phil Jones," 48.

9. John Dewey, *Art as experience*, 170.

10. From Csikszentmihalyi's perspective, the origin of well-being is to be found in particular forms of not necessarily consistent interaction, and therein lays the motivation for studying Flow. See François Pachet, "Creativity studies and musical interaction," 351.

11. John Dewey, *Art as experience*, 170.

12. Cecilia Hultberg points to Vygotsky's view that "interaction between cultural participants working at different levels of expertise activates learners' 'zones of proximal development' (ZPD). When learners work with others more expert in their ZPD they tend to perform at higher levels than they would have managed on their own." See Cecilia Hultberg, "Making music or playing instruments," 118.

13. See Ingrid Monson, *Saying something*, 2.

14. See, for example, Mary-Anne Mace, cited in Matthew Peacock, "Constructing creativity," 248.

15. Ericsson and his colleagues define this term as "effortful activity designed to optimize improvement." See K. Anders Ericsson et al., "The role of deliberate practice," 363.

16. According to Boden, a valuable idea is P-creative if the person in whose mind it arises could not have had it before. See Margaret Boden, "What is creativity?" 76.

17. Roger Chaffin et al., "Spontaneity and creativity in highly practised performance," 201.

18. Vlad Petre Glăveanu, "Paradigms in the study of creativity," 10.

19. Ibid., 8–12. Such a brief summation inevitably omits the nuance necessary to explain the accounts given us by Michael Pickering, Donald Winnicott, Howard Gruber, and Keith Negus. Glăveanu offers a fuller explanation of the thinking of these individuals in this area. See Vlad Petre Glăveanu, "Paradigms in the study of creativity."

20. This useful term collapses and encompasses the outdated distinction between the functions of composer and performer. It appears to be gaining currency in the literature.

21. Sarah Thornton cited in Justin Williams, *Rhymin' and stealin'*, 27–28.

22. All music creation seems to me to be on the increase, with the performance element arguably increasing with less rapidity than other dimensions of creation. There is much anecdotal evidence, however, to support Sarah Thornton's view that the *performed* component in contemporary recording is in decline in real terms. For her, performance has declined "as both the dominant medium of music and the prototype for recording" (Thornton, cited in Justin Williams, *Rhymin' and stealin'*, 27–28). The discrepancy might be explained in part if we distinguish between, on the one hand, the decline of the big budget, high performance content, commercial recording sessions of the predigital era, and, on the other, the rise of the low budget, low performance content, typically self-financed home recording session of the subsequent postdigital era. Both views are dependent on highly nuanced interpretations of performance and must remain a matter of speculation; both have profound implications for the drummer.

23. Alexandra Lamont, "Emotion, engagement and meaning," 589.

24. See Amy Blier-Carruthers, *The performer's place*, for an account of performance anxiety within classical music.

25. Richard Florida, cited in Margaret Barrett, "Troubling the creative imaginary," 212.

26. See Raymond Nickerson, "Enhancing creativity," 401–2, for a review of the debate so far. Personal experience suggests that the expensive process of brainstorming in music rehearsals has mixed results, an approach that has anyway fallen into disuse under financial constraints. An improved strategy built around "light-touch" guidance, scarcely more than the provision of a suitable performance space and a blueprint for action, may yield more consistently creative results.

27. See, for example, Teresa Amabile, *Creativity and innovation in organizations*, or Frank Barrett, "Coda—creativity in jazz and organizations."

28. David Bastien and Todd Hostager, "Jazz as a process of organizational innovation."

29. Pamela Burnard, *Musical creativities in practice*, 44.

Chapter 4

1. John Dewey, *Art as experience*, 99.

2. See Allan Moore, *Song means*, 51–52, for a longer engagement with this standard beat that Moore sees as part of the "almost innate vocabulary" of most contemporary musicians. Others have formulated views on this basic beat. Williams, for example, defines it as a "structural layer or core layers of the musical complement that change little for a significant duration of the song." He also references the work of, in particular, Robert Fink and Adam Krims in this area. See Justin Williams, *Rhymin' and stealin'*, 174, n7.

3. Carol Dweck identifies two loci of control: internal and external. Broadly, those with an internal locus tend to display "mastery oriented" behavior such as persistence in overcoming setbacks. Those with an external locus tend to feel that circumstances are beyond their control. See Carol Dweck, *Self-theories*.

4. Igor Stravinsky allegedly wanted only execution, not interpretation, from the performer. Nicholas Cook, "Music as performance," 204.

5. Keith Negus and Michael Pickering, *Creativity, communication, and cultural value*, 19.

6. This phenomenon is described in, for example, Alf Gabrielsson, *Strong experiences with music*, or Elina Hytönen-Ng, *Experiencing Flow*.

7. Jenny Boyd, *Musicians in tune*, 172.

8. Jeff Pressing is quoted in Paul Berliner, *Thinking in jazz*, 798, n39.

9. Igor Stravinsky and Robert Craft, *Expositions and developments*, 147–48.

10. The composer Donnacha Dennehy, for example, finds inexplicability rather than explicitness to be an essential attribute of the creative musical act. Dennehy is cited in Pamela Burnard, *Musical creativities in practice*, 132. See also Alfonso Montuori, cited in Vlad Petre Glăveanu, "Habitual creativity," 35.

11. This has been noted by Keith Simonton, "Creativity as a constrained stochastic process."

12. The phrase "oscilloscopic prurience" is not mine, and I regret I am unable to identify its author. I trust she or he will forgive my borrowing; it neatly connotes an evangelical or Puritan strain among early adopters of computer-based recording technology that, while it may now have begun to dissipate, was very much present in the last two decades of the last century and the first of this.

13. Allan Moore, *Song means*.

14. There are parallels here with theater actors who perform the same play every night for extended periods. Audience expectations of a well-honed optimal reading that the individual actor (and collectively, the cast) replicates on each subsequent performance may clash with the actor's desire to vary dimensions of the performance (such as line delivery) to try to find new wrinkles to the character.

15. This strategy has echoes of Sudnow's phenomenological account of learning how to play jazz piano. See David Sudnow, *Ways of the hand*.

16. The advent of electronic drums in live performance is discussed in some depth in Bill Bruford, *The autobiography*, 77–83.

17. Much of the data on performance contexts chimes with Teresa Amabile's intrinsic motivation principle (Amabile 1996), which suggests that the intrinsic motivation involved in self-directed or shared performance might be seen as conducive to creativity. Conversely, the controlling extrinsic motivation associated with externally directed functional performance may be seen as detrimental to creativity. The enabling extrinsic motivation embedded within the close relationship of a benevolent leader who "allows me to be me" may be seen as potentially conducive, particularly if initial levels of intrinsic motivation are high. See Amabile in Mary Ann Collins and Teresa Amabile, "Motivation and creativity."

18. Matthew Peacock, "Constructing creativity," 180.

19. For instance, the Geneplore model brought forward by Thomas Ward et al. examines this approach in greater depth. See Thomas Ward et al., "Creative cognition," 191.

20. Johannella Tafuri, "Processes and teaching strategies," 151.

21. Giovanni De Poli, "Methodologies for expressive modelling," 1.

22. Creativity in music performance is frequently linked to expression, a musical activity interpreted by Palmer as an aggregate of "large and small variations in timing, intensity, or dynamics, timbre, and pitch that form the microstructure of a performance and differentiate it from another performance of the same music." Musicians have been found to be able to replicate their expressive patterns of timing and dynamics for a given musical piece with high precision, but measurements of performance expression sometimes differ across studies, making comparisons difficult. See Caroline Palmer, "Music performance," 118, and Patrik Juslin, *From mimesis to catharsis*, 87.

23. Erik Lindström et al. cited in Patrik Juslin, *Emotion in music performance*, 378.

24. With regard to pulse and meter, see Jonathan Pieslak, "Re-casting metal," or Robin Attas, "Meter as process"; for more on metric dissonance, see Matthew Butterfield, "Variant timekeeping patterns," or Nicole Biamonte, "Formal functions of metrical dissonance." I have borrowed from Anne Danielsen's *Musical rhythm*, Milton Mermikides's "Changes over time," and Mark Doffman's "Feeling the groove," all in the areas of swing, beat, and groove. I am appreciatively indebted to these authors.

25. Patrik Juslin, *From mimesis to catharsis*, 88.

26. Gareth Dylan Smith, *I drum, therefore I am*, 112.

27. Valerie Wilmer, cited in Gareth Dylan Smith, *I drum, therefore I am*, 88.

28. Alf Gabrielsson, "The relationship between musical structure and perceived expression," 143.

29. Trumpeter Bobby Shew, who performed in Rich's band, described the leader's drumming in these terms: "He had a habit of rushing the beat, and he'd change the tempo." See Marc Myers, "Bobby Shew on Buddy Rich."

30. Blair Sinta, "Capturing the 4th Street feeling," 72. The term "negotiated time" in-

dicates any performance made without recourse to the clock-time generated from a computer, or any otherwise automated click track. The tempo is "negotiated" live between the performers with important implications for swing, groove, and placement of the beat.

31. Gareth Dylan Smith, "I drum, therefore I am?" 148.

32. Bill Bruford, *The autobiography*. Jazz drummer Warren "Baby" Dodds, an icon of the 1930s swing era, also saw the drummer as "the conductor in the band." Valerie Wilmer, cited in Gareth Dylan Smith, *I drum, therefore I am?* 149.

33. For a full examination of the microstructure of musical timing, see Milton Mermikides, "Changes over time."

34. One author who has shed light in this area is Anne Danielsen. See her book *Musical rhythm*.

35. Further examples of the convenience to the producer or recording engineer of having a consistent tempo are provided by Simon Zagorski-Thomas, "Real and unreal performances," 206.

36. I have noted this previously in *Bill Bruford: The autobiography*, 308.

37. Approaching this topic from his background in record production, Zagorski-Thomas uses the word "consistency" frequently. Representing the dominant discourse, he asserts that dynamic and timbral consistency are necessary to maintain the intensity of emotion and excitement associated with rock music, and that "dynamic compression is the principal technique used in record production" to achieve it. He defines compression as "an electronically controlled process whereby the dynamic range of a performance is reduced": its use, perhaps intentionally so, serves to limit and constrain the drummer's self-expression. See Simon Zagorski-Thomas, "Real and unreal performances," 204.

38. Anne Danielsen, *Musical rhythm*.

39. As observed by Simon Zagorski-Thomas in "Real and unreal performances," 206.

40. An examination of the various points of intersection between attitudes to "consistency," "accuracy," and "perfection" in drum performance are unfortunately beyond the scope of the present discussion. Zagorski-Thomas, however, accurately refers to consistency as a "cult" that has developed since the 1980s. Simon Zagorski-Thomas, "Real and unreal performances," 209.

41. For a longer engagement with musical identity, see Raymond MacDonald et al., "Musical identities," and with specific regard to drummers, Gareth Dylan Smith, *I drum, therefore I am*.

42. As documented by Sini Wirtanen and Karen Littleton, "Collaboration, conflict and the musical identity work of solo piano students." I tend to interpret musical identities as plural, relational, ongoing, and dynamic. This accords with my inability to find a single musical "home" (identity) and thus my creation of several homes (identities) along the highway between sublimation and projection in functional and compositional practice. For more, see *Bill Bruford: The autobiography*.

43. See Björn Merker, "Layered constraints," 37, n1.

44. See Milton Mermikides, "Changes over time," 134, for an analysis of the time-feel negotiation in a Michael Jackson rehearsal. This offers an excellent "real world" example of the level of precision involved when this is enacted in performance.

45. Philip Tagg, *Music's meanings*, 296.

46. Regarding embodiment and shared processes, see Mark Doffman, "Feeling the groove." With regard to shared knowledge, see Lawrence Zbikowski, "Modelling the

groove." For more on groove patterns, see Stan Hawkins, "Feel the beat come down." Jones's phrase is to be found in LeRoi Jones, "The changing same."

47. Mark Doffman, "Feeling the groove."

48. Ingrid Monson, *Saying something*, 68.

49. Charles Keil, "Participatory discrepancies." Better scholars than I will have already noted two parallel tendencies within Western music cultures. The one seeks to remove such participatory discrepancies on the grounds that they inhibit or prevent the functionality and enjoyment of the music. The other seeks to remove what we may call, in this context, auditory discrepancies. These comprise "extraneous" extramusical sounds, such as the buzzing and rattling of the beads around an m'bira, or the "excessive" harmonics flying from a progressive rock drummer's snare drum. In many non-Western music cultures, such auditory and participatory discrepancies tend to be valorized as part of the aural experience and seen as the seat of the music's meaningfulness.

50. Harris Berger, *Stance*, xiii.

51. Robin Attas, "Meter as process," 39.

52. Proponents of this idea might include Mark Katz in *Groove music* or Joseph Schloss in *Making beats*.

53. See Anne Danielsen, *Musical rhythm*, for further discussion in this area.

54. Jon Frederickson, "Technology and music performance," 212.

55. James Baldwin cited in Vlad Petre Glăveanu, "Habitual creativity," 14.

56. The organization Turn Me Up! is a nonprofit music industry organization working with a group of artists and recording professionals devoted to bringing dynamic range back to popular music. See Paul Lamere, "The loudness war analyzed," or Adam Sherwin, "Why music really is getting louder." For more on repetition, see Yizhao Ni et al, "Hit song science once again a science?"

57. Simon Zagorski-Thomas, "Real and unreal performances."

58. See Ronald Wilson, "Melodic drum set compositions," for discussion and analysis in this area.

59. These are the major seventh, the dominant seventh, the minor seventh, the half-diminished seventh, and the fully diminished seventh.

Chapter 5

1. Vlad Petre Glăveanu, *Distributed creativity*, 76.

2. This point has been made elsewhere by, most notably, Aaron Williamon et al., "Creativity, originality, and value in music performance."

3. See John Covach, "Progressive rock, "Close to the Edge" and the boundaries of style," 11-14, for a discussion of the use of this device in Yes, and Jonathan Pieslak, "Recasting metal," for its use in Meshuggah.

4. In this respect, Doffman found that "the unbridled pursuit of virtuosity tends to be frowned upon within both jazz and rock unless married to an aesthetic that values a performed integrity." See Mark Doffman, "Feeling the groove," 154. Williamon et al. take a similar view in Aaron Williamon et al., "Creativity, originality, and value in music performance," 161.

5. Such as those performances, for example, analyzed in Roger Chaffin et al., "Spontaneity and creativity in highly practised performance."

6. Simon Zagorski-Thomas, "Real and unreal performances," 206–10.

7. Roger Chaffin et al., "Spontaneity and creativity in highly practiced performance," 200.

8. Thomas Ward et al., "Creative cognition," 191.

9. Todd Lubart, "Creativity across cultures," 339.

10. A specimen of one of Rich's legendary tirades is available at https://www.youtube.com/watch?v=t8-u0TD4fMQ

11. Matthew Peacock's 2008 research on the creative practice of scientists and writers has identified a similar approach to the writing of fiction. It might be summarized as "write what you would want to read rather than what you think other people will want to buy." Matthew Peacock, 2015, private correspondence.

12. Tony Allen and Michael Veal, *Tony Allen*, 17.

13. Irène Deliège and Marc Richelle, "Prelude," 2.

14. Howard Gruber and Doris Wallace, "The case study method and Evolving Systems approach," 109.

15. Raymond MacDonald et al., "Improvisation as a creative process," 246.

16. T. S. Eliot, Preface to *Transit of Venus*.

17. See, for example, Sami Abuhamdeh and Mihaly Csikszentmihalyi, "The artistic personality," in this regard.

18. As noted, creativity in this sphere is generally located in the recombination of existing elements rather than in the pursuit of newness for its own sake. One might surmise, with Cottrell, that there are strongly pragmatic reasons for this; employment opportunities within popular music as much as classical music tend to encourage the pursuit of "better" while discouraging the pursuit of "different." See Stephen Cottrell, *Professional music-making*, 58–59, for more on employment opportunities.

19. This has been a common enough pathway to individuation throughout popular music practice; one that was followed, for example, by Elvis Presley when he yelled "I don't sound like nobody" at an early recording session. The phrase is taken as the title of Albin Zak's account of the transformation of American popular music in the 1950s. Albin Zak, *I don't sound like nobody*.

Chapter 6

1. See Mihaly Csikszentmihalyi, *Flow: The psychology of optimal experience*.

2. Brian Wilshere, "The drummer as composer," 21.

3. John Dewey, *Art as experience*, 28.

4. Margaret Barrett, "Musical communication and children's communities of musical practice."

5. Ibid., 263.

6. Margaret Barrett, *A cultural psychology of music education*.

7. Etienne Wenger, *Communities of practice*, 80.

8. David Hiles, "Cultural psychology and the centre-ground of psychology."

9. Donald Polkinghorne, *Narrative knowing*, 7.

10. Michael Cole, *Cultural psychology*, 109.

11. Donald Polkinghorne, *Narrative knowing*.

12. Jeff Pressing, "Psychological constraints on improvisational expertise," 36.

13. Bill Bruford, *The autobiography*, 141.

14. This point has been made by Michael Crotty in *The foundations of social research*, 64.

15. Carl Ratner, "Three approaches to cultural psychology," 7.

16. Michael Cole, *Cultural psychology*, 328.

17. Ibid., xiv.

18. Lutz Eckensberger, "From cross-cultural psychology to cultural psychology," 37.

19. Michael Cole, *Cultural psychology*, 8.

20. Ibid.

21. The embattled drum hero tends to be passed on by cultural elders and accepted unquestioningly by acolytes. Gene Krupa and Buddy Rich were two of the most commonly cited drumming influences among Smith's respondents, a fact that Smith connects to the pervasive influence of the two drummers' 1952 recording of a "drum battle." See Gareth Dylan Smith, *I drum therefore I am?*, 204.

22. Jeff Pressing, "Psychological constraints on improvisational expertise," 62.

23. The term is used as the title for drummer Ginger Baker's 2010 autobiography, *Hellraiser*.

24. Effectively portrayed by (1) a person in a gorilla suit playing a drum kit for a 2007 Cadbury Schweppes TV ad, and by (2) the house drummer called "Animal" on the popular TV show *The Muppets*.

25. Simon Frith identifies a process of what he calls "double enactment" whereby popular musicians "enact both a star personality (their image) and a song personality, the role that each lyric requires, and the pop star's art is to keep both acts in play at once." Although more diffuse among instrumentalists than singers, it is not too fanciful to suggest that the drumming in this instance embodied exactly the sort of double enactment that Frith identifies. Frith is cited in Philip Auslander, "Performance analysis," 6.

26. Silvano Arieti, *Creativity*, 308.

27. This understanding follows Monson's approach to ideology: Ingrid Monson, *Saying something*, 120–21.

28. The term, synonymous with "drummer," was coined by drummer Stewart Copeland in the mid-1980s for an album, film, and DVD of that name.

29. On Hill's account, different cultures have different beliefs concerning which types of people have the ability to be musically creative. See Juniper Hill, "Imagining creativity."

30. See Ted Gioia, "Jazz and the primitivist myth," for further discussion in this area.

31. Simon Frith, *Performing rites*, 27–35. Both drumming and the popular music that embodies it are generally seen as fun. We are wired to respond to sound and particularly rhythmic sound. See also Donald Hodges, "Bodily responses to music," 126.

32. Simon Frith, *Performing rites*, 125.

33. Peter Stadlen, "The aesthetics of popular music," 353. Stadlen is quoted in Simon Frith, *Performing rites*, 125.

34. I am indebted to Matthew Brennan for this insight. Krehbiel is cited in Brennan's "'Instruments of a lower order.'"

35. Ted Gioia, "Jazz and the primitivist myth."

36. This argument has been promoted most notably by Simon Frith in *Performing rites*, 127.

37. Such an approach has been identified within an "occupational culture" by sociologist Howard Becker in his book *Outsiders*.

38. Copeland is quoted in Phil Sutcliffe, "The Police"; italics added. Fleetwood is cited in Johnny Black, "Mick Fleetwood interview." For more in this area, see also Cohen's study of Liverpool bands: Sara Cohen, *Rock culture in Liverpool*.

39. Patrick Burke, "Clamor of the Godz," 38.

40. Christopher Small, *Musicking*, 121.

41. Roger Hargreaves, *Mr. Noisy*.

42. Something of an agreement emerged from the interviewees in two respects. First, influential others (teachers, parents, friends) and even some participants considered an unpitched musical instrument insufficient or incomplete in some way. Second, it was almost uniformly suggested to interviewees during their formative years that they should play a second instrument to compensate for this perceived insufficiency.

43. Sandra Jovchelovitch, *Knowledge in context*, 71.

44. See, for example, Margaret Barrett, "Musical communication and children's communities of musical practice," or *A cultural psychology of music education* by the same author.

45. Etienne Wenger, *Communities of practice*, 63.

46. See Wilfred Drath and Charles Palus, *Making common sense*.

47. See Stephen Cottrell, *Professional music-making*, for more on this topic.

48. For example, see Raymond MacDonald and Graeme Wilson, "Musical identities of professional jazz musicians," and "Constructions of jazz," by the same authors.

49. This assertion borrows from Etienne Wenger's *Communities of practice*.

50. See Edward Lazear, "Culture and language," for a deeper engagement with this topic.

51. Etienne Wenger, *Communities of practice*, 70.

52. Sandra Jovchelovitch, *Knowledge in context*.

53. Lori Custodero, "The call to create," 372.

54. Vlad Petre Glăveanu, "Principles for a cultural psychology of creativity," 160.

55. Sara Cohen, *Rock culture in Liverpool*, 225.

56. Wilfred Drath and Charles Palus, *Making common sense*, 13.

57. Ibid., 10.

58. Harris Berger, *Stance*, xiv.

59. This point is noted by Elina Hytönen-Ng, *Experiencing "Flow" in jazz performance*, 51.

60. Anecdotal evidence supports Matt Dean's view that most drummers learn by watching other, more senior members of the community. Matt Dean, *The drum*.

61. Keith Negus and Michael Pickering, *Creativity, communication and cultural value*, 32.

62. Ibid., 22–23.

63. Ibid., 24. Viewed from this position, all effective creativity is ultimately collaborative creativity between, at a minimum, addresser and addressee. See also Matthew Peacock, "Constructing creativity," 252–53.

64. Robert Weisberg speculates that it is only the highest level of instrumentalists, which he defines as "those who have achieved careers as soloists," who may be considered to offer creative performance, because they are capable of "communicating emotion to their listeners." Robert Weisberg, "Creativity and knowledge," 235.

65. See Benjamin Bloom, *Developing talent in young people*, cited in Robert Weisberg, "Creativity and knowledge," 235. Bloom reports how, in the final stage of training, his

small group of high-achieving classical pianists was taught how to develop a personal style of communicating emotion.

66. See Erik Lindström cited in Patrik Juslin, *Emotion in music performance*, 378.

67. See, for example, Patrik Juslin and Erik Lindström, "Musical expression of emotions."

68. A full engagement with the body in performance is beyond the scope of this study, but Davidson offers an overview of important insights in the context of the perception of musical intention and the possibilities for sharing and participation. See Jane Davidson, "Bodily communication in musical performance" and "Movement and collaboration in musical performance."

69. "Two hearts . . ." is borrowed from Lutz Neugebauer and David Aldridge, cited in Gary Ansdell and Mercédès Pavlicevic, "Musical companionship," 199. For "Mutual coordination . . ." see Gary Ansdell and Mercédès Pavlicevic, cited in Dorothy Miell et al., *Musical communication*, 199.

70. See Ricardo Pinheiro, "The creative process in the context of jazz jam sessions," 3, or Fred Seddon, "Empathetic creativity," for discussion on intersubjective engagement.

71. This has been noted by Raymond MacDonald and Graeme Wilson in "Constructions of jazz," 59, and Ricardo Pinheiro in "The creative process in the context of jazz jam sessions."

72. Thornton argues that "liveness," as "a distinct musical value," dominated notions of authenticity in the period of the mid-1950s to the mid-1980s, roughly the period in which our interviewees spent their formative years. We have already noted her view that performance is in decline as both the dominant medium of music and the prototype for recording. The end date is selected presumably in view of the arrival and mass acceptance of the computer as a music tool. See Sarah Thornton, cited in Justin Williams, *Rhymin' and stealin'*, 27–28.

73. Los Angeles–based drummer Aaron Sterling recommends that all drummers learn audio engineering and production skills: "Everyone expects you to have your own studio. Whether drummers like it or not, they need to learn the engineering aspect of it—if they want to survive." Michael Dawson: *Aaron Sterling's sound of sterloid.*

74. Margaret Barrett, *A cultural psychology of music education*, 45.

75. Ibid., 160. Barrett suggests that such a collaborative approach exemplifies the interactive, intersubjective pedagogy advocated by Jerome Bruner in which he suggests "works-in-progress create shared and negotiable ways of thinking in a group."

76. Keith Sawyer, *Group genius*, 125.

77. Eva Vass, "Understanding collaborative creativity," 79–84.

78. In this view, for example, a piece of new music constructed by composers Francis Scott Key and John Stafford Smith (e.g., "The Star-Spangled Banner," c. 1814) might thus be transformed into new knowledge in performance (by the Jimi Hendrix Experience in 1969).

79. Vera John-Steiner, *Creative collaboration.*

80. Ibid., 189–90.

81. The review of literature searches is to be found in Paul Paulus and Bernard Nijstad, "Group creativity." The findings within large groups are attributable sequentially to Joseph McGrath, *Groups*; Irving Janis, *Groupthink*; and Charlan Nemeth and Brendan Nemeth-Brown, "Better than individuals?"

82. Pamela Burnard and Keith Sawyer, for instance, adopt this view. See Keith Sawyer in Pamela Burnard, *Musical creativities*, 137–38.

83. Keith Sawyer, "Group creativity," 153.

84. Ibid., 157–60.

85. Raymond MacDonald et al., "Creativity and flow in musical composition."

86. Keith Sawyer, "The interdisciplinary study of creativity in performance."

87. The story is told of the northern club owner in the United Kingdom who had booked a (singer) Shirley Bassey tribute act. The real Bassey had a hole in her tour schedule on the same night, and on hearing that the club had booked the tribute act, Bassey's agent rang the owner and offered the services of the real thing. There were no other considerations and any price differential was of no consequence. The owner declined the services of the real Bassey, going on to explain, to the agent's astonishment, that the tribute act singer "sounds just like her . . . she's probably better than her." The idea that the tribute act can be "better" than the original is incomprehensible until rephrased in terms that incorporate the idea that in some areas of music performance it is more fun, interesting, or entertaining to watch a good tribute performer trying to emulate the real thing than it is watching the real thing. The anecdote is reported by Dave Spikey in "Eyes down on club land," BBC Radio 4 Extra, at approximately 04′40″.

88. Cottrell's classical musicians considered that "many of the audience cannot distinguish an excellent performance and a poor one." Stephen Cottrell, *Professional musicmaking*, 166.

89. Lisa Gjedde and Bruno Ingemann, *Researching experiences*, 2.

90. Simon Frith, "Creativity as a social fact," 64–65.

91. Frank Zappa cited in Bill Milkowski, "Frank Zappa," 1.

92. John Dewey cited in Jeanne Bamberger, "How the conventions of music notation shape musical perception and performance," 143. James Lull broadens the discussion when he suggests that culture in the widest sense is evidenced by "shared values, assumptions, rules, and social practices that make up and contribute to personal and collective identity and security." Lull is cited in Margaret Barrett, *A cultural psychology of music education*, 42.

93. Donald Polkinghorne, *Narrative knowing*, 6.

94. The advertisement is available at https://www.youtube.com/watch?v=TnzFRV1LwIo

95. Anthony Giddens is cited in Donald Polkinghorne, *Narrative knowing*, 6.

96. Harris Berger, *Stance*, ix.

97. Bill Bruford, *The autobiography*, 316.

98. For more on these communities, see Trevor Harvey, "Virtual garage bands."

99. Thomas Csordas, "Somatic modes of attention."

100. Greg Corness, "The musical experience," 21.

101. Eric Clarke cited in Allan Moore, *Song means*, 248.

102. Michael Szekely, "Gesture, pulsion, grain," section 5, paragraph 5.

103. Roland Barthes cited in Michael Szekely, "Gesture, pulsion, grain," section 5, paragraph 5.

104. Allan Moore, *Song means*, 4.

105. Mark Doffman, "Feeling the groove," 1 and 11.

106. John Sloboda et al., "Choosing to hear music," 431.

107. In popular music culture, this aspect manifests itself in work songs, sea shanties, military music, and so forth. See Martin Clayton, "The social and personal functions of music."

108. See Eviatar Zerubavel, *Social mindscapes*; Shinobu Kitayama, "Culture and basic psychological processes."

109. Lori Custodero, "The call to create," 371.

110. See, respectively, Alf Gabrielsson, *Strong experiences with music*; Keith Sawyer, "Group creativity"; Elina Hytönen-Ng, *Experiencing Flow*.

111. Mihaly Csikszentmihalyi, *Flow*, 217.

112. Ibid.

113. John Dewey cited in Vlad Petre Glăveanu et al., "Creativity as action," 2–3.

114. Elina Hytönen-Ng, *Experiencing Flow*, 155.

115. Becker and Geer, for example, link the sharing of problems to culture. The "organised whole" of the solutions to shared problems is the culture of the group. See Howard Becker and Blanche Geer, "Latent culture," 305.

116. Matt Brennan, 2013, personal correspondence.

117. Regarding "standing apart . . . ," see Ingrid Monson, *Saying something*, 27, or Gareth Dylan Smith, *I drum, therefore I am*. Drummers' lack of recognition has been noted by Tony Allen and Michael Veal, *Tony Allen*, 3.

118. Lawrence Levine, *Highbrow/lowbrow*, 136.

119. Keir Keightley, "Taking popular music (and Tin Pan Alley and jazz) seriously," 91.

120. Quoted in Burt Korall, *Drummin' men*, 97.

121. Quoted in Stanley Crouch, "Max Roach," 106.

122. John Murph, "Joe Chambers."

123. This phrase was used by Milton Mermikides in personal correspondence, 2015.

124. Hollin Jones details some of the ways the sterility of contemporary online collaboration may only now be beginning to lift. See http://www.musictech.net/2015/08/on line-collaboration/ (accessed March 4, 2016).

125. In Aymeric Zils et al., *Automatic extraction of drum tracks from polyphonic music signals*, the authors found homogeneity of tempo and meter in a substantial majority of the titles of a rock music catalog but produced little evidence for why this might be so. Gary Tamlyn, in "The Big Beat," an exhaustive enquiry into the prevalence of the backbeat in early swing, rhythm and blues, and rock and roll, found remarkable stylistic consistency within drumming, but the book tells us little about anything after 1960.

126. See Daniel Levitin et al., "Musical rhythm spectra from Bach to Joplin," and Yizhao Ni et al., "Hit song once again a science?", for further discussion in the area of rhythmic predictability and homogeneity.

127. Joan Serrà et al., "Measuring the evolution of contemporary Western popular music," 5.

128. David Blake, "Timbre as differentiation in Indie music," 1.

129. Recent studies show that supposedly "metronomic" styles like funk actually contain significant and meaningful tempo variations between sections (see Simon Millward, "Feel-good factor"). Milton Mermikides has examined the subtlety of rhythm under the powerful microscope that modern technology affords in "Changes over time."

130. See Allan Moore, *Song means*, 29–44.

131. For example, see Michael Tomasello, "The human adaptation for culture"; or Ralph Holloway, "Culture."

Chapter 7

1. Clifford Geertz cited in Michael Cole, *Cultural psychology*, 122.
2. Vlad Petre Glăveanu, "Principles for a cultural psychology of creativity," 153–54.
3. Teresa Amabile cited in Jonathan Plucker and Joseph Renzulli, "Psychometric approaches," 45. Emphasis added.
4. This echoes the observation made in Bill Bruford, *The autobiography*, 242–43.
5. Private correspondence, June 8, 2016. See Matthew Peacock, "Constructing creativity."
6. See Mary Ann Collins and Teresa Amabile, "Motivation and creativity," 304.
7. Monson cited in Nicholas Cook, "Beyond creativity?" 457.
8. Stephen Cottrell, *Professional music-making*, 113.
9. Allan Moore, *Song means*, 3.
10. The assumption within the culture that any active member will be aware of all and any significant developments that might change the way she or he does things may be unrealistic but retains considerable traction.
11. Glăveanu, for example, identifies mastery as "the uppermost expression of habitual practice, at which action has been so well exercised and internalised that it often becomes associated with advanced forms of creative expression." Vlad Petre Glăveanu, "Habitual creativity," 4.
12. One unattributed anecdote comes from a musician who worked with Jones. The pianist describes playing with the drummer as like "lighting a cigarette in a hurricane."
13. This observation echoes the idea that one of the indicators of a creative piece of work or idea is that one cannot deduce how it came about from what came before it.
14. My guides here were Todd Lubart and Jacques-Henri Guignard. See "The generality-specificity of creativity," 52.
15. Nicholas Cook, "Beyond creativity?," 457.
16. Harrison's approach is elucidated in Gavin Harrison, *Rhythmic illusions*.
17. These two examples are borrowed, with gratitude, from Sheila Henderson, "Inventors," 104.
18. See Pete Lockett, *Indian rhythms for drumset*.
19. Pamela Burnard, *Musical creativities*, 223.

Chapter 8

1. See the Introduction to this volume.
2. Allan Moore, *Song means*, 215.
3. See, for example, Bruno Nettl, *The study of ethnomusicology*, and Eric Clarke, "Creativity in performance."
4. This view is embodied in Brian Eno and Peter Schmidt's "Oblique Strategies." See Charles Amirkhanian, "Interview with Brian Eno."
5. The experience described echoes the Zone of Proximal Development identified by Vygotsky within the educational psychology literature. This seems to be an adult instance. See this volume, chapter 3.
6. See Peggy Phelan, *Unmarked*, 146. Phelan's influential work on the ontology of

performance identified it as that which "cannot be saved, recorded, documented, or otherwise participate in the circulation of representations of representations." Building on this, Will Shüler observes how theater and performance studies scholars encourage us to revisit, revise, and contest how "ephemerality" relates to performance, asking: What remains? What haunts? What lasts? In short, what legacies does performance leave behind?" (personal communication). From Phelan's theoretical orientation, the recording session might thus be viewed as a performance *only part of which* is recorded for circulation.

7. See Keith Sawyer, *Group genius*, for further discussion in this area.

8. Bill Bruford, *The autobiography*, 289.

9. See, for example, Jenny Boyd, *Musicians in tune*, or Elina Hytönen-Ng, *Experiencing "Flow."*

10. See, for example, Keith Sawyer, "Improvisational creativity," 257. Vlad Petre Glăveanu et al.'s "Creativity as action" connects the pragmatism of Dewey to the action-theory of Boesch and Eckensberger within a cultural psychology framework, but it does not address the fluidity of performance in which functionality, usefulness, and validation is construed as being "in the moment."

11. Bill Bruford, *The autobiography*, 151.

12. Jason Toynbee, *Making popular music*, 35.

13. Interestingly, Robert Weisberg notes that success and failure may be equally valuable in an assessment of creativity, and there is nothing in systems models per se that insists that the creative act requires a successful outcome, merely a valuable one. See Robert Weisberg, *Creativity: Beyond the myth of genius*.

14. Doffman develops a masterly account of meaning-making within music performance that clarifies how the simple act of being in time together yields such significance for musicians. Mark Doffman, *Feeling the groove*.

15. This is consistent with Lori Custodero, who draws on perspectives from music education when she adopts "a model of creativity involving an individual's active construction of musical meaning through responsive interaction with [culturally understood] musical materials" to support the notion of learning through creating. See Lori Custodero, "The call to create," 370.

16. See Mark Doffman, "Feeling the groove," for further discussion of entrainment.

17. Schubert asserts, for example, that "positive feeling—whether it be delight, pleasure, ecstasy, immersion, flow—is an essential part of the creative experience." See Emery Schubert, "Spreading activation and dissociation," 132. See also Mihaly Csikszentmihalyi, *Flow: The psychology of optimal experience*; Elina Hytönen-Ng, *Experiencing "Flow"*; and Keith Sawyer, *Group genius*, for further discussion.

18. The fundamental traits of Flow are elucidated by Mihaly Csikszentmihalyi and Isabella Csikszentmihalyi in François Pachet, "Creativity studies and musical interaction," 351–52.

19. See Martin Seligman, Acacia Parks, and Tracy Steen cited in Alexandra Lamont, "Emotion, engagement and meaning," 575.

20. See Andrew Evans, *The secrets of musical confidence*; or Richard Ryan et al., cited in Alexandra Lamont, "Emotion, engagement and meaning," 575. Both authors echo this line of thinking.

21. Melissa Dobson, "Insecurity, professional sociability and alcohol."

22. Emery Schubert, "Spreading activation and dissociation."

23. Etienne Wenger, *Communities of practice*.

24. Pamela Burnard, *Musical creativities*, 68.

25. See, for example, Jerome Bruner, "The conditions of creativity," or Bruce Ellis Benson, *The improvisation of musical dialogue*. In his discussion of the necessary conditions for creativity, Bruner decides that "an act that produces effective surprise—this I shall take as the hallmark of a creative enterprise" (Bruner, cited in Ian Fillis and Andrew McAuley, "Modeling and measuring creativity at the interface," 9). In a similar vein, McLean proposes that creativity be understood, implicitly or explicitly, as "the processual encompassment by culture of the contingent, the new, and the unforeseen." Stuart McLean, "Stories and cosmogonies," 214.

26. Other investigators warn against mistaking real creativity for a "pseudocreativity" derived, for instance, from ignorance or lack of discipline: see Raymond Cattell and Harold Butcher, cited in David Cropley and Arthur Cropley, "Elements of a universal aesthetic of creativity," 156, or a "quasicreativity" (Gottfried Heinelt, cited on the same page of the same source), which may have many of the elements of genuine creativity but only a tenuous connection with reality.

27. Margaret Boden, *The creative mind*, 163.

28. Gregory Feist, "The evolved fluid specificity," 74.

29. Donald Polkinghorne, *Narrative knowing and the human sciences*, 36.

30. Ernst Boesch, "Symbolic action theory," 479–80.

31. Ibid., 482.

32. Ibid., 480.

33. Creativity continues to have a spiritual dimension for a minority of participants. Their perceptions reflected a small but significant and surprisingly tenacious adherence to the "lone genius" paradigm of creativity, indicating a residual traction to a conception of creativity that the discourse within modern psychology has long since debunked. This constitutes an example of the way research tends to have neglected the voices of those for whom the paradigm retains substantial resonance.

34. Jonathan Smith et al., *Interpretative phenomenological analysis*, 16–17.

35. Boesch cited in Lìvia Simão, "Boesch's symbolic action theory," 489.

36. Hard compositional jazz drummer Antonio Sanchez describes himself as "comfortable being uncomfortable." Michael Parillo, "Antonio Sanchez," 43.

37. Bill Bruford, *The autobiography*, 306.

38. The potential outcome of such an involvement has been characterized by Keith Sawyer as a "'combinatorial explosion' of potential interactions" resulting in "unpredictable emergence." See Sawyer, cited in Nicholas Cook, "Beyond Creativity?" 452.

39. Boesch cited in Walter Lonner and Susanna Hayes, *Discovering cultural psychology*, 329.

40. Seeking to go beyond Wenger's "community of practice" in his search for a collective noun to frame the identity of drummers as a group, Gareth Smith proposes use of the word "web," which I borrow here (Gareth Smith, *I drum, therefore I am*, 168–69). The metaphor has also been brought into play earlier in the Weberian image of man as an animal suspended in a self-spun web of significances. See this volume, chapter 7.

41. Boesch cited in Walter Lonner and Susanna Hayes, *Discovering cultural psychology*, 329.

Chapter 9

1. This line of thinking can be found in Donald Treffinger, "Creative problem solving," and Thomas Ward et al., "Creative cognition," 189.

2. Johannella Tafuri, "Processes and teaching strategies," 135.

3. See Raymond MacDonald et al., "Creativity and flow in musical composition," 293, for an example of research in this area.

4. Nicholas Cook, "Beyond creativity?" 458.

5. This area is explored, for example, by Lori Custodero, "The call to create"; Pamela Burnard, *Musical creativities*; and Margaret Barrett, *A cultural psychology of music education*.

6. See Alexandra Lamont, "Emotion, engagement and meaning," 579, for details of this research.

7. Michael Crotty, *The foundations of social research*, 64.

8. François Pachet, "Creativity studies and musical interaction," 347.

9. Alexandra Lamont, "Emotion, engagement and meaning," 589.

10. Anne Danielsen, *Musical rhythm*.

11. See http://www.musictech.net/2015/08/online-collaboration/ for further discussion (accessed March 4, 2016).

12. The cohort of interviewees generally prioritizes creativity over virtuosity.

13. Examples of this research can be found in Milton Mermikides, "Changes over time"; Paul Lamere, "The loudness war analyzed"; and Anne Danielsen, *Musical rhythm*. In their analysis of expert drummer Jeff Porcaro's iconic performance of "I Keep Forgettin'" by Michael McDonald, Esa Räsänen et al. found that such fluctuations led to a "favoured listening experience." See Esa Räsänen et al., "Fluctuations of hi-hat timing."

14. Drummers may, however, be a special case in the sense that the "making it work/matter" is often done at the functional polarity of the FCC in a somewhat covert, "invisible" manner, anonymous in terms of authorship, and constrained by the dimensions of the drum cultural psychology.

15. James Greeno is cited in Göran Folkestad, "Digital tools," 196.

References

Abuhamdeh, S., and M. Csikszentmihalyi. 2004. "The artistic personality: A systems perspective." In *Creativity: From potential to realization*, edited by R. J. Sternberg, E. L. Grigorenko, and J. L. Singer, 31–42. Washington, DC: American Psychological Association.

Allen, T., and M. E. Veal. 2013. *Tony Allen: An autobiography of the master drummer of Afrobeat*. Durham, NC: Duke University Press.

Amabile, T. M. 1996. *Creativity and innovation in organizations*. Boston: Harvard Business School.

Amirkhanian, C. 1980. "Interview with Brian Eno, KPFA Radio, Berkeley, CA." http://www.rtqe.net/ObliqueStrategies/OSintro.html. Accessed October 20, 2015.

Ansdell, G., and M. Pavlicevic. 2005. "Musical companionship, musical community: Music therapy and the process and value of musical communication." In *Musical communication*, edited by D. Miell, R. MacDonald, and D. Hargreaves, 193–213. Oxford: Oxford University Press.

Arieti, S. 1976. *Creativity: The magic synthesis*. New York: Basic Books.

Armstrong, V. 2011. *Technology and the gendering of music education*. Farnham: Ashgate.

Attas, R. E. S. 2011. "Meter as process in groove-based popular music." PhD thesis, University of British Columbia.

Auslander, P. 2004. "Performance analysis and popular music: A manifesto." *Contemporary Theatre Review* 14 (1): 1–13. http://dx.doi.org/10.1080/1026716032000128674. Accessed June 2, 2014.

Baker, G. 2010. *Hellraiser: The autobiography of the world's greatest drummer*. London: John Blake Publishing.

Balliett, W. 1959. *The sound of surprise: 46 pieces on jazz*. New York: Dutton.

Bamberger, J. 2005. "How the conventions of music notation shape musical perception and performance." In *Musical communication*, edited by D. Miell, R. MacDonald, and D. Hargreaves, 143–70. Oxford: Oxford University Press.

Barrett, F. 1998. "Coda—creativity in jazz and organizations: Implications for organizational learning." *Organization Science* 9 (5): 605–22.

Barrett, M. S. 2005. "Musical communication and children's communities of musical practice." In *Musical communication*, edited by D. Miell, R. MacDonald, and D. Hargreaves, 261–80. Oxford: Oxford University Press.

Barrett, M. S., ed. 2011. *A cultural psychology of music education*. Oxford: Oxford University Press.

Barrett, M. S. 2012. "Troubling the creative imaginary: Some possibilities of ecological thinking for music and learning." In *Musical imaginations: Multidisciplinary perspectives on creativity, performance and perception*, edited by D. Hargreaves, D. Miell, and R. MacDonald, 206–19. Oxford: Oxford University Press.

Barrett, M. S., and J. E. Gromko. 2007. "Provoking the muse: A case study of teaching and learning in music composition." *Psychology of Music: Society for Education, Music and Psychology Research* 35 (2): 213–30.

Barthes, R. 1977. *Image-music-text*. Translated by S. Heath. London: Fontana.

Bastien, D. T., and T. J. Hostager. 1988. "Jazz as a process of organizational innovation." *Communication Research* 15 (5): 582–602.

Becker, H. 1963. *Outsiders: Studies in the sociology of deviance*. New York: Free Press.

Becker, H., and B. Geer. 1960. "Latent culture: A note on the theory of latent social roles." *Administrative Science Quarterly* 5 (2): 304–13. http://www.jstor.org/stable/2390783. Accessed July 24, 2012.

Bennett, A. 1999. "Subcultures or neo-tribes? Rethinking the relationship between youth, style and musical taste." *Sociology* 33 (3): 599–617.

Benson, B. 2003. *The improvisation of musical dialogue: A phenomenology of music*. Cambridge: Cambridge University Press.

Berger, H. M. 2009. *Stance*. Middletown, CT: Wesleyan University Press.

Berliner, P. F. 1994. *Thinking in jazz*. Chicago: University of Chicago Press.

Biamonte, N. 2014. "Formal functions of metric dissonance in rock music." *Music Theory Online* 20 (2). http://www.mtosmt.org/issues/mto.14.20.2/mto.14.20.2.biamonte.html. Accessed July 7, 2016.

Black, J. 1995. "Mick Fleetwood Interview." *Mojo*, December. http://www.rocksbackpages.com/article.html?ArticleID=9164&SearchText=drumming. Accessed January 24, 2012.

Blake, D. 2012. "Timbre as differentiation in Indie music." *Music Theory Online* 18 (2). http://www.mtosmt.org/issues/mto.12.18.2/mto.12.18.2.blake.html. Accessed May 25, 2015.

Blier-Carruthers, A. 2013. *The performer's place in the process and product of recording*. Paper presented at the Performance Studies Network International Conference, Cambridge, UK, April 2.

Bloom, B. S., ed. *Developing talent in young people*. New York: Ballantine.

Boden, M. 1994. "What is creativity?" In *Dimensions of creativity*, edited by M. Boden, 75–117. Cambridge: MIT Press

Boden, M. 2004. *The creative mind: Myths and mechanisms*. 2nd ed. London: Routledge.

Boesch, E. E. 1987. "Cultural psychology in action-theoretical perspective." In *Growth and progress in cultural psychology*, edited by Ç. Kağitçibaşi, 41–51. Lisse, Netherlands: Swetts and Zeitlinger.

Boesch, E. E. 2001. "Symbolic action theory in cultural psychology." *Culture & Psychology* 7: 479–83. http://cap.sagepub.com/content/7/4/479. Accessed October 23, 2014.

Boesch, E. E., W. J. Lonner, and S.A. Hayes. 2007. *Discovering cultural psychology: A profile and selected readings of Ernest E. Boesch*. Charlotte, NC: Information Age Publishing.

Boyd, J. 1992. *Musicians in tune*. New York: Simon and Schuster.

Brannick, T., and D. Coghlan. 2007. "In defense of being "native": The case for insider academic research." *Organizational Research Methods* 10 (1): 59–74.

Brennan, M. 2013. "'Instruments of a lower order': Historicizing the double status of the drum kit and drummers." Paper presented at the International Association for the Study of Popular Music 17th Biennial Global Conference, University of Oviedo, Asturias, Spain, June 25. Forthcoming as part of *The drum kit: A social history*.

Bruford, B. 2009. *Bill Bruford: The autobiography*. London: Jawbone Press.

Bruner, J. 1962. "The conditions of creativity." In *Contemporary approaches to creative thinking*, edited by H. Gruber, G. Terrell, and M. Wertheimer, 1–30. New York: Atherton Press.

Bruner, J. 1986. *Actual minds, possible worlds*. Cambridge: Harvard University Press.

Bruner, J. 1996. *The culture of education*. Cambridge: Harvard University Press.

Burnard, P. 2012. *Musical creativities in practice*. Oxford: Oxford University Press.

Burke, P. 2011. "Clamor of the Godz: Radical incompetence in 1960s rock." *American Music* 29 (1): 35–63. http://www.jstor.org/stable/10.5406/americanmusic.29.1.0035?seq=1#page_scan_tab_contents. Accessed January 23, 2012.

Butterfield, M. 2010. "Variant timekeeping patterns and their effects in jazz drumming." *Music Theory Online* 16 (4).

Chaffin, R., A. Lemieux, and C. Chen. 2006. "Spontaneity and creativity in highly practised performance." In *Musical creativity: Multidisciplinary research in theory and practice*, edited by I. Deliège and G. Wiggins, 200–17. Hove, Sussex: Psychology Press.

Clarke, E. 2012. "Creativity in performance." In *Musical imaginations: multidisciplinary perspectives on creativity, performance and perception*, edited by D. Hargreaves, D. Miell, and R. MacDonald, 17–30. Oxford: Oxford University Press.

Clayton, M. 2009. "The social and personal functions of music in cross-cultural perspective." In *The Oxford handbook of music psychology*, edited by S. Hallam, I. Cross, and M. Thaut, 35–44. Oxford: Oxford University Press.

Clayton, M., T. Herbert, and R. Middleton,. eds. 2003. *The cultural study of music: A critical introduction*. New York: Routledge.

Cohen, S. 1991. *Rock culture in Liverpool: Popular music in the making*. Oxford: Clarendon Press.

Cole, M. 1996. *Cultural psychology: A once and future discipline*. Cambridge: Harvard University Press.

Collins, M. A., and T. M. Amabile. 1999. "Motivation and creativity." In *Handbook of creativity*, edited by R. J. Sternberg, 297–312. Cambridge: Cambridge University Press.

Cook, N. 2003. "Music as performance." In *The cultural study of music: A critical introduction*, edited by M. Clayton, T. Herbert, and R. Middleton, 204-15. New York: Routledge.

Cook, N. 2012. "Beyond Creativity?" In *Musical imaginations: Multidisciplinary perspectives on creativity, performance and perception*, edited by D. Hargreaves, D. Miell, and R. MacDonald, 451–59. Oxford: Oxford University Press.

Corness, G. 2008. "The musical experience through the lens of embodiment." *Leonardo Music Journal* 18: 21–24.

Cottrell, S. 2004. *Professional music-making in London*. Aldershot: Ashgate Publishing.

Covach, J. 1997. "Progressive rock, 'Close to the Edge,' and the boundaries of style." In *Understanding rock: Essays in musical analysis*, edited by J. Covach and G. M. Boone, 3–31. New York: Oxford University Press.

Cropley, D., and A. Cropley. 2008. "Elements of a universal aesthetic of creativity." *Psychology of Aesthetics, Creativity, and the Arts* 2 (3): 155–161.

Crotty, M. 1998. *The foundations of social research: Meaning and perspective in the research process*. London: Sage.

Crouch, S. 1979. "Max Roach: Drums Unlimited." *Village Voice*, December 17, 106–7.

Csikszentmihalyi, M. 1988. "Society, culture and person: A systems view of creativity." In *The nature of creativity: Contemporary psychological perspectives*, edited by R. Sternberg, 325–39. New York: Cambridge University Press.

Csikszentmihalyi, M. 1990. *Flow: The psychology of optimal experience*. New York: Harper and Row.

Csikszentmihalyi, M. 1992. *Flow: The classic work on how to achieve happiness*. New York: Harper and Row.

Csikszentmihalyi, M. 1997. *Creativity: Flow and the psychology of discovery and invention*. New York: Harper Collins.

Csikszentmihalyi, M. 1999. "Implications of a systems perspective for the study of creativity." In *Handbook of creativity*, edited by R. Sternberg, 313–35. Cambridge: Cambridge University Press.

Csordas, T. J. 1993. "Somatic modes of attention." *Cultural Anthropology* 8 (2): 135–56.

Custodero, L. 2012. "The call to create: Flow experience in music learning and teaching." In *Musical Imaginations: Multidisciplinary perspectives on creativity, performance and perception*, edited by D. Hargreaves, D. Miell, and R. MacDonald, 369–84. Oxford: Oxford University Press.

Danielsen, A. 2010. *Musical rhythm in the age of digital reproduction*. Farnham: Ashgate Publishing.

Davidson, J. 2005. "Bodily communication in musical performance." In *Musical communication*, edited by D Miell, D. J. Hargreaves, and R. MacDonald, 215–38. New York: Oxford University Press.

Davidson, J. 2009. "Movement and collaboration in musical performance." In *The Oxford handbook of music psychology*, edited by S. Hallam, I. Cross, and M. Thaut, 364–76. Oxford: Oxford University Press.

Dawkins, R. 1976. *The selfish gene*. Oxford: Oxford University Press.

Dawson, M. 2016. "Aaron Sterling's Sound of Sterloid Vol. 1." *Modern Drummer*, (September): 86.

Dean, M. 2012. *The drum: A history*. Plymouth, UK: Scarecrow Press.

Deliège, I., and M. Richelle. 2006. "Prelude: The spectrum of musical creativity." In *Musical creativity: Multidisciplinary research in theory and practice*, edited by I. Deliège and G. Wiggins, 1–6. Hove, Sussex: Psychology Press.

Denzin, K., and Y. Lincoln, eds. 2000. *The Sage handbook of qualitative research*. 2nd ed. Thousand Oaks, CA: Sage Publications.

Denzin, K., and Y. Lincoln, eds. 2011. *The Sage handbook of qualitative research*. 4th ed. Thousand Oaks, CA: Sage Publications.

DeVeaux, S. 1997. The birth of bebop: A social and musical history. Berkeley: University of California Press.

Dewey, J. 1934. *Art as experience*. New York: Penguin Books.

Dobson, M. C. 2010. "Insecurity, professional sociability, and alcohol: Young freelance musicians' perspectives on work and life in the music profession." *Psychology of Music* 39 (2): 240–60. http://pom.sagepub.com/content/39/2/240. Accessed January 12, 2012.

Doffman, M. 2008. "Feeling the groove: Shared time and its meanings for three jazz trios." PhD thesis, Open University.

Drath, W., and C. Palus. 1994. *Making common sense: Leadership as meaning-making in a community of practice.* Greensboro, NC: CCL Press.

Dweck, C. S. 2000. *Self-theories: Their role in motivation, personality and development.* Hove, Sussex: Psychology Press.

Dwyer, S. C., and J. L. Buckle. 2009. "The space between: On being an insider-outsider in qualitative research." *International Journal of Qualitative Methods* 8 (1): 54–63.

Eckensberger, L. 1990. "From cross-cultural psychology to cultural psychology." *Quarterly Newsletter of the Laboratory of Comparative Human Cognition* 12 (1): 37–52.

Eckensberger, L. 1995. "Activity or action: Two different roads towards an integration of culture into psychology." *Culture and Psychology* 1: 67–80.

Eliot, T. S. 1931. Preface to *Transit of Venus*, poems by Harry Crosby. Paris: Black Sun Press.

Ericsson, K. A., R. T. Krampe, and C. Tesch-Römer. 1993. "The role of deliberate practice in the acquisition of expert performance." *Psychological Review* 100 (3): 363–406.

Evans, A. 1994. *The secrets of musical confidence: How to maximise your performance potential.* London: Thorsons.

Feist, G. J. 2004. "The evolved fluid specificity of human creative talent." In *Creativity: From potential to realization*, edited by R. Sternberg, E. Grigorenko, and J. Singer, 57–82. Washington, DC: American Psychological Association.

Fillis, I., and A. McAuley. 2000. "Modeling and measuring creativity at the interface." *Journal of Marketing Theory and Practice* 8 (2): 8–17. http://www.jstor.org/stable/40469989?seq=1#page_scan_tab_contents. Accessed July 20, 2012.

Florida, R. 2002. *The rise of the creative class.* New York: Basic Books.

Folkestad, G. 2012. "Digital tools and discourse in music: The ecology of composition." In *Musical Imaginations: Multidisciplinary perspectives on creativity, performance and perception*, edited by D. Hargreaves, D. Miell, and R. MacDonald, 193–205. Oxford: Oxford University Press.

Frederickson, J. 1989. "Technology and music performance in the age of mechanical reproduction." *International Review of the Aesthetics and Sociology of Music* 20 (2): 193–220.

Frith, S. 1996. *Performing rites: Evaluating popular music.* Oxford: Oxford University Press.

Frith, S. 2012. "Creativity as a social fact." In *Musical imaginations: Multidisciplinary perspectives on creativity, performance and perception*, edited by D. Hargreaves, D. Miell, and R. MacDonald, 62–72. Oxford: Oxford University Press.

Fulton, J., and E. Paton. 2016. "The systems model of creativity." In *The creative system in action*, edited by P. McIntyre, J. Fulton, and E. Paton, 27-43. New York: Palgrave Macmillan.

Gabrielsson, A. 2003. "Music performance research at the millennium." *Psychology of Music* 31 (3): 221–72.

Gabrielsson, A. 2009. "The relationship between musical structure and perceived expression." In *The Oxford handbook of music psychology*, edited by S. Hallam, I. Cross, and M. Thaut, 141–50. Oxford: Oxford University Press.

Gabrielsson, A. 2011. *Strong experiences with music*. Oxford: Oxford University Press.

Gardner, H. 1993. "Seven creators of the modern era." In *Creativity*, edited by J. Brockman, 28–47. New York City: Simon and Schuster.

Gioia, T. 1989. "Jazz and the primitivist myth." *Musical Quarterly* 73 (1): 130–43. http://www.jstor.org/stable/741862?loginSuccess=true&seq=5#page_scan_tab_contents. Accessed May 31, 2015.

Gitler, I. 1985. *Swing to bop*. 1st ed. New York: Oxford University Press.

Gjedde, L., and B. Ingemann. 2008. *Researching experiences: Exploring processual and experimental methods in cultural analysis*. Newcastle: Cambridge Scholars Publishing.

Gladwell, M. 2008. *Outliers: The story of success*. Lebanon, IN: Little, Brown and Company.

Glăveanu, V. P. 2010a. "Paradigms in the study of creativity: Introducing the perspective of cultural psychology." *New Ideas in Psychology* 28 (1): 79–93. http://eprints.lse.ac.uk/29334/. Accessed September 14, 2012.

Glăveanu, V. P. 2010b. "Principles for a cultural psychology of creativity." *Culture and Psychology* 16 (2): 147–63. http://cap.sagepub.com/content/16/2/147. Accessed April 3, 2012.

Glăveanu, V. P. 2012. "Habitual creativity: Revising habit, reconceptualizing creativity." *Review of General Psychology* 16 (1): 78–92.

Glăveanu, V. P. 2014. *Distributed creativity: Thinking outside the box of the creative individual*. Heidelberg: Springer Science & Business Media.

Glăveanu, V. P., T. Lubart, N. Bonnardel, M. Botella, P-M. de Biaisi, M. Desainte-Catherine, A. Georgsdottir, K. Guillou, G. Kurtag, C. Mouchiroud, M. Storme, A. Wojtczuk, and F. Zenasni. 2013. "Creativity as action: Findings from five creative domains." *Frontiers in Psychology* 13 (4): article 176. http://journal.frontiersin.org/article/10.3389/fpsyg.2013.00176/full. Accessed May 31, 2015.

Glennie, E. 2003. "How to truly listen." TED Talk. At approximately 3'17." http://www.ted.com/talks/evelyn_glennie_shows_how_to_listen.html. Accessed April 15, 2012.

Gracyk, T. 1996. *Rhythm and noise: An aesthetics of rock*. London: I. B. Tauris.

Greeno, J. G. 1989. "A perspective on thinking." *American Psychologist* 44 (2): 134.

Gridley, M. 1983. "Clarifying labels: Jazz, rock, funk and jazz-rock." *Popular Music and Society* 9 (2): 27–34. http://www.tandfonline.com/doi/citedby/10.1080/03007768308591211. Accessed June 6, 2012.

Gruber, H. 1989. "The Evolving Systems approach to creative work." In *Creative people at work: Twelve cognitive case studies*, edited by D. Wallace and H. Gruber, 3–24. Oxford: Oxford University Press.

Gruber, H., and D. Wallace. 1999. "The case study method and evolving systems approach for understanding unique creative people at work." In *Handbook of creativity*, edited by R. J. Sternberg, 93–115. Cambridge: Cambridge University Press.

Hargreaves, D., R. MacDonald, and D. Miell. 2005. "How do people communicate using music?" In *Musical communication*, edited by D. Miell, R. MacDonald, and D. Hargreaves, 1–26. Oxford: Oxford University Press.

Hargreaves, R. 1997. *Mr. Noisy, the musician*. Paris: Hachette Livre.

Harrison, G. 1999. *Rhythmic illusions*. Van Nuys, CA: Alfred Press.

Harvey, T. 2009. "Virtual garage bands: Collaborative cyber communities of Internet musicians." PhD thesis, Florida State University. http://diginole.lib.fsu.edu/island ora/object/fsu%3A182386/datastream/PDF/view. Accessed July 25, 2012.

Hawkins, S. 2003. "Feel the beat come down: House music as rhetoric." In *Analyzing popular music*, edited by A. F. Moore, 80–102. Cambridge: Cambridge University Press.

Hayes, J. 1989. "Cognitive processes in creativity." In *Handbook of creativity*, edited by J. Glover, R. Ronning, and C. Reynolds, 135–45. New York: Plenum.

Helmholtz, H. V., and R. Kahl. 1971. *Selected writings of Hermann von Helmholtz*. Middletown, CT: Wesleyan University Press.

Henderson, S. J. 2004. "Inventors: The ordinary genius next door." In *Creativity: From potential to realization*, edited by R. Sternberg, E. Grigorenko, and J. Singer, 103–25. Washington, DC: American Psychological Association.

Hennessey, B. 2003. "Is the social psychology of creativity really social? Moving beyond a focus on the individual." In *Group creativity: Innovation through collaboration*, edited by P. Paulus and B. Nijstad, 181–201. New York: Oxford University Press.

Hiles, D. 1996. "Cultural psychology and the centre-ground of psychology." *International Journal of Psychology* 31 (3–4): 1525–40.

Hill, J. 2012. "Imagining creativity: An ethnomusicological perspective on how belief systems encourage or inhibit creative activities in music." In *Musical imaginations: Multidisciplinary perspectives on creativity, performance and perception*, edited by D. Hargreaves, D. Miell, and R. MacDonald, 87–104. Oxford: Oxford University Press.

Hodges, D. 2009. "Bodily responses to music." In *The Oxford handbook of music psychology*, edited by S. Hallam, I. Cross, and M. Thaut, 121–30. Oxford: Oxford University Press.

Holloway, R. 1969. "Culture: A human domain." *Current Anthropology* 10 (4): 395–412. http://www.jstor.org/stable/2740553. Accessed June 13, 2013.

Hope Mason, J. 2003. *The value of creativity: The origins and emergence of a modern belief*. Aldershot: Ashgate.

Howkins, J. 2001. *The creative economy: How people make money from ideas*. London: Penguin.

Hultberg, C. 2011. "Making music or playing instruments: Secondary students' use of cultural tools in aural- and notation-based instrumental learning and teaching." In *A cultural psychology of music education*, edited by M. Barrett, 115–42. Oxford: Oxford University Press.

Hytönen-Ng, E. 2013. *Experiencing "Flow" in jazz performance*. Farnham: Ashgate.

Impett, J. 2009. "Making a mark: The psychology of composition." In *The Oxford handbook of music psychology*, edited by S. Hallam, I. Cross, and M. Thaut, 403–12. Oxford: Oxford University Press.

Janis, I. L. 1982. *Groupthink: Psychological studies of policy decisions and fiascos*. Boston: Houghton Mifflin.

John-Steiner, V. 2000. *Creative collaboration*. New York: Oxford University Press.

Jones, L. [Baraka, A.]. 1971. "The changing same (R&B and new black music)." In *The black aesthetic*, edited by A. Gayle Jr., 112–25. Garden City, NY: Doubleday.

Jovchelovitch, S. 2007. *Knowledge in context: Representations, community and culture*. London: Routledge.

Juslin P. N.. 2005. "From mimesis to catharsis: Expression, perception and induction of emotion in music." In *Musical communication*, edited by D. Miell, R. MacDonald, and D. Hargreaves, 85–115. Oxford: Oxford University Press.

Juslin P. N. 2009. "Emotion in music performance." In *The Oxford handbook of music psychology*, edited by S. Hallam, I. Cross, and M. Thaut, 377–89. Oxford: Oxford University Press.

Juslin, P. N., and E. Lindström. 2010. "Musical expression of emotions: Modelling listeners' judgements of composed and performed features." *Music Analysis* 29 (1–3): 334–64.

Katz, M. 2012. *Groove music: The art and culture of the hip-hop DJ*. New York: Oxford University Press.

Kaufman, S. B., and J. C. Kaufman. 2007. "Ten years to expertise, many more to greatness: An investigation of modern writers." *Journal of Creative Behavior* 41 (2): 114–24.

Keepnews, P. 2007. "Max Roach, a founder of modern jazz, dies at 83." *New York Times*, August 16. http://www.nytimes.com/2007/08/16/arts/music/16cnd-roach.html?ei=5090&en=48adf94b947bc225&ex=1344916800&emc=rss&pagewanted=all&_r=1&. Accessed November 27, 2011.

Keightley, K. 2010. "Taking popular music (and Tin Pan Alley and jazz) seriously." *Journal of Popular Music Studies* 22 (1): 90–97.

Keil, C. 1987. "Participatory discrepancies and the power of music." *Cultural Anthropology* 2 (3): 275–83. http://onlinelibrary.wiley.com/doi/10.1525/can.1987.2.3.02a00010/full. Accessed February 28, 2013.

King, K. 2016. "Phil Jones: The perfect gig." *Drumhead* (September/October): 46–51.

Kitayama, S. 2002. "Culture and basic psychological processes—toward a system view of culture: Comment on Oyserman et al.." *Psychological Bulletin* 128 (1): 89–96.

Korall, B. 2002. *Drummin' men: The heartbeat of jazz; The bebop years (Vol. 2)*. New York: Oxford University Press.

Lamere, P. 2009. "The loudness war examined." *Music Machinery*, http://musicmachinery.com/2009/03/23/the-loudness-war/. Accessed August 23, 2013.

Lamont, A. 2012. "Emotion, engagement and meaning in strong experiences of music performance." *Psychology of Music* 40 (5): 574–94. http://pom.sagepub.com/content/40/5/574. Accessed July 19, 2013.

Lazear, E. P. 1995. "Culture and language." No. 5249, National Bureau of Economic Research. Cambridge, MA: NBER.

Levine, L. W. 1990. *Highbrow/lowbrow: The emergence of cultural hierarchy in America*. Cambridge: Harvard University Press.

Levitin, D., P. Chordia, and V. Menon. 2012. "Musical rhythm spectra from Bach to Joplin obey a 1/f power law." *PNAS* 109 (10): 3716–20. http://www.pnas.org/content/109/10/3716.full. Accessed May 6, 2012.

Limb, C. 2010. "Your brain on improvisation." TED talk. http://www.ted.com/talks/charles_limb_your_brain_on_improv.html. Accessed July 25, 2016.

Lock, G. 2011. "Musical creativity in the mirror of Glăveanu's five principles of cultural psychology." *Culture and Psychology* 17 (1): 121–36. http://cap.sagepub.com/content/17/1/121. Accessed February 7, 2012.

Lockett, P. 2008. *Indian rhythms for drumset*. New York: Hudson Music.

Lubart, T. I. 1999. "Creativity across cultures." In *Handbook of creativity*, edited by R. Sternberg, 339–50. Cambridge: Cambridge University Press.

Lubart, T., and J-H. Guignard. 2004. "The generality-specificity of creativity: A multivariate approach." In *Creativity: From potential to realization*, edited by R. Sternberg,

E. Grigorenko, and J. Singer, 43–56. Washington, DC: American Psychological Association.

MacDonald, R.A.R., C. Byrne, and L. Carlton. 2006. "Creativity and flow in musical composition: An empirical investigation." *Psychology of Music* 34 (3): 292–307. http://pom.sagepub.com/content/34/3/292.abstract. Accessed June 10, 2015.

MacDonald, R.A.R., D. Hargreaves, and D. Miell. 2009. "Musical identities." In *The Oxford handbook of music psychology*, edited by S. Hallam, I. Cross, and M. Thaut, 462–70. Oxford: Oxford University Press.

MacDonald, R.A.R., and G. B. Wilson. 2005. "Musical identities of professional jazz musicians: A focus group investigation." *Psychology of Music* 33 (4): 395–417.

MacDonald, R.A.R., and G. B. Wilson. 2006. "Constructions of jazz: How jazz musicians present their collaborative musical practice." *Musicae Scientiae* 10 (1): 59–83.

MacDonald, R., G. Wilson, and D. Miell. 2012. "Improvisation as a creative process within contemporary music." In *Musical imaginations: Multidisciplinary perspectives on creativity, performance and perception*, edited by D. Hargreaves, D. Miell, and R. MacDonald, 242–56. Oxford: Oxford University Press.

Mace, M-A. 1998. "Modelling the creative process: A grounded theory analysis of creativity in the domain of art-making." PhD thesis, Canterbury University.

Marton, F. 1988. "Phenomenography: A research approach to investigating different understandings of reality." In *Qualitative research in education: Focus and methods*, edited by R. Sherman and R. Webb, 141–161. Lewes: Falmer Press.

Mattingly, R. 2008. "Max Roach." *Percussive Arts Society Online, Hall of Fame*, http://www.pas.org/About/the-society/halloffame/RoachMax.aspx. Accessed July 2, 2016.

Maykut, P., and R. Morehouse. 1994. *Beginning qualitative research: A philosophical and practical guide*. Washington, DC: Falmer.

McGrath, J. 1984. *Groups: Interaction and performance*. Vol. 14. Englewood Cliffs, NJ: Prentice-Hall.

McIntyre, P. 2011. "Rethinking the creative process: The systems model of creativity applied to popular songwriting." *Journal of Music, Technology and Education* 4 (1): 77–90.

McIntyre, P. 2012. *Creativity and cultural production: Issues for media practice*. Basingstoke: Palgrave Macmillan UK.

McIntyre, P., J. Fulton, and E. Paton, eds. 2016. *The creative system in action: Understanding cultural production and practice*. Basingstoke: Palgrave Macmillan UK.

McLean, S. 2009. "Stories and cosmogonies: Imagining creativity beyond 'nature' and 'culture.'" *Cultural Anthropology* 24 (2): 213–45.

Merker, B. 2006. "Layered constraints on the multiple creativities of music." In *Musical creativity: Multidisciplinary research in theory and practice*, edited by I. Deliège and G. Wiggins, 25–41. Hove, Sussex: Psychology Press.

Mermikides, M. 2010. "Changes over time: The analysis, modelling and deployment of jazz improvisational and time-feel mechanisms." PhD thesis, University of Surrey.

Miell, D., R. MacDonald, and D. Hargreaves, eds. 2005. *Musical communication*. Oxford: Oxford University Press.

Milkowski, B. 1983. "Frank Zappa: Guitar Player." *Downbeat*, February. http://wiki.killuglyradio.com/wiki/Frank_Zappa:_Guitar_Player. Accessed July 24, 2015.

Millward, S. 2001a. "Feel-good factor: Giving your MIDI tracks a live feel, part 1." *Sound on Sound*, July.

Millward, S. 2001b. "Feel-good factor: Giving your MIDI tracks a live feel, part 2." *Sound on Sound*, August.

Monson, I. 1996. *Saying something: Jazz improvisation and interaction*. Chicago: University of Chicago Press.

Moore, A. F. 2013. *Song means: Analyzing and interpreting popular song*. Farnham: Ashgate.

Moran, S., and V. John-Steiner. 2004. "How collaboration in creative work impacts identity and motivation." In *Collaborative creativity: Contemporary perspectives*, edited by D. Miell and K. Littleton, 11–25. London: Free Association Books.

Munson, C. 2012. "Max Roach: 'Blues for Big Sid' transcription and analysis." *Percussion Sessions*, February. Reprinted in Bill Bruford, *Making it work: Creative music performance and the Western kit drummer*, 295–96, PhD thesis, University of Surrey, 2016.

Murph, J. 2012. "Joe Chambers: The big picture." *Jazz Times*, November. http://jazz times.com/articles/62657-joe-chambers-the-big-picture. Accessed February 3, 2013.

Myers, M. 2010. "Bobby Shew on Buddy Rich (part 2)." *Jazzwax.com*. http://www.jazz wax.com/2010/02/bobby-shew-on-budy-rich-part-2.html. Accessed June 9, 2017.

Nardi, B. A. 1996. "Studying context: A comparison of activity theory, situated action models, and distributed cognition." In *Context and consciousness: Activity theory and human-computer interaction*, edited by B. A. Nardi, 35–52. Cambridge: MIT Press.

Negus, K., and M. Pickering. 2004. *Creativity, communication, and cultural value*. London: Sage Publications.

Nemeth, C. J., and B. Nemeth-Brown. 2003. "Better than individuals? The potential benefits of dissent and diversity for group creativity." In *Group creativity: Innovation through collaboration*, edited by P. B. Paulus and B. Nijstad, 63–84. New York: Oxford University Press.

Nettl, B. 1983. *The study of ethnomusicology: 29 issues and concepts*. Urbana: University of Illinois Press.

Ni, Y., R. Santos-Rodriguez, M. McVicar, and T. De Bie. 2011. "Hit song science once again a science?" Paper presented to the 4th International Workshop on Machine Learning and Music, December 17, Sierra Nevada, Spain. http://citeseerx.ist.psu. edu/viewdoc/download?doi=10.1.1.412.9732&rep=rep1&type=pdf. Accessed February 27, 2012.

Nickerson, R. S. 1999. "Enhancing creativity." In *Handbook of creativity*, edited by R. J. Sternberg, 392–431. Cambridge: Cambridge University Press.

O'Brien, M., and M. Walton. 2011. "Music and creativity." *National Science Foundation Online*. http://www.nsf.gov/news/special_reports/science_nation/musiccreativity. jsp. Accessed May 26, 2015.

Pachet, F. 2006. "Creativity studies and musical interaction." In *Musical creativity: Multidisciplinary research in theory and practice*, edited by I. Deliège and G. Wiggins, 347–58. Hove, Sussex: Psychology Press.

Palmer, C. 1997. "Music Performance." *Annual Review of Psychology* 48: 115–38. http:// www.annualreviews.org/doi/abs/10.1146/annurev.psych.48.1.115. Accessed June 21, 2012.

Parillo, M. 2015. "Antonio Sanchez." *Modern Drummer* (August): 36–48.

Paulus, P., and B. Nijstad. 2003. "Group creativity: An introduction." In *Group creativity: Innovation through collaboration*, edited by P. Paulus and B. Nijstad, 3–11. New York: Oxford University Press.

Peacock, M. 2008. "Constructing creativity: A discursive examination of innovative scientists and authors of fiction talking about creativity." PhD thesis, University of Bath.

Phelan, P. 1993. *Unmarked: The politics of performance.* London: Routledge.

Pieslak, J. 2007. "Re-casting metal: Rhythm and meter in the music of Meshuggah." *Music Theory Spectrum* 29 (2): 219–45. http://mts.oxfordjournals.org/content/29/2/219.short. Accessed January 23, 2012.

Pinheiro, R. 2010. "The creative process in the context of jazz jam sessions." *Journal of Music and Dance* 1 (1): 1–5. http://www.academicjournals.org/journal/JMD/edition/January_2011. Accessed June 4, 2014.

Plucker, J. A., and J. S. Renzulli. 1999. "Psychometric approaches to the study of creativity." In *Handbook of creativity*, edited by R. J. Sternberg, 35–61. Cambridge: Cambridge University Press.

Poincaré, H. (1908) 1985. "Mathematical creation." In *The creative process: A symposium*, edited by B. Ghiselin, 22–31. Berkeley: University of California Press.

Poli, G. D. 2004. "Methodologies for expressiveness modelling of and for music performance." *Journal of New Music Research* 33 (3): 189–202.

Polkinghorne, D. 1988. *Narrative knowing and the human sciences.* Albany: SUNY Press.

Pressing, J. 1998. "Psychological constraints on improvisational expertise and communication." In *In the course of performance: Studies in the world of musical improvisation*, edited by B. Nettl and M. Russell, 47–67. Chicago: University of Chicago Press.

Räsänen, E., O. Pulkkinen, T. Virtanen, M. Zollner, and H. Hennig. 2015. "Fluctuations of hi-hat timing and dynamics in a virtuoso drum track of a popular music recording." *PloSone* 10 (6):e0127902.http://journals.plos.org/plosone/article?id=10.1371/journal.pone.0127902. Accessed August 30, 2016.

Ratner, C. 1999. "Three approaches to cultural psychology: A critique." *Cultural Dynamics* 11: 7–31. http://cdy.sagepub.com/content/11/1/7.full.pdf+html. Accessed May 17, 2012.

Rink, J., ed. 1995. *The practice of performance: Studies in musical interpretation.* Cambridge: Cambridge University Press.

Rogers, A. 2003. "Miles Davis: The complete *In a Silent Way* sessions." *All about Jazz.* http://www.allaboutjazz.com/php/article.php?id=11942#.UidZYH-Voyc. Accessed September 4, 2013.

Santamaría, A., C. Mercedes, and M. de la Mata. 2010. "Thinking as action: Theoretical and methodological requirements for cultural psychology." *Theory and Psychology* 20 (1): 76–101. http://tap.sagepub.com/content/20/1/76. Accessed December 10, 2012.

Sawyer, R. K. 1992. "Improvisational creativity: An analysis of jazz performance." *Creativity Research Journal* 5 (3): 253–63.

Sawyer, R. K. 1998. "The interdisciplinary study of creativity in performance." *Creativity Research Journal* 11 (1): 11–19.

Sawyer, R. K. 2003. *Group creativity: Music, theater, collaboration.* Mahwah, NJ: Lawrence Erlbaum.

Sawyer, R. K. 2006. "Group creativity: Musical performance and collaboration." *Psychology of Music* 34 (2): 148–65. http://pom.sagepub.com/content/34/2/148. Accessed May 14, 2013.

Sawyer, R. K. 2007. *Group genius: The creative power of collaboration.* New York: Basic Books.

Schloss, J. 2004. *Making beats: The art of sample-based hip-hop.* Middletown, CT: Wesleyan University Press.

Schubert, E. 2012. "Spreading activation and dissociation: A cognitive mechanism for creative processing in music." In *Musical imaginations: Multidisciplinary perspectives on creativity, performance and perception,* edited by D. Hargreaves, D. Miell, and R. MacDonald, 124–40. Oxford: Oxford University Press.

Seashore, C. (1938) 1967. *Psychology of music.* New York: Dover.

Seddon, F. 2004. "Empathetic creativity: The product of empathetic attunement." In *Collaborative creativity: Contemporary perspectives,* edited by D. Miell and K. Littleton, 65–78. London: Free Association Books.

Serrà, J., Á. Corral, M. Boguñá, M. Haro, and J. L. Arcos. 2012. "Measuring the evolution of contemporary western popular music." *Scientific Reports* 2: 521.

Shannon, C. E., and W. Weaver. 1949. *The mathematical theory of communication.* Urbana: University of Illinois Press.

Sherwin, A. 2007. "Why music really is getting louder." *London Times,* June 4. http://elliott-randall.com/2011/06/why-music-really-is-getting-louder/. Accessed August 13, 2015.

Simão, L. M. 2001. "Boesch's symbolic action theory in interaction." *Culture & Psychology* 7 (4): 485–93. http://cap.sagepub.com/content/7/4/485. Accessed October 23, 2014.

Simonton, D. K. 2004. "Creativity as a constrained stochastic process." In *Creativity: From potential to realization,* edited by R. J. Sternberg, E. L. Grigorenko, and J. L. Singer, 83–101. Washington, DC: American Psychological Association.

Sinta, B. 2012. "Capturing the 4th Street feeling." *Drumhead* 34: 72–77. http://www.brettsimons.com/frames/press/Drumhead_Sinta_Simons_Etheridge.pdf. Accessed August 22, 2016.

Sloboda, J. A. 2001. *Generative processes in music: The psychology of performance, improvisation and composition.* Oxford: Oxford University Press.

Sloboda, J., A. Lamont, and A. Greasley. 2009. "Choosing to hear music: Motivation, process and effect." In *The Oxford handbook of music psychology,* edited by S. Hallam, I. Cross, and M. Thaut, 431–40. Oxford: Oxford University Press.

Small, C. 1998. *Musicking: The meaning of performance and listening.* Hanover, NH: Wesleyan University Press.

Smith, J. A., P. Flowers, and M. Larkin. 2009. *Interpretative phenomenological analysis: Theory, method and research.* London: Sage Publications.

Smith, G. D. 2011. "I drum, therefore I am? A study of kit drummers' identities, practices and learning." PhD thesis, University of London.

Smith, G. D. 2013. *I drum, therefore I am: Being and becoming a drummer.* Farnham: Ashgate.

Spikey, D. 2016. "Eyes down on club land." *BBC Radio 4 Extra,* January 12.

Stadlen, P. 1962. "The aesthetics of popular music." *British Journal of Aesthetics* 2 (4): 351–61.

Starko, A. J. 2001. *Creativity in the classroom: Schools of curious delight.* 2nd ed. Mahwah, NJ: Lawrence Erlbaum.

Sternberg, R. J., and T. I. Lubart. 1999. "The concept of creativity: Prospects and paradigms." In *Handbook of creativity,* edited by R. J. Sternberg, 3–15. Cambridge: Cambridge University Press.

Stravinsky, I., and R. Craft. 1962. *Expositions and developments.* London: Faber.

Sudnow, D. 1978. *Ways of the hand: The organisation of improvised conduct*. Cambridge: Harvard University Press.

Sutcliffe, P. 2008. "The Police." *Mojo*, August. http://www.rocksbackpages.com/Library/Article/the-police/. Accessed January 25, 2012.

Szekely, M. D. 2006. "Gesture, pulsion, grain: Barthes' musical semiology." *Contemporary Aesthetics* 4. http://quod.lib.umich.edu/c/ca/7523862.0004.005/--gesture-pulsion-grain-barthes-musical-semiology?rgn=main;view=fulltext. Accessed August 4, 2015.

Tafuri, J. 2006. "Processes and teaching strategies in musical improvisation with children." In *Musical creativity: Multidisciplinary research in theory and practice*, edited by I. Deliège and G. Wiggins, 134–57. Hove, Sussex: Psychology Press.

Tagg, P. 2013. *Music's meanings: A modern musicology for non-musos*. Larchmont, NY: Mass Media Music Scholars' Press.

Tamlyn, G. 1998. "The big beat: Origins and development of snare backbeat and other accompanimental rhythms in rock'n'roll." PhD thesis, University of Liverpool. http://www.tagg.org/xpdfs/TamlynPhD2.pdf. Accessed June 2, 2012.

Tedlock, B. 1991. "From participant observation to the observation of participation: The emergence of narrative ethnography." *Journal of Anthropological Research* 47 (1): 69–94.

Tomasello, M. 1999. "The human adaptation for culture." *Annual Review of Anthropology* 28: 509–29. http://www2.psych.ubc.ca/~ara/Teaching%20407/psych407%20readings/Tomasello1999.pdf. Accessed June 13, 2013.

Toynbee, J. 2000. *Making popular music: Musicians, creativity and institutions*. London: Arnold.

Treffinger, D. 1995. "Creative problem solving: Overview and educational implications." *Educational Psychology Review* 7 (3): 301–12.

Valsiner, J. 1997. *Culture and the development of children's action: A theory of human development*. New York: Wiley.

Vass, E. 2004. "Understanding collaborative creativity: Young children's classroom-based shared creative writing." In *Collaborative creativity: Contemporary perspectives*, edited by D. Miell and K. Littleton, 79–95. London: Free Association Books.

Vygotsky, L. S. 1974. *Thought and language*. Edited and translated by E. Haufmann and G. Vakar. Cambridge: MIT Press.

Vygotsky, L. S. 1980. *Mind in society: The development of higher psychological processes*. Edited by M. Cole, V. John-Steiner, S. Scribner, and E. Souberman. Cambridge: Harvard University Press.

Wallas, G. 1926. *The art of thought*. New York: Harcourt Brace.

Ward, T. B., S. M. Smith, and R. A. Finke. 1999. "Creative cognition." In *Handbook of creativity*, edited by R. Sternberg, 189–212. Cambridge: Cambridge University Press.

Webster, P. R. 2002. "Creative thinking in music: Advancing a model." In *Creativity in music education: Research to practice*. CMWA Biennial Series. http://www.peterrwebster.com/pubs/WillinghamBook.pdf. Accessed September 19, 2012.

Weisberg, R. 1993. *Creativity: Beyond the myth of genius*. New York: W. H. Freeman and Company.

Weisberg, R. 1999. "Creativity and knowledge: A challenge to theories." In *Handbook of creativity*, edited by R. Sternberg, 226–50. Cambridge: Cambridge University Press.

Wenger, E. 1998. *Communities of practice: Learning, meaning, and identity*. New York: Cambridge University Press.

Wertsch, J. 1998. *Mind as action*. New York: Oxford University Press.

Williamon, A., S. Thompson, T. Lisboa, and C. Wiffen. 2006. "Creativity, originality, and value in music performance." In *Musical creativity: Multidisciplinary research in theory and practice*, edited by I. Deliège and G. Wiggins, 161–80. Hove, Sussex: Psychology Press.

Williams, J. 2013. *Rhymin' and stealin': Musical borrowing in hip-hop*. Ann Arbor: University of Michigan Press.

Wilshere, B. 2002. "Brian Wilshere: The drummer as composer." PhD thesis, Goldsmiths College, University of London.

Wilson, R. 2003. "Melodic drum set compositions: A study of Max Roach and Terry Bozzio." MA thesis, William Paterson University, NJ.

Wirtanen, S., and K. Littleton. 2004. "Collaboration, conflict and the musical identity work of solo-piano students: The significance of the student-teacher relationship." In *Collaborative creativity: Contemporary perspectives*, edited by D. Miell and K. Littleton. London: Free Association Books.

Zagorski-Thomas, S. 2010. "Real and unreal performances: The interaction of recording technology and rock drum kit performance." In *Musical rhythm in the age of digital reproduction*, edited by A. Danielsen, 195–212. Farnham: Ashgate.

Zak, A. 2010. *I don't sound like nobody: Remaking music in 1950s America*. Ann Arbor: University of Michigan Press.

Zbikowski, L. M. 2009. "Modelling the groove: Conceptual structure and popular music." *Journal of the Royal Musical Association* 129 (2): 272–97. http://www.jstor.org/stable/3557507. Accessed August 14, 2013.

Zerubavel, E. 1997. *Social mindscapes: An invitation to cognitive sociology*. Cambridge: Harvard University Press.

Zils, A., F. Pachet, O. Delerue, and F. Gouyon. 2002. "Automatic extraction of drum tracks from polyphonic music signals." In *Proceedings of the 2nd International Conference on Web Delivering of Music* (WedelMusic2002), Darmstadt, Germany, December 9–11, 179–83. https://csl.sony.fr/downloads/papers/2002/ZilsMusic.pdf. Accessed February 28, 2013.

Discography

Etheridge, Melissa. 2012. "4th Street Feeling." New York: Island Records.

Collins, Phil. 1985. "One More Night." London: Virgin Records.

Collins, Phil. 1990. "Do You Remember?" London: Virgin Records.

Collins, Phil. 1993. "Can't Turn Back the Years." London: Virgin Records.

Fleetwood Mac. 1976. "Go Your Own Way." Los Angeles: Warner Brothers.

Gaye, Marvin. 1968. "I Heard It through the Grapevine." New York: Motown Records.

Charlie Parker Quintet 1953. *Jazz at Massey Hall*. Album. New York: Debut Records.

Roach, Max. 1966. "Big Sid," from the album *Drums Unlimited*. Album. New York: Atlantic Records.

Rollins, Sonny. 1957. *Freedom Suite*. Album. California: Riverside Records.

Index

Note: Italicized page numbers indicate figures, while page numbers with an italicized *n* indicate notes.

actions and action-choices: analysis of, 4, 237*n*6; individual, creativity and, 10; involuntary component of, 242*n*30; making meaning of lived experience through, 35; relationship in, 28–29; social matrix of people, artifacts and, 15; Strønen on differentiation and, 115

action theory: activity theory and, 27; creativity and meaning and, 36–37; creativity studies and, 8; cultural products and artifacts of human mind and, 131–32; drummers' community of practice and, 136–37; Flow and, 157

action theory of creativity (ATC), 29–30

activity theory, 27, 29

additive processes, 73, 74, 109

African and African American legacy, 124, 134, 159–60

agency in performance, selection and, 84

allowing, in creative performance, 18, 62, 193–94

Amabile, Teresa, 166, 247*n*17

Arieti, Silvano, 36, 133, 190

artifacts: drum culture and, 28, 204, 258*n*40; human mind, cultural products and, 15, 131–32

assessments: arbiters of significance and, 165–70; attributing significance to self and others, 173–80; of creativity, 17; diverging, 36; overview, 165; personal creativity and, 170–73; in SDCA framework, *23*, 24; success or failure of creativity in, 257*n*13; summary, 180–81

audiences, communication with, 146–53, 166–67, 188, 254*n*87–88

authorship: compositional practice and, 46–47; functional practice and, 44

Barrett, Margaret, 129, 136, 144, 190, 253*n*75

bass players, 243*n*8

being in the zone, 240*n*61. *See also* Flow; "in the moment"; slightly altered state

Berger, Harris, 103, 139, 154, 155

Big-C creativity, 9, 21, 49–50, 51. *See also* historical creativity

Björk, 27–28

Blackman Santana, Cindy: African American legacy and, 124; on audience reception, 147, 150, 151; on change and transformation, 121; on collaborative communication, 142–43, 145; on creativity within, 69–70, 71, 172–73, 183–84; on differentiation, 109, 115; on enabling creativity, 118; ethical drivers for, 93–94; expert perspective of, 6; on expressive intentions, 97, 98–99; on fun of drumming, 187; on going further, 122; on leader imposing creativity limitations, 57; on musical interpretation, 86–87; on performing as a leader, 66, 67; on performing with a leader, 62; self-imposed constraints for, 95; on significance of others, 177; on stick control, 89; on stylistic appropriateness, 85; on trusting, 195–96

Boden, Margaret, 46, 71, 139, 199, 245*n*16

bodily communication, 141, 253*n*68

body at work, 27–28

Boesch, Ernst: action theory of, 8, 15, 28, 207; on culture, 129, 131, 201; Glăveanu's action theory and, 30; on reciprocal interaction, 156; Soviet activity theory and, 29

bone conduction, sound reinforcement system and, 28, 241*n*28

Boulez, Pierre, 12, 46

Bozzio, Terry, 46, 72, 106, 180

Brennan, Matthew, 158, 214

Bruford, Bill: audience on groove and, 103; on connecting, 199; on disconnectedness of performers and audience, 170; expert perspective of, 6–7; keyboard player duo and, 72; motivational constraints, 92; overdub session recording, 202–3; on performing as a leader, 68; timbral color and, 105–6; timekeeping by, 100

178; on stick control, 89; on studio performances, 74; on surprise, 200
Hytönen-Ng, Elina, 158

identity: construction of, meaningfulness and,
201–2; timekeeping and, 101–2. *See also* musical identity
IMCM (integrated model of the circulation of
meaning): audience reception and, 151; creative
experience and, 201; differentiation and, 120–
21; domain-level meaning, goal-oriented action
and, 32, *32*; drum culture and, 130; drummers
making meaning of lived experience, 33–35, *34*;
existing models' shortcomings and, 30–31;
individual-level meaning circulation, 33, *33*; introduction of, 15; as localized application of
cultural psychology, 36; sharing meaning and,
154; shortcomings of, 36; as situated action
model, 31–37, 207
improvisation, surprise and, 199
indefinite pitch: instruments of, 17, 237n4; practitioners, 136. *See also* unpitched instruments
indeterminate pitch, 207, 237n4. *See also* unpitched instruments
individual-level meaning, in IMCM, 32, 33, *34*, 35,
36
intellect, drummers' downplay of, 134–35, 136
internal locus of control, 83, 246n3
internal negative constraints, 94
interpretation, in popular music, 109–10. *See also*
functional/compositional continuum
"in the moment," 4, 30, 188–90, 240n61, 257n10
intra-performers, 103, 141, 168–69. *See also* co-
performers
intrinsic motivation principle, 247n17
invisible composer, functional performer as, 43–
44

jazz: change and transformation in, 121; character-
izing, 80; collaborative communication in, 141;
compositional practice and, 40, 46; performance creativity in, 13–14, 87; players listening
during, 169; temporal lever of control and, 101
Jazz at Massey Hall (Charlie Parker's quintet), 49
Jones, Elvin, 99, 177–78, 256n12
Jones, Jo, 42, 243n7

King Crimson, 36, 86, 132
Kravitz, Lenny, 147, 196
Krupa, Gene, 123, 251n21

Lamont, Alexandra, 77–78, 212
language, common culture and, 137–38

Lave, Jean, 28–29
leadership, collaborative performance and, 54
learning, 58, 257n15
listeners, 97, 156, 167–68. *See also* audiences
little-c (psychological) creativity, 9, 21–22
live performance, 73–78, 81, 247n16, 247n22,
253n72
Lock, Gerhard, 38, 240n49
Lockett, Pete, 180

making it matter, 17, 18, 206, 259n14
making it work: arbiters of significance and, 170;
brainstorming in music rehearsals and, 80,
246n26; communication and, 26; as core function, 18; as creativity, 17, 206, 259n14; functionally before compositionally, 81; functional practice and, 80; performing for a leader and, 55, 60,
61; performing with a leader and, 62; solo concerts and, 68; studio musicians and, 41–42
Marton, Ference, 7–8
McIntyre, Phillip, 10, 182, 239n36
meaning (meaningfulness): in action, 201–4;
drummers, creative performance and, 209; live
performance and, 191–93; sharing of, 154–56
meaninglessness in performance, 202–3
mediated action, 3, 35, 242n48
Mehldau, Brad, 72, 76–77
melodic drumming, 3
memes, Roach's domain-changing creativity and,
244n28
Mermikides, Milton, 41, 160, 255n129
meter, control and, 102–4, 109, 247n24
microgenesis, definition of, 239n37
mind/body split: drum ideology and, 17, 133–34,
136; drummer denigration and, 159
Monson, Ingrid, 69, 169
Moore, Allan, 156, 162, 174, 182; standard rock
beat and, 83, 99–100, 246n1
Morrison, Van, 63, 64
motivational constraints, 92–96, 247n17
Musical Creativities in Practice (Burnard), 21
musical identity: appropriate performance and,
112; consistency and, 101, 248n37; going further
and, 125–26, 250n18–19; performing with a
leader and, 65; solo piano students and,
248n42; timekeeping and, 101–2
musical taste groups, 43, 243n12
music creativity, as network of people cooperating, 10
music education, on creative process, 210
music inventors, 74, 245n20
music technology: drummer marginalization and,
160–61, 214, 255n124; dynamic compression